Shaping an Urban Future:
Essays in Memory of Catherine Bauer Wurster

The MIT Press
Massachusetts Institute of Technology
Cambridge, Massachusetts, and London, England

Shaping an Urban Future:
Essays in Memory of Catherine Bauer Wurster
EDITED BY BERNARD J. FRIEDEN AND WILLIAM W. NASH, JR.

Preface

Catherine Bauer Wurster's untimely death in 1964 left her many personal friends and professional colleagues temporarily uncertain of the best way to express their grief over the loss of this great lady. The series of memorial lectures that served as the basis for this volume grew out of conversations among her many admirers on the faculties of City and Regional Planning at the Massachusetts Institute of Technology and the Harvard Graduate School of Design. It was Lloyd Rodwin of M.I.T., however, who first expressed the idea of a lecture series to the editors who then gave it its present form.

The resulting lecture series would have been impossible without using financial resources made available by the Richard King Mellon Trusts. Nor would it have been as successful as it was without the dedicated handling of administrative details by Miss Camilla Moon of Harvard and Mrs. Colene Abramson of M.I.T. Miss Susan Crystal prepared the bibliography of works by Catherine Bauer Wurster, and Mrs. Kelley Sutherland assisted with editorial and production work. We are grateful also for the advice and assistance our colleagues have given us in planning and managing the lecture series.

Bernard J. Frieden
Massachusetts Institute of Technology
William W. Nash, Jr.
Harvard University

Contents

Shaping an Urban Future:
Essays in Memory of Catherine Bauer Wurster

Editors' Introduction

The essays in this book have been assembled to honor the memory of
Catherine Bauer Wurster, although her most enduring memorial
will consist always of her own achievements in housing and community
planning both in the United States and overseas. Her remarkable
career as policy adviser, author, lobbyist, educator, and philosopher of
urbanism spanned the period from the late 1920's to 1964 and reflected
an extraordinary range of interests. As author of the pioneering book
Modern Housing; as adviser to Presidents Roosevelt, Eisenhower,
and Johnson; and as a leader of the National Housing Conference,
she contributed directly to the development of national housing
policy. In her work for the United Nations and in India, she helped
formulate strategies for guiding urban growth in developing countries.
As a faculty member of Harvard University and then, together with her
husband, Dean William Wilson Wurster, of the University of
California, she shaped the thinking of a generation of students in
city and regional planning. Her continuing concern for the social
purposes to be served by urban development did much to direct the
attention of the planning profession to the unresolved issues of social
policy in urban America.

 Although Catherine Bauer Wurster was an important contributor
to the scholarly literature of urbanism, her career focused primarily
on programs, policy, and action. The papers in this book were
commissioned in the hope of carrying forward this spirit in her work.
Their common purpose is to explore the choices open to us in planning
and building tomorrow's urban environment. None are memorial
essays in the sense that they review past achievements or summarize
the current state of knowledge. Instead, they question trends now
under way and argue for new approaches or for reconsideration of
currently accepted ideas. They share a common assumption that urban
development today poses problems that need to be resolved by means
of public action. In debating possible policies and their consequences,
they follow the pathway that Catherine Bauer Wurster explored. In
one of her last essays she wrote:

 Modern metropolitan trends have destroyed the traditional concept of
 urban structure, and there is no new image to take its place. Blind forces
 push in various directions, while urban environments are being shaped
 by decisions which are neither based on any real understanding of cause-
 and-effect nor geared to consistent purposes. But the problems are steadily

mounting, and all levels of government are called in to solve them. Public actions and expenditures of many kinds play an ever-increasing role in shaping the urban and regional environment. But the problems cannot be solved piecemeal by *ad hoc* decisions unrelated to any clear consensus about public purposes. Costly conflicts must be resolved, alternative directions identified, and the nature of the big choices, which tend to come in packages, thoroughly understood.[1]

This book, then, is an exploration of possible urban futures and the choices that would have to be made to bring them into existence. As we move into the greatest period of city-building that this country and the entire world have ever experienced, we know that the world of the future will be an urban world. The authors represented here address themselves primarily to issues of public policy and action that will influence the character of this world. They approach the task initially in a critical frame of mind, questioning and evaluating the way we are now managing urban growth. But they move beyond criticism to propose new goals and, perhaps more important, new strategies that will advance us toward these goals.

These strategies are developed by dealing with specific issues of urban development, all of which were of major interest to Catherine Bauer Wurster. Lisa Peattie and Charles Abrams propose new policies for coping with housing problems of the poor. Abrams turns his attention also to the special housing needs of low-income Negroes and to relationships between housing patterns and race. Thomas Pettigrew focuses more directly on the problems of the Negro as the most critical issue confronting American cities today. Edward P. Eichler evaluates and rejects a favorite solution that has been proposed for meeting the housing needs of growing urban populations: the development of planned New Communities by private investors. Lowdon Wingo, Jr., explores the links between urbanization and economic growth in developing countries. Norman Beckman examines the changing role of government in managing urban development in the United States. Finally, Britton Harris suggests a process by which planners and the public may explore developmental alternatives and jointly invent the future metropolis.

In the first of these essays, Lisa Peattie reverses the usual flow of

[1] Catherine Bauer Wurster, "The Form and Structure of the Future Urban Complex," in Lowdon Wingo, Jr., ed., *Cities and Space: The Future Use of Urban Land* (Baltimore: John Hopkins Press, 1963), pp. 73–74.

technical aid by considering what the United States can learn from developing countries about ways to meet the housing needs of low-income families. Drawing on personal experience gained while living in squatter housing in Venezuela, Mrs. Peattie finds that the less developed housing arrangements of Latin America serve the low-income immigrant population better than our own more tightly organized cities. Despite the low physical housing standards of the barrios of Caracas—recognized as such by the residents—she finds considerable optimism to exist and concludes that these are "slums of hope." In contrast, the slums of American cities, with their higher housing standards, are often "slums of despair."

These differences result in large part from the complex role that housing plays in the lives of the poor. Housing is not always a high-priority item for people struggling to establish themselves in the city. Housing *standards,* in particular, are often less important than other considerations. The squatter housing that people are able to provide for themselves in Latin America meets several important needs. It provides a familiar social environment. Its location offers access to city opportunities. As a form of home ownership, it provides a source of economic security. With no fixed rent to pay, the squatter has considerable flexibility in his limited and uncertain resources: in times of reduced income he can curtail his building activities, rent part of his house, or even sell it to raise funds. The process of piecemeal home building enables the squatter family to acquire construction skills which it can use to enter the urban labor market.

The more tightly regulated American city does not allow for such informal solutions to low-income housing problems. In designing housing policies, however, Mrs. Peattie argues that we should build in more sensitivity to the same needs for easy access to jobs and services, flexibility in budgeting, and economic security. Recognizing that morale is influenced by a range of social opportunities, not just housing conditions, we should move beyond preoccupation with housing standards toward housing policies that will strengthen other opportunities for the poor. As illustrations, she notes the importance of keeping housing costs down, rewarding rather than penalizing extra income-producing effort by families in public housing, facilitating home ownership and housing improvement by low-income residents, and providing supporting services together with housing improvements.

In a related paper, Charles Abrams questions the rigidities that have
become built into housing policies in the United States and proposes
a program of home ownership for low-income people. Federal urban
programs still reflect very strongly the conditions and assumptions
of the 1930's and the compromises made at that time. These policies,
he argues, have not yet been revised to cope successfully with current
problems of race relations, the deterioration of central cities, and
the limited fiscal capacity of these core cities to meet the pressing needs
of their low-income populations.

Abrams challenges several preconceptions that underlie present
housing programs: that home ownership is risky and unwise for
low-income families; that there is always a wide gap between what the
poor can afford and the cost of decent housing on the private market;
and that Negroes, in particular, are always forced to pay too high a
price for private housing. To substantiate this, he cites information
from a recent study he conducted in Philadelphia. With the exodus
of large numbers of middle-income families from the city, housing
prices have fallen to the point where a large number of old houses on
the private market, in move-in condition, are available to Negroes
and whites for less than $5,000. Many low-income families could afford
to own these houses with only limited assistance from a public program.
Nevertheless, the Philadelphia Housing Authority has proceeded to
buy many of these cheap houses, invest heavily in elaborate renovation
that prices them beyond the means of the poor, and rent them under
their public housing program. Abrams contends that the result has
been to ignore an important opportunity for change and, instead,
to establish a permanently subsidized, permanently supervised, and
permanently dependent tenantry. He urges, instead, that federal and
local housing officials undertake ongoing studies of current conditions
of housing and use this information to revise existing policies. [As
this book goes to press, Congress has enacted new legislation to
authorize a low-income home ownership program and other innovations
in federal housing policy, reflecting several of the changing conditions
and priorities that Abrams has noted here.]

To many analysts of urban affairs, the overwhelming urban problem
in the United States today is the problem of racial inequality.
Thomas Pettigrew's paper approaches this subject in a perspective
that illustrates the current broadening of urban development policy

beyond the physical environment of the cities. In blending physical planning strategies with other policy proposals and in proposing strategies
on a metropolitan-wide basis, this paper follows directly in the line of
Catherine Bauer Wurster's work on racial issues. Writing in 1963, she
posed prophetic questions about racial patterns in urban areas:

> Will the restrictions of the housing market continue to force most low-
> income and minority households to live in the old cities, whether in
> successive blighted areas or in heavily subsidized public housing projects?
> Will the Negroes use their rising political power for greater integration
> throughout the metropolitan area or for separatist strength within
> the central cities?[2]

Pettigrew stresses that the great migration of American Negroes to
the cities has had both positive and negative results. He examines
problems of police-community relations, housing, employment,
and education and proposes a number of short-term and long-term
remedies. In the case of police-community relations, Pettigrew
calls for improvement in police training, in procedures for handling
citizen complaints, and increased recruitment of Negroes for the
force. Long-term solutions, however, will require changes in housing,
employment, and education, and these are the main subjects of the
paper.

The limited and inadequate housing supply available to Negroes
results from several interacting causes, including: discrimination in the
sale and rental of housing, leading virtually to separate housing
markets for Negroes and whites; a general shortage of housing for
low-income families; and widespread suburban exclusion of Negroes
and the poor. Pettigrew argues that to counteract these forces, new
housing strategies must be metropolitan in scope; must be related
carefully to other components of urban structure, mass transit, education,
and employment opportunities; and must provide satisfactory conditions
for interracial exchange.

In analyzing employment problems, Pettigrew notes a growing split
within the Negro community between those who are making significant
economic progress and the great majority who are slipping further
behind white income levels. His proposals are directed at bringing
the lower two thirds, "the other Negro America," into the economic
mainstream. As with housing, the remedies must be metropolitan-wide,

---

[2] *Ibid.,* pp. 85–86.

systematic, and mutually interactive. They include national policies to maintain a tight labor market and to provide governmentally financed employment where necessary, creation of metropolitan job councils, strategically patterned legal action to eliminate job discrimination, reform of the welfare system to provide work incentives and encourage family stability, and improvements in public transportation linking Negro communities to suburban job centers.

Finally, Pettigrew presents, in detail, the case for school integration as a national educational goal. He reviews the evidence of social scientists in support of school integration as a way to improve academic achievement, ameliorate racial prejudice in the early years, and prepare children to live in the interracial world of the future. In formulating integration strategies, he distinguishes between "small ghetto" and "big ghetto" situations. In cities with small Negro populations, such devices as redistricting, pairing schools, and locating new and larger schools outside the ghetto can often cope successfully with school segregation. For the major cities with very large Negro ghettos, Pettigrew proposes a metropolitan school park plan in which the central city and one or more suburbs would jointly develop a school complex serving a racially balanced population. This proposal is a particularly vivid illustration of the close connection between the spatial pattern of metropolitan development and the social issues that confront us today.

Many critics of urban development in the United States have turned to planned New Communities as a solution to the shortcomings of suburbia. In contrast to suburbia, New Communities are seen as a way of providing housing for a balanced population—including low-income groups and Negroes—and as a way of building a more varied, stimulating, and attractive environment with a full range of services available in every community. Edward P. Eichler's article reports the findings of a study of over forty large New Communities being developed by private investors. All these communities are being planned and built with a view toward both applying the best current standards of design and including a combination of residential, commercial, industrial, and public facilities together with many features not normally found in new suburbs. His findings constitute a severe reappraisal of the merits of New Communities as a solution to urban development problems.

Although there clearly are a number of community builders who accept the challenge to provide a viable alternative to suburbia, Eichler concludes that their finished projects will be virtually indistinguishable from the traditional suburban pattern surrounding them, except perhaps for their greater array of recreation facilities. The reasons for this conclusion read like a condemnation of the contemporary American institutions and values that shape urban life. No single government has the power to give New Communities a separate identity by enfolding them in greenbelts or to infuse them with jobs by directing industrial location. Demand for houses in New Communities comes almost exclusively from families with incomes over $8,000 a year who value planning only insofar as it promises to screen out all undesirable neighbors. Undesirable neighbors are defined as low-income, particularly black, families and noxious industries. The profit-seeking investor must acquiesce to these desires, in spite of initial good intentions, especially since past experience shows that the risks of building a New Community are high, the payoffs come only many years after the land is first acquired, and the eventual rates of return on massive outlays of capital are very modest.

Eichler argues that if New Communities were to be built in great numbers, they would only exacerbate racial and class separation. Further, like suburbs, New Communities would be built at high unit cost and low density to accommodate market demand. As a result, the prevailing suburban pattern would continue. Eichler contends that the federal aid now authorized for New Community development will not materially change this picture and will benefit only the landowner, the developer, or the middle- and upper-class residents. He suggests that a possible justification for federal aid would be the support of development corporations to undertake technological experimentation in providing public facilities within New Communities.

Eichler concludes that present New Communities are not only unexciting but, even worse, irrelevant to contemporary urban problems. His evaluation of privately built New Communities should prompt a reconsideration of the public benefits that might be achieved by this type of development.

Lowdon Wingo, Jr., writes of urbanization in developing countries, particularly of the relationship between central planning and local and regional development. On the basis of Latin American experience, he argues against relying exclusively on central planning for national development. His essay examines the major links between patterns of urbanization and economic growth: internal migration flows, private investment patterns, and the creation of public infrastructure. He describes each link, analyzes interrelationships among them, and concludes that much more reliance must be placed on semiautonomous local and regional planning or "subnational development" if continuing economic gains are to be made.

This conclusion arises from several considerations. First, the prevalence of a single, dominant, "primate" city in most developing countries will persist for sound economic reasons. Two development factors mutually reinforce the growth of this single city. Improved agricultural productivity will free a seemingly endless labor reservoir, and public and private investments made in the dominant urban area will continue to attract these laborers.

In spite of the advantages of a primate city, in time it will begin to act as a drag against rapid national development. A point is reached where further investments in public infrastructure are uneconomic. This is particularly true since improvements in public goods and services appear to accelerate population growth and to raise demand for even higher service standards.

Although there is no satisfactory evidence to support claims for an optimum size of city, Wingo is convinced that an urbanization policy which supports the growth of several cities, each of which is involved in a healthy competition for its share in the national economy, would benefit total national growth. There is some movement in this direction in Latin America. The continuing reliance on central planning, however, resulting partly from tradition and partly from severe limitations of trained personnel, has retarded almost every regional economic development program.

Wingo concludes his paper by calling for basic reforms in governmental institutions to facilitate the development of capable regional and local governments charged with subnational development responsibilities. More fundamentally, however, competent national and regional administrative groups must be educated and equipped with detailed information about the nature of interdependent patterns of urban growth and economic development.

Norman Beckman's essay focuses on the changing structure of

government in urban areas of the United States. He notes that the role of government is often slighted in current literature on urban problems. Yet this role is a vital one for resolving conflicts in urban development, for equalizing social and economic opportunities, and for protecting public interests. The most apparent feature of urban government has been its fragmentation into many independent decision-making units, with a consequent dispersal of responsibility for urban policy and with formidable problems of coordination. Beckman's paper, however, also analyzes governmental change in the broad context of forces tending toward centralization of decisions as well as the more evident trend toward dispersal. He describes many coordination efforts which have been obscured and many adjustments to enable governments to cope more effectively with urban problems.

Beckman identifies three sets of trends toward dispersal of decision making in urban government and countervailing forces toward consolidation. The first of these is the great proliferation of separate federal aid programs for urban development, offset in part by efforts to coordinate them through metropolitan planning, state offices of local government, and consolidated city development agencies. A second fragmentizing force has been the separation of government administration into specialized program and professional channels; this separation has been countered in part by various forms of federal interagency cooperation and program linkages. Finally, lack of state involvement in urban affairs has encouraged a dispersal of decision making to local units; this trend is increasingly offset by the reapportionment of state legislatures, by emerging federal-state-local relationships, by state constitutional reform, and by increasing state aid for urban development.

The emphasis in Beckman's review is not on sweeping restructuring of government but on pragmatic adaptations to handle changed responsibilities or to cope with new problems. Beckman suggests that the evolutionary path toward governmental reform is producing important results. He proposes further changes—greater fiscal equalization, development programs on a metropolitan basis, metropolitan organization of political parties, and greater public use of the private sector—for guiding urban development in accord with public policy.

The essay by Britton Harris dissects the planner's inability to cope with the mounting problems of metropolitan growth and recommends a new type of planning to invent the future metropolis. Harris draws a distinction between "nonplanning" problems, such as billboards and auto junkyards, and planning issues having to do with the total organization of the metropolis and with the separation and distribution of functions within it. While the former can be handled by means of regulation, solutions to true planning problems must begin with extremely explicit definitions. In fact, Harris argues, part of the planner's inability to solve problems of the metropolis can be traced to a continuing inability to define them with sufficient precision.

Harris points out the need for a new social science which will recognize that history is shaped by the constant shifting of public values under the pressure of new ideas. Therefore, it would be hopelessly inadequate to continue projecting past trends in order to identify emerging urban problems. Instead, the new social science should blend the rigors of the scientific method with a humanistic understanding of social values in a system for identifying future problems and inventing their possible solutions. This new science, by drawing on the strengths of several disciplines concerned with the urban environment, can help innovate workable value systems with the full participation of an increasingly aware public. These value systems, in turn, can be translated into imaginative social and physical alternatives to our present cities.

Although Harris explicitly avoids a full discussion of the implementation of plans, he points out that any inventive process must control the short-run gain aspirations of private investors, adapt decision rules to recognize a pluralistic society, and, above all, be based on a more complete understanding of metropolitan dynamics.

Harris cites three approaches which must be blended in the process of invention: willingness to be utopian; the habit of sketching many future alternatives; and the discipline of a guiding set of concepts, or master plan, to provide a framework for the selection of alternative futures. Further, the invention process must recognize the uncertainty of the future and be continuous. It must, however, offer not a series of sequential choices but rather the big choices of total future patterns. It must accept constant trade-offs between the present exploitation of resources and their preservation for future generations. The consequences of alternative plans must be assessed through careful benefit-cost studies and the results disseminated for public debate in order to make reasoned choices possible.

Planning would then become an activity requiring close identification with the values and objectives of society, powerful means of analyzing alternatives, and creativity to imagine future possibilities and to organize interaction with other professions and the public. Thus, the invention of the future metropolis would proceed as a partnership of environmental experts with a pluralistic public.

It is striking that all these essays call first for a fundamental exploration of public attitudes and values, only then paralleled by revised professional methods and techniques. This is directly in the spirit of Catherine Bauer Wurster's philosophy of effective action: that urban policies must be based firmly on a realistic understanding of people's current and emerging needs and a willingness to meet them. Only then can we expect to reshape the urban world for the better.

1.

Social Issues in Housing
Lisa R. Peattie

The person who has had occasion to discuss some topic with anthropologists is likely to have encountered that exasperating comparative ploy to which anthropologists are prone. He starts to discuss with them a particular social phenomenon and finds the ground suddenly shifted under him; all at once he is discussing something else—like the first situation in some ways, but different from it in others. He raises the subject of what to do about American teen-agers, and finds himself hearing about puberty rites among the Kwoma.

As an anthropologist, I shall run true to form. I want to set forth what I see as some issues in housing in the United States by considering housing in a very different sort of social situation, the cities of the developing countries of Latin America. I shall discuss Latin American slums and try to use an analysis of those slums as an intellectual lever for prying into some aspects, which I believe want investigation, of our more sophisticated slums.

The concept of a "slum" seems to be, actually, a rather complex one containing, in somewhat unclear relationship, elements of land use, density, building condition, and social attributes of people. The *American College Dictionary* defines a "slum" as "A thickly populated, squalid part of a city, inhabited by the poorest people." In an earlier, less sophisticated age, this relationship between people and building seems to have been thought of as a kind of natural state of congruence of species and habitat. A slum was the way that the lower orders lived. As slums began to be seen as a "social problem," the slummy state of the lower classes came to seem less inevitable. In one view, which might be identified as the "coal in the bathtub" school of thought, the slumminess of the buildings was seen as produced by the slum residents. A high school civics textbook in use in the thirties gave as one of the obligations of immigrants to the United States that "they should not crowd themselves into unsightly slums." Liberal thought turned the relationship around, regarding the poor immigrants as forced into and deformed by the slums. The reversal gave us the movement for slum clearance, which has been struggling against fearful obstacles ever since.

In any case, all agree that a slum is not just a state of buildings but a state of people as well, and that there is some important relationship between the state of the buildings and the state of the people. To some commentators, the nature of this relationship appears obvious. A recent paper states, "The effects of overcrowding, squalor, filth and other aspects of slum housing on family welfare are well known. Poverty, bad housing, family breakdown and social disorganization form an all too familiar vicious circle."[1] Yet, I would maintain that despite the clear visibility of a correlation between poor, crowded housing, poor people, and other sorts of "social problems," the dynamics of the relationship still want looking at. Indeed, I believe that despite a good deal of relevant research, most of the questions as to the nature of the relationship raised by Catherine Bauer Wurster more than a decade ago[2] are still unanswered. A look at the slums of Caracas does not answer those questions and perhaps raises others, but it may be a way to begin the discussion afresh.

SLUMS OF HOPE IN CARACAS

The slums of Caracas are far worse physically than the slums of Boston or New York. Something over a fourth of the population of the city live in ranchos—shacks of wattle and daub, of boards, of tin, even of flattened boxes, usually with thin sheet-aluminum roofs. During a quarter-century oil boom, Venezuela became transformed from a nation two-thirds rural to a nation two-thirds urban; and during that rush to the cities, the capital grew fastest of all, trebling its population in a single decade. New migrants to Caracas, a city squeezed between mountains, crowded themselves onto every patch of vacant and undefended land. Some ranchos have beautiful sites. The Barrio "Child Jesus" is a neighborhood which spreads over hills and broad valleys at the west end of the city, and the air blows clean. Others are jammed into airless pockets. In the Barrio "Ear of Corn" at the other end of Caracas people are living—some of them paying rents—in shacks packed as densely together as physically possible on both sides of a narrow valley; at the bottom a small slowly running stream carries the waste which drains into it from all those dwellings, and the entire settlement is pervaded by an unspeakable odor of sewage. Other ranchos are clustered together under bridges; you may not even notice their presence until you happen to see a child carrying a loaf of bread duck down and disappear under the viaduct. Last spring I noticed that some enterprising families had built in masonry under

[1] Astrid Monson, "Slums, Semi-Slums and Super-Slums," *Marriage and Family Living,* Vol. 17:2 (1955), p. 118.
[2] Catherine Bauer, *Social Questions in Housing and Town Planning* (London: University of London Press, 1952).

one of the elevated superhighways, creating a sort of tiny, multistory dwelling under the traffic. In 1965 the housing expert of the Joint Center for Urban Studies project in Venezuela walked out of his glass-walled Caracas living room into his garden and, looking down, saw that a man was constructing a rancho just below him on a narrow strip of land next to the drainage canal. When the housing expert's children climbed down to investigate, the rancho builder sent back with them a gift of limes, as from one neighbor to another.

Some ranchos are in better locations than others, and some are better constructed than others, but they are almost without exception below any adequate housing standard, not only to the middle-class observer but (and I think this is important) to their residents. They are generally too small, they are generally poorly constructed, and they are built in locations and under circumstances which tend to ensure that they will be lacking what we hopefully call minimal services. Since an electric line is relatively easy to string, up- or downhill, these lines do make their way into the barrios, and it usually does not take long for the people farther up the hill to tap the lines below them. Water is more difficult. If the terrain permits a road on which trucks can pass, the rancho dweller is lucky, for this means that the water truck can come by and—if the truck gets there, if the supply is not exhausted in the early part of the route, if the rancho dweller is at home, and if he has the money to pay—he can buy water to fill his fifty-gallon water drum. There may be a jerry-built system of public water spigots. The nearest spigot may be far away, and women may have to pick their way up or down narrow steps or earth slopes to carry water. Sewage lines are almost nonexistent. A garbage collection truck would be exotic. Since the ranchos are generally built on the steep slopes rejected by regular builders, the very earth on which they perch is an inadequate base; every year when the heavy annual rains come, the rancho dwellers pick their way up and down slithery clay, and every year numbers of ranchos simply become detached and slide down the hills.

The circumstances which have produced the rancho settlements of Caracas are those characteristic of developing countries. The ranchos are the product, on the one hand, of a lag in the development of institutions relative to need. They have sprung up in a nation which is unable to enforce the edicts it periodically issues against irregular building and which lacks the public or private institutions for planning, financing, and building regulated, low-income housing. They express also the unbalanced economic development pattern typical of developing nations. There is a sharp rise in productivity and in wages in the narrow, developed sector and a focusing of economic activity and of public services in the city, which makes it an irresistible magnet. At the same time urban unemployment runs at levels unthinkable in the United States—28 per cent in Caracas in 1961.[3] Those rancho dwellers in Caracas are perching uncomfortably on their hillsides to participate in a vast urban shape-up for jobs. In this shape-up, they stand a good chance of losing out.

The rancho settlements of Caracas are, then, slums in which people are suffering from a rate of unemployment probably greater than that in Watts, while living in physical conditions far worse than Watts. It is somewhat of a shock, then, to find morale a great deal better. A recent writer says, "[the ranchos] are not expressions of despair, but of hope and activity and courage."[4] One finds in these slums, says another writer, a strongly developed "sense of personal freedom" and a "common belief that the road for social and economic advancement is open."[5] A survey carried out in 1963 found only 32 per cent of a national sample of rancho dwellers regarding their situation as worse than it had been five years previously. A substantial majority, 69 per cent, expected it to be better in five years more. An even higher proportion (87 per cent) believed that children of today have greater opportunities for advancement than those of earlier times. Those rancho dwellers had a sense of open opportunities which is quite astonishing: 85 per cent thought that "any capable person" might become an owner of a large enterprise; 89 per cent thought that "any capable person" might become a lawyer; 90 per cent thought that "any capable person" might eventually occupy a high government post.[6] One day when I was lending a hand on a self-help sewer construction project in a particularly unattractive Caracas barrio (board shacks on bare earth, and 1,200 children without a school), I was struck by the fact that residents to whom I spoke gave such self-improving reasons for moving there. The commonest were to own their own

[3] Foreign Area Studies Division Special Operations Research Office, The American University, *U.S. Army Area Handbook for Venezuela* (February 1964), p. 54.
[4] Emrys Jones, "Aspects of Urbanization in Venezuela," *Ekistics,* Vol. 18:109 (December 1964), p. 424.
[5] Talton Ray, "The Political Life of the Venezuelan Barrios," unpublished manuscript.
[6] Centro de Estudios del Desarrollo, Universidad Central de Venezuela, *Estudio de Conflictos y Consenso,* Serie de Resultados parciales (Caracas: Imprenta Universitaria, 1967).

homes and to exercise better control over their children than had been possible in the multifamily dwellings of the central city.

THE CONTEXT OF HOUSING

The rancho dwellers of Caracas, then, have extremely bad housing, but they experience this bad housing differently from the way the slum dwellers of Boston experience their bad housing. It is important not to summarize and dismiss this difference as a "difference in values" which makes the rancho dwellers "not care." The rancho dwellers of Caracas also value good housing. They demonstrate it by improving their housing as rapidly as they can. The tin or pressed-board wall gets replaced by one of concrete block. Rooms get added on. The concrete block gets plastered. The plaster gets painted. The windows get covered by an ornamental metalwork grille. A little garden is enclosed at the front. The shack has become a *quintica,* a workingman's version of the rich man's luxury housing or *quinta.* All this has to be done in spare time with the money extracted from a small income subject to out-of-work stoppages and personal emergencies, and it may take many years. But when you look at any Caracas barrio which has been long established (and in the Caracas context, long means on the order of twenty years), the process is manifest through a stratigraphy which, as in archaeology, expresses evolutionary change through time by sequence of levels and forms. At the bottom of the hill the dwellings are plastered and painted masonry; just above come rough block walls; at the top are the board and tin shacks. To climb the hill is to run a developmental history backwards.

It seemed to me that the members of the Venezuelan working class, once established, housed themselves astonishingly well considering their incomes. I do not consider this evidence of the sudden appearance of a new value on housing, but I believe rather that good housing was something which they appreciated even in the stage when they were living in ranchos. But then it was a value they could not practically satisfy.

The difference in attitude toward housing is, then, not a difference in values per se, so much as it is a difference in relevance and context. The rancho dwellers would like to have good housing, but they are willing to put the satisfaction of that value aside while they try to satisfy some other more pressing values.

A house is a machine for living—a place for eating and sleeping and talking to friends and making love and sewing clothes and helping children with their homework—but it is also an aggregation of resources. People's resources are limited. At any given time they must deploy them as well as they can to solve the problems which are for them at that point most pressing. Sometimes other problems are more pressing than having an agreeable home, and people put that off. During the years my husband and I were in graduate school, we lived in several striking slums. Although I found it unpleasant to have to put on an overcoat to get up at night to nurse the baby, this appeared to be the price which I had to pay for us to continue studying. It was not that my values set studying above comfort at all times and places, but for that time, that selection of priorities seemed appropriate.

The first point, then, which seems to come out of the comparison between the Caracas slums and the American slums is that housing must be thought of in its whole social context. It is not merely that "other cultures" and other styles of life are reflected in other kinds of housing preferences; it is that preferences as to housing themselves gain or lose salience depending on the terms set by the social situation in which people are trying to make their lives. For housing experts and for some planners, housing is always a central issue; for some people housing is and must be a peripheral issue. Particularly, it is true that housing *standards* are in many situations a peripheral issue; other aspects of housing may be more important.

The comparison also suggests that people's sense of mastery and satisfaction is likely to be less strongly affected by the quality of their housing per se than it is by other factors which may be associated with a particular kind of housing. A distinction has been made between two kinds of slums: "slums of hope" and "slums of despair."[7] The Barrio "Child Jesus" in Caracas is a "slum of hope"; Watts is a "slum of despair." The housing in Barrio "Child Jesus" is vastly inferior to that in Watts. Indeed, the point has been made, in categorizing areas of poor housing as "slums of hope" and "slums of despair," that there is likely to be an inverse correlation between housing quality and social morale. A typical "slum of despair" is the urban "gray area" in which once-good housing is being occupied by poor people, and in which it is said that "the neighborhood is going down."

---

[7] Charles J. Stokes, "A Theory of Slums," *Land Economics*, Vol. 38:3 (August 1962), pp. 187–197.

The shacks of the hopeful entrants into the urban economy are typical "slums of hope"; their occupants are people who feel that they are going up. It is not the housing which makes the difference; it is the thrust of the social forces affecting its residents or, at any rate, the way they perceive those social forces. In Watts the housing is not so bad, but everything conspires to make people feel (realistically) that in occupying those houses they are being trapped at the bottom of society.

HOUSING AND ACCESS TO OPPORTUNITY

A consideration of the Caracas squatter settlements points up, further, that a house, besides being a place to live, is a base of operations. The most rudimentary ranchos are hardly more than that. When the squatter first sets up his framework of poles and lays over them a few sheets of corrugated roofing, he is hardly creating a dwelling; what he is doing is staking a claim—a claim to be there, to sit in at the urban-industrial game. For this squatter, housing standards are much less crucial than access to opportunity. Peter Marris has made this point with great clarity in his study of the social consequences of central-city redevelopment in Lagos.[8] When the Nigerian government decided to rebuild the center of Lagos, a main focus of the project was the elimination of the eyesore represented by the shacks of the poor— the people who, as in Venezuela, had been drawn into the margins of the urban economy, subsisting by various kinds of occasional and low-paid labor and commerce. When the shacks were taken down, the residents were offered housing which was greatly superior from the point of view of housing standards, neat little low-rent masonry houses with basic services. But this new housing, even though low-rent, was not low-rent enough for many of those people, and, worse still, it was on the outskirts of the city. In all the technical skills and social *expertise* needed to survive in the labor markets of Lagos, the people of the shacks were at the margins. Now they were physically at the margins, too. To be moved away from the center, where the income opportunities were, was enough to push many of them right to the edges of possibility. Their housing standard had been improved, but they had been dealt an overwhelming or almost-overwhelming blow. The case of Watts makes this point, too. Watts is a "slum of despair" partly because it is isolated; it does not give adequate access to

[8] Peter Marris, *Family and Social Change in an African City: A Study of Rehousing in Lagos* (London: Routledge & Kegan Paul, 1961).

opportunity. Either its people should be closer to the jobs, or an efficient low-cost public transit system should put the jobs within reach.

The case of Caracas, the case of Lagos, and the case of Watts make the same point. What the people at the bottom of the system need especially is not so much better housing as a better chance. They need a way of getting close to good jobs and good schools and the other things which make up social opportunity. It is easy to pass over this point when considering other factors going into housing strategy—on the one hand, the problems of getting low-rent housing provided at all in our tight institutional structure and, on the other, the financial problems of the central city and the cost of social services to low-income people—but the point is clear enough. Social policy should not focus on housing standards but rather on provision of opportunity through housing strategy.

UNCERTAINTY AND BUDGET FLEXIBILITY

The Latin American squatter settlements suggest another element in the housing situation which can easily take precedence over housing standards. This is resource maneuverability. In discussion of housing need, we often use figures of ability to pay based on a standard percentage of income. Such figures quite inadequately represent the level at which a fixed expenditure for housing should be allowed to bite into many people's incomes. This kind of figure may serve very well as an index of ability to pay for some sorts of people with regular incomes and regular lives. It works well, for example, for the kind of middle-class families in Park Forest who, as Whyte suggests,[9] really prefer to buy on time payments so as to regularize their monthly expenditures. It does not work well for the sorts of people who populate the squatter settlements of Latin American cities. A recent study of rancho dwellers in Bogotá,[10] for example, found that the rancho inhabitants had for the most part left much superior housing in the same city for their shacks. From the point of view of standards, this was a step down so striking that the writer refers to it as "de-urbanization"; at the same time, rather to the writer's surprise, the people of the ranchos appeared satisfied with the trade. Their

[9] William H. Whyte, *The Organization Man* (New York: Doubleday Anchor Books, 1957), p. 356–357.
[10] Charles Barstow Turner, Jr., *Squatter Settlements in Bogotá* (Bogotá: Bogotá Centro Interamericano de Vivienda y Planeamiento, 1964).

satisfaction was based primarily on their escape from the burden of city rents.

Rent is a fixed expense which locks individuals in. In New York and in Boston, as well as in Caracas and in Bogotá, there are people who need very badly not to be locked in by rents. A woman interviewed in New York as part of an evaluation of a rehabilitation project there[11] expressed in her interview the same theme which appears in the Bogotá study. She likes the physical improvement, but her income is so undependable that the rent increment, small as it is ($13 a month), frightens her. This tenant is a sewing machine operator. "My job is very peculiar," she says. "It's seasonal. Sometimes I'll make $6 a day, sometimes $15 a day; sometimes I am laid off for two weeks. I have to make sure my money is spread out, otherwise I'll starve. When I collect unemployment, I get $22 a week. I figure $45 to $50 per week year around average. I don't work full time. I had a stroke a few years ago and I have to take it easy. I can't run to my children every time I need money."

People who sell minimal skills in a labor market oversupplied with unskilled workers, people whose physical strength is precarious, people who want to spend chunks of time doing nonpaying things like painting or sculpting or writing or bumming around have the same kind of problem; they must be able to survive layoffs. They must have a style of life which allows retrenchment and maneuverability of income. They have to have some way of hanging on in the city through periods of unemployment, while awaiting the next dollop of income. A substantial rent makes it impossible to retrench effectively. It makes it difficult to maneuver. The people at the bottom need maneuverability even more than the economically established do. Thus, those at the bottom—who in our system frequently pay a much higher proportion of income for rent than the middle class—should, by and large, be paying the lowest proportion. In a society like that of Venezuela, where the people at the bottom have to do a tremendous amount of balancing and maneuvering to get along in the city at all, there are numbers of people whose housing cost should really be zero. The squatter settlements make this arrangement possible.

---

[11] Richard Bolan *et al.*, Project to evaluate New York Rent and Rehabilitation Administration Low-Cost Housing Demonstration Project (Cambridge: Joint Center for Urban Studies of M.I.T. and Harvard University; New York City Housing and Development Administration, LIHD No. 3, unpublished data).

HOUSING AS SECURITY

The figures on percentage of income for housing pass over another important consideration. This is the question of whether the payments are going into rent or ownership. If we are thinking of the "housing problem" merely as a problem of providing people with places to live, it is not crucial whether those places are owned or are rented by those who live in them. But if we think of the "housing problem" as part of the whole problem of deploying resources to handle a given situation in life, the difference between rental and ownership can be extremely important.

One of the writers previously quoted as identifying in the Venezuelan barrios a "sense of personal freedom" and a "belief that the road for social and economic advancement is open" goes on to attribute this general sense of potency and optimism to the fact that in the Venezuelan barrios a large proportion of the shacks are built and owned by the residents.

The lack of acute concern with social inequalities is also the result of the special characteristic of barrio living—that people have "property." A ranchito is a man's private house and it rests on land that he considers to be his own. He can convert it into a dancehall and paint it orange and black to attract customers. With money he can construct a sturdy block home, and if space permits, add rooms as the family grows. Or, if he needs cash he can sell all this and move on.

The spirit created by this freedom for improvement and expansion is vastly different from that which is characteristic of the slums in the industrialized cities of more developed countries. There, working class families live in buildings which belong to absentee landlords and pay high rent for shabby quarters. Physical improvements have to wait for the landlord's initiative and tenants are evicted at his discretion. The psychological effect of this relationship on families who are not able to enjoy the advantages of a developing economy is well known.[12]

The sense of potency and optimism in the Venezuelan ranchos is all the more notable since, in almost all cases, the ownership in question does not extend to the land on which the houses are built. Most rancho owners are "squatters," occupying land which they do not own and which would not be for sale to them if they were to try to buy it. But ownership of a dwelling—or of other improvements such as fences or fruit trees—is not dependent on ownership of the land where the improvements stand. More than that, ownership of land,

[12] Ray, "The Political Life of the Venezuelan Barrios."

in custom if not in law, becomes very rapidly established through use. Rights to plots of land in the form of title to the improvements on the land are in fact bought and sold all the time. The limits to the sense of ownership are set not so much by the formal legal situation of a given plot or barrio as by the amount of pressure exerted by the government to state its claim against the rancho owner. There are barrios in which rancho owners are subject to pressure from government agents who tell the people that they should not repair their dwellings, much less add to them, since they are where they have no right to be. In such barrios, the spirit of "freedom for improvement and expansion" cannot develop. In many other barrios, the government has in effect decided to cede its claim, to let well enough alone, and to allow people to live as if they were owners. In such areas, the question of legal ownership becomes moot, and people build, buy, sell, and rebuild real property without regard for the legal niceties of land title. They act and feel like owners.

The possibility of home ownership at a very low level of income has more than just psychological consequences; it has important economic and social ones as well. In the Venezuelan barrio I know best—and where, for three years, I was myself the owner of a rancho built on municipal land—I became interested in people's use of house ownership as a means of consolidation.

Once someone gets into the city and enters the modern economy—once a man, for example, gets a job as a laborer with the steel mill or the oil company—he has got himself a toehold. But it is a precarious toehold. He is perpetually in danger of losing it and of dropping back into the great mass of workers struggling to find a place in a society which cannot open up new opportunities fast enough to give places to all the recruits coming in. His next task after getting started is to find a way to consolidate his grip on the new system. There seem to be two basic consolidation strategies: acquisition of skills, and investment and capital accumulation.

Some individuals succeed in their own lifetimes in acquiring marketable skills which give them a base of security. The man across the street from me in my barrio, for example, had started as a laborer with the United States Steel subsidiary and had learned on the job to be an electrician; by the time I knew him, he had a foreman's job in the steel mill. Another way is a kind of two-generation process in which one manages to hold on just enough to see that one's children get through school and get established at a level above the unskilled mass. This pattern I saw also in my barrio.

The consolidation of mobility through acquiring skills, especially when it takes place over two generations, is often supplemented and supported by the alternative pattern of consolidation by investment. The investment strategy is quite general; it would be a mistake to suppose that people with minimal income do not invest. One takes one's earnings, especially the earnings which come in the form of lump sums for annual bonus or termination pay, and starts some sort of small business. Invested in this way, savings will not necessarily make much of a profit. The small shops begun in this way seem to flourish in a context in which the opportunity cost to the entrepreneur is virtually zero. But at least they will not be dissipated in immediate consumption or in helping out struggling friends and relatives, and to be a business owner, even at the tiny scale at which business runs in the barrio (five shops for less than five hundred poor people in mine), is to give oneself a sort of position in the community.

A special kind of investment is house building and owning. To build a house for oneself is to acquire permanent capital. There is a character in one of E. M. Forster's novels who says, "We all stand on islands of five hundred pounds a year." To own one concrete-block house in a working-class barrio is not to stand on an island of any great size, but it is *a* place to stand, a sort of rock on which to perch. Many people in my barrio had extended their base by becoming the owners of several houses. One of the most respected men in the community, for example, had worked "for the companies" for some years but had not had a wage-labor job since the Iron Mines Company released him at forty years of age; he may have derived a small profit from selling beer to those who came to play pool on a battered table in his shop (although I am not convinced that this enterprise did better than break even); his main source of income was the rent from three houses he owned in town. During the time of my residence in the barrio, several people built houses there specifically for rental. House ownership is, then, a way in which people at the bottom can acquire capital and a social base.

House ownership probably has both economic and psychological functions in the social mobility and social consolidation processes which go into urbanization and industrialization. In a study of social mobility in nineteenth-century Newburyport, Stephan Thernstrom quotes a New England newspaper of 1856: "The man who owns the roof that is over his head and the earth under his dwelling can't help thinking that he's more of a man though he had nothing, with poverty upon his back and want at home; and if he don't think so, other people will."[13] Thernstrom points out that "property mobility" through home ownership was of very considerable importance in converting what had been in Newburyport an unskilled, often illiterate, proletarian class, mainly migrants from New England farms and Irish villages, into something quite different.

By 1880 the undifferentiated mass of poverty-stricken laboring families, the "lack-alls" who seemed at mid-century to be forming a permanent class, had separated into three layers. On top was a small but significant elite of laboring families who had gained a foothold in the lower fringes of the middle class occupational world. Below them was the large body of families who had attained property mobility while remaining in manual occupations, most often of the unskilled or semiskilled variety; these families constituted the stable, respectable home-owning stratum of the Newburyport working class. At the very bottom of the social ladder was the impoverished, floating lower class. . . .[14]

This description seems to fit very handily what is happening in Venezuela now.

HOUSING AS ECONOMIC OPPORTUNITY

In nineteenth-century Newburyport and in Venezuela today, housing had another function which seems to have nearly disappeared in our own present-day society. To see this function requires looking at housing from a different point of view, from the standpoint of production as well as of consumption. From this standpoint, as a business, housing is still tremendously important in our economy. But our housing business is organized differently from that of Venezuela, and in its difference of organization serves somewhat differently. Construction work seems to be a classic route into the labor market in developing societies. It is a way of earning and of learning salable skills. House building requires a high ratio of labor to capital; it involves skills which are relatively easy to master; in a society like Venezuela it is practiced in a decentralized, small-group way which makes movement up from

---

[13] Stephan Thernstrom, *Poverty and Progress: Social Mobility in a Nineteenth Century City* (Cambridge: Harvard University Press, 1964), p. 164.
[14] *Ibid.,* p. 158.

skill level to skill level relatively easy. Shortly after I arrived in
Venezuela, for example, I met in Ciudad Guayana a man building
a house for his family who, five years before, had lived on a farm
in the Delta and had known no trade but farming. Coming to the city,
he had gotten a job as an unskilled construction laborer. By the time
I met him, he considered himself a skilled mason. He believed that
in a year or so he would be ready to be a contractor in his own right.
A contractor in that setting needs not have either capital or substantial
bookkeeping *expertise*; all he requires is the technical and organizational
skills involved in putting together a house of concrete blocks.

UNITED STATES COUNTERPARTS

In respect to this particular social function of housing, the comparison
between the Latin American rancho settlements and the low-cost
housing of the United States points out how we have organized some
possibilities *out* of our society and suggests with regard to the whole
comparison between Caracas and the United States a rather odd
generalization. The generalization is this: The evidently wretched
standard of housing in the rancho settlements masks certain benefits
which the rancho residents derive from the inadequacies of
organization which helped bring about that low standard. In the
absence of social institutions which would solve his housing problem
for him or help him with it the rancho builder must use his small
resources of skill and capital to solve his housing problem by individual
effort; acting so, he is not able to build much of a house. But, from
his freedom to maneuver as an individual in this area, he derives
some considerable advantages. The socially mobile individual can use
the possibilities of ownership and improvement as ways of tightening his
hold on the development escalator. The nonmobile individual benefits
by the possibility of a no-rent housing solution which leaves him maximum use of his even narrower economic resources. It is some of this
freedom to maneuver that we have organized out of our major cities.

In some ways, our institutions do less well in serving the people at
the bottom of the ladder than do the "less developed" institutions of
the Latin American countries. Our general level of housing standards
is better, but standards, I believe, are not as relevant to the people
at the bottom as are some other aspects of housing: housing as a
means of access to opportunity; housing at costs such as to make
income maneuverability possible; house ownership as a means of

economic and social consolidation; house construction as a path of entry into the skilled labor market for the unskilled worker. All these requirements the rancho settlement satisfies quite neatly. In our more tightly organized cities it is much more difficult to produce a solution of such flexibility. There are only occasional and partial parallels.

As a college student, I had an experience with something like the Caracas barrios in an American setting when I took part in a survey of people living in trailer camps in Chester County, Pennsylvania. The war was on, and Chester was a shipyard town bursting at the seams with war workers. The overflow had spilled out into a series of trailer camps outside town. The trailer camps were depressing enough to look at: public water taps and electricity were the public services offered; living quarters were cramped; when it rained, the trailers sat glumly in the mud. There was some concern over the unfortunate trailer residents, and our survey was the result. I can still remember clearly the sense of surprise we felt at finding that most people in the trailers, while not altogether delighted with their style of life, and certainly with no intention of keeping it up forever, still found it distinctly preferable to paying high rents for crowded apartments in town. This way, they were at least saving money against the war's end. It was a little like the ranchos, without the possibility of improvement and increasing equity.

Later, as graduate students, my husband and I occupied an actual rancho for several years in Chicago. Here was a situation in which, supposedly, public policy had long organized rancho building out of possibility; this one just slipped through the meshes. A few blocks from the University of Chicago, Mr. Hrapek, owner of a decaying four-story brick building, built for some friends of ours, poor-as-churchmice students, a rancho in the back yard of his house. We inherited this rancho when our friends moved on to the University of Kansas. Lacking a building permit, Mr. Hrapek had done construction in the guise of repairing a toolshed, which was later carried out, board by board, from the center of the completed dwelling. The foundation was of bottles set in concrete. The walls and roof were of boards covered with tar paper, and they were thin. When time came for us to move and we unscrewed a loudspeaker we had mounted on the ceiling (for want of other space), we could see clouds through the screw holes; and once in the winter when I left off mopping the kitchen floor for an hour, I had, on my return to the job, great difficulty in detaching the mop from the wall, to which it had frozen fast. Mr. Hrapek's shack offered certain daily-life challenges, but its very low rent gave me, in compensation, the financial leeway for a master's degree and a year off work to enjoy a first baby. On the other hand, it must be admitted that, as a solution to the student housing problem, Mr. Hrapek's shack had its evident defects. These defects were both of adequacy of standard and of the possibility of generalization—of use of the solution on a large scale. There are good reasons why the city of Chicago does not allow the building of ranchos, and why one of the first things which happened when the University neighborhood underwent redevelopment was the razing of Mr. Hrapek's anomaly.

REFOCUSING PUBLIC POLICY

Mr. Hrapek's rancho and the trailer camps are isolated North American instances of housing solutions in something like the Latin American rancho style. But they have to be atypical. There is no use pining after the rancho-building squatter settlement solution to the low-cost housing problem in American cities—even if it were a better solution than it is. Our cities are organized in a way which makes that sort of solution generally impossible for us. We are committed to solving our low-cost housing problem within our own institutional context. Thus we must leave the topic of what the poor do for themselves in a society which leaves them to cope with their housing problem individually and turn to the question of what our kinds of institutions can do for the poor. What the Caracas comparison does is to point up some of the things we should be getting our institutions to deliver.

By and large, I think it would be generally agreed that, as things now stand, the people at the bottom are not well served by our institutions, either public or private. Lacking money and lacking political power, the people at the bottom are without adequate means of shaping either category of institution to their needs. As Charles Abrams and others have cogently pointed out, urban renewal programs aimed at "slum clearance," ostensibly in the interest of the poor, have frequently operated directly counter to the interests of the low-income tenant because other needs which the programs were to satisfy conflicted with the needs of the poor and operationally took precedence over them.

Another set of difficulties evidently inhere in our rather complicated ideas about what it is proper for government to do. It can subsidize farmers through a variety of price-support programs and can, unchallenged, build roads for automobile owners to drive on. But only with great discomfort do we entertain the idea of government providing goods or services directly to individuals. Thus, programs of public housing and rent subsidy are undertaken grudgingly and hemmed about with elaborate regulations and procedures designed to determine "need." Our discomfort with such programs has also led us to design some of them in such a way as to stigmatize the recipients. The drab design of public housing projects seems to serve functions somewhat similar to the unbecoming orphanage uniforms of an earlier generation. The peculiarities of the American context in this respect may be suggested by comparing our policy with that of the Swedes, who appear to handle housing very nearly as a public utility.

It also seems likely that the failure of middle-class people to focus clearly on the housing needs of the poor, to see what is involved in "making it" at the bottom, is one basis for the inadequacy of our institutions designed to satisfy those needs. For middle-class people are in a position to demand different sorts of things from their housing. Housing is much less directly tied to job locations; not only can the salaried worker better afford to commute, but his ability to get the job is less directly tied to being on the job spot. He has his channels of communication and influence built up through his personal and professional contacts; he may use the house to be near *those*, which may be far from the work place. With a stable and dependable income, he can more readily commit himself to fixed expenditures for rent. The middle-class individual, while perhaps finding house ownership a convenient means of handling capital, has in his skills and social position another sort of capital which may make the home less crucial as an aggregation of wealth than it would be for the just-established workers. If he does any building, it is to practice a recreational hobby, rather than a job skill. On the other hand, for the middle-class individual the standard of housing, not only in comfort but also in appearance, becomes much more salient and indeed becomes a crucial part of the handling of his social role.

Besides that, it appears to be a tendency for many of the most civic-conscious of the middle class, precisely in that they *are* civic-conscious, to regard the whole city rather as an extension of their own social world: to treat the city as though it were their own larger living room. The "public image" of the city is important to them. They speak of the slum dwellings as "blight" on the community, rather than as bad, overpriced housing for the families who live in them, and they speak of "improving neighborhoods" as if a neighborhood could be identified with its buildings. In this context, "slum clearance" or "neighborhood rehabilitation" can easily become a sort of cleanup campaign managed by the middle classes which sweeps away poor tenants along with the local eyesores. This sort of focus can make rehabilitation and renewal efforts shape up as rather more sophisticated and long-lasting versions of the system which, I am told, is used in Addis Ababa to clean up the capital's streets when a foreign delegation is in the offing: a truck drives about the city collecting all beggars and deposits them in a barracks outside the city.

When one adds to the factor of difference in intellectual focus between the poor and those who dominate the housing institutions all the practical difficulties involved in producing low-cost housing under present conditions and all the varying social, economic, and political interests which enter into any program concerning urban housing, it is not remarkable that the needs of the poor often seem to be lost to sight.

The first step to make our institutions serve the housing needs of the people at the bottom would appear to be a clear recognition of some simpleminded facts. Most people who live in slums do so because they cannot afford better housing. Their basic trouble is poverty, not poor housing. They need better housing, but they also need better health services, better food, better education. If our institutions have the effect of raising housing standards but make the poor pay the costs in increased rents, we are doing the poor a dubious service. Whatever name we give to what we are doing—"renewal," "rehabilitation," "improvement"—if it forces the poor to live beyond their limited means, if it forces them to pay for a certain standard of housing whether or not they wish to do so, we are making poverty more of a box than before.

Everyone knows this, of course. It would seem unnecessary to state these obvious facts, except that they seem so often to be forgotten. I note, for example, that the large and imaginative public program for doing away with slums proposed by a committee recently formed under the sponsorship of the Commission on Religion and Race of the National Council of Churches talks only of new building and of

rehabilitation and their cost magnitudes.[15] It is an exciting thought
to suppose that we might decide, as a nation, to foot the bill to do
away with slum dwellings. But then what? Does this mean that all
housing will be kept up to some minimum standard by public policy
at public cost? If public policy is to underwrite the replacement of the
slums, will any part of the cost be paid by the building owners or by
the tenants? And how much of what we call the slum problem is in fact
a physical problem? How much is a lack-of-opportunity problem?
If we rehabilitate the ghettos, does this mean they still remain ghettos?

Our public policies will have to deal with such questions. If they do
not, our urban poor will be at the mercy of private institutions which
can push low-income tenants beyond the reach of urban opportunity
as effectively as any federal bulldozer project pointed to by the foes
of urban renewal. Indeed, one year when I was helping a group of
M.I.T. graduate students try to develop an "advocacy plan" for a
low-income neighborhood in Cambridge, the students began to feel
that a sort of rehabilitation-and-improvement strategy for the area might
transform it into one suitable for the professional staff of the adjacent
universities and research centers and thereby displace the low-income
people whom they had taken as their "clients." The group joked about
helping keep the area slummy to hold rent levels down and concluded
that only considerable public intervention to produce and protect
low-rent housing in the area would make it possible for the poor to
stay there.

If we want the poor of our cities to live at "decent" housing levels
and if, in some cases, we may even want to protect their chance to be in
reach of the centers of opportunity, we will evidently have to underwrite
their chances. Why not? The underwriting of opportunities is a policy
to which our public institutions have been committed for a long
time. I think merely that it is important for us to consider our public
policies and institutions relating to housing in such a way as to make
sure that we are underwriting opportunities, not being custodial. I
think we realize that our policies in this area have been too niggling and
too stigmatizing. In the context of our political and social institutions,

---

[15] Steering Committee of the Pre–White House Conference, Commission on Religion
and Race, *A Strategy for the Next Stage in Civil Rights: Metropolitan Development for
Equal Opportunity* (National Council of Churches, 475 Riverside Drive, New York,
December 1965).

some of this is probably inevitable; for example, it is probably impossible for us to subsidize housing in such a way as to make possible for some individuals (as the Latin American rancho settlement solution does) an "abnormally" low rent. But I think that we could provide the programs and policies to keep rent levels down so that families can have a greater proportion of disposable income, to reward instead of penalizing income-producing extra effort by public housing tenants and their children, to make possible new creative approaches to house ownership and housing improvement by tenants at the low-income level.

The recent Model Cities legislation seems to be an attempt to make possible, within the existing framework of our kind of institutions, a more flexible approach to the problem of the slums. It attempts to shift the focus of policy from housing per se to a more general packaging of services relevant to the city dweller, to make possible a series of programs particularly tailored to local conditions, to work in a framework giving a greater degree of expression to the needs of low-income people, and to develop institutions within which ownership of housing by the tenants becomes more possible at a below middle-class level. We do not know how this legislation will turn out in practice, but it does look like a more flexible way of working.

This legislation, at any rate, has grown out of a somewhat new direction in thinking about what public policy should do for urban people. It is the beginning of an attempt to treat housing in its whole social context and to attend to what that social context is.

I have merely brought forward the rancho settlement–American slum comparison to suggest what a useful direction this may be for thinking and planning. I believe it is a direction which we will have to pursue further. We will have to shift from a focus on buildings to one on people and social institutions and social trends, from a focus on housing standards to one on housing needs, to one which treats housing not simply as an economic and social material, but also as an economic and social resource. And then we will have the sizable job of designing and creating the institutions which will do what needs to be done.

Until we have done that, let us not be too sorry for the Latin Americans—or at any rate, let us not commiserate over their rancho settlements until we have constructed out of our more sophisticated institutions a housing solution of equal flexibility.

2.

Housing Policy—1937 to 1967
Charles Abrams

The mid-1930's produced some well-defined theories about the slum and the housing problem, some of which were carried over from England, some spawned in the settlement houses of New York, and some originated in Congress. What emerged was a composite which could be summarized as follows: The slum is a building that is old, decrepit, and lacks essential amenities. The best way to get rid of it is to tear it down. As it goes down, so will the rate of TB, crime, and delinquency. The new units built should be in self-contained projects large enough to create their own environment; otherwise, the adjoining slums will overtake them. The dwelling units in the projects should be rented to the qualified poor, who cannot afford to own their own homes and would be better off as tenants of a public overseer. When a project family's income goes up beyond prescribed limits, the family should be asked to go elsewhere. Projects should be built to minimal standards and at limited cost per room. Otherwise, they would be too good for the poor and would compete with private enterprise. The projects, just like schools or roads, should be owned perpetually by public agencies; only the public agency can deal with the problems of poor families, keep them from "putting coal in their bathtubs," and keep them prompt in their rent payments as well as clean and well-behaved. The public housing authorities owning the projects should be independent entities, removed from the corruptive influences of Tammany and its counterparts in Boston and Chicago.

When these theories were formed, the Negro problem had not yet arisen, so that when President Franklin D. Roosevelt referred to the "one-third of a nation" that was ill-housed, he was referring to an economic, not a racial group, and a group that was predominantly white. Moreover, public housing had been spawned as a stimulus to the building industry; not until 1937 did it shed this motivation and acquire a social purpose. By that time, the housing illuminati were fed up with the way Harold Ickes had been tackling the housing program, and they fought to have it turned over to the cities, which they felt could do the job quicker, cheaper, and better than his federal bureaucracy.

There was objection by the stargazers of the period to the rigid cost and income limitations of the new units, to the low physical standards prescribed for the projects, and to compulsory slum demolition. But they had no choice except to compromise; it was all thought to be an experiment anyway. In retrospect, I believe that the compromises that

were made in the 1937 debate on the public housing measure lastingly
impaired it and will ultimately contribute to its demise. In many
cities, slum elimination reduced, equivalently, the supply of housing
available to the slum dweller and raised the rents of remaining slums.
In new units, income limits made tenure uncertain, forced out the
families who contributed leadership to community life, and made the
projects way stations instead of communities. The low income limits
also brought a larger number of Negro families into the projects,
creating racial imbalance in the neighborhood schools. Cost limits,
coupled with the generally higher expenses entailed in public building
operations, necessitated cutting standards and emphasized massiveness
of structures instead of livability.

There were other consequences which could not be foreseen at the
time. Substituting local control for federal control speeded operations
and got rid of the supercautious Mr. Ickes, but it destroyed what might
have been an opportunity to build public housing in suburbs as well
as in the cities. Also, the feeling that projects should be self-contained
influenced the building of extensive building complexes. The public
housing program resulted in demolition of a considerable number
of houses owned by low-income families, many of whom preferred
ownership even if it meant owning a substandard home. As public
ownership of projects increased, even the friends of the program began
to dread the idea of a monolithic landlord who might ultimately own
all the shelter available to the nation's low-income class.

Soon public housing began to lose popularity. The number of white
applicants declined. Neighborhood opposition to public housing made
site selection more difficult. In New York State appropriations under
the state program were voted down by the electorate. That the federal
program survives today is due less to its general popularity than to
the support it has received from the official housing agencies, from the
backers of urban renewal, and from the Wall Street investment houses
which have been floating its tax-exempt bonds.

SOCIAL VERSUS ECONOMIC PURPOSE

There were other housing programs which were adopted at about the
same time as public housing but which lacked even a semblance of
social motivation. Their objective was solely to revive the building
industry and the private mortgage market. These programs included the

Home Loan Bank System (set up a few years before the New Deal), the Federal Housing Administration, and later the Veterans Administration housing program and the Federal National Mortgage Association. The philosophy behind them was that the mortgage market was the mainstay of private building operations and that it was in the national interest to keep mortgage money flowing even to the extent of pledging the full faith and credit of the federal government to mortgage lenders. With the same motivation, the federal government assured the savings and loan associations of liquidity, insured their depositors against loss, and bought up sour mortgages totaling more than three billion dollars from lending institutions.

The mortgage market, however, did not generally operate in areas occupied by poorer families, so that the very generous aids provided were not shared by the families who needed help most. For instance, the FHA guarantee did not reduce interest rates on homes, nor was it felt that it should. Under FNMA, mortgage-lending institutions were assured of a federal bail-out of their mortgage paper, but this was of no benefit to lower-income families, nor was it intended to be. FHA permitted builders to make fortunes without staking a penny of investment, but as one high FHA official put it, "FHA is a sales tool for realtors."

The feeling in Congress was that social welfare was not the purpose of these housing programs, that a line should be drawn between social and economic purpose and that the economic purpose agencies should not get involved with the nation's social obligations.

As the years went on, and as the federal udder became more widely accepted as the main source of housing credit, other beneficiaries sought suction from it—colleges, speculators, mobile park owners, war veterans, tract builders, privately sponsored cooperatives, and nursing home entrepreneurs. Hardly a segment of the housing industry was excluded from the federal benefits.

URBAN RENEWAL

Urban renewal, spawned in 1949, is in a class by itself. It is a hybrid creature both public and private, profit and nonprofit. Its target was the city slum which, it was felt, could be torn down and replaced with a paying enterprise by the private builder if only the land cost were subsidized. As originally conceived, the slum would be demolished and the cleared land resold at a bargain price to the builder, while public housing would provide the alternative shelter for the displaced slum dwellers.

Urban renewal is like a lady with a past who has been unable to live it down. Her early sins consisted of large-scale displacement of Negro families, inadequate relocation of the evicted families, the ousting of small businesses, and the demolition of buildings whose sites have never found buyers. Though the lady sins less often and has recently demonstrated some creditable virtues, her past excesses continue to be cited with remorseless irrelevance.

Contrary to the original intention of its congressional sponsors, urban renewal has veered in its motivation from slum clearance to city regeneration. It is now reclaiming downtown store areas, building middle- and high-rent housing, getting industries to stay in the cities, drawing back those that have left them, and getting new ones to come in. This shift in emphasis has paralleled a recent concern about the plight of cities by the President, by Senate committees, and by the big-city press.

While urban renewal is helping a number of cities with some of their problems, it is not meeting the main problems and is even diverting public attention from them. The cities are in deep financial and social trouble. They can no longer afford to educate and train their underprivileged, support their unemployed and elderly poor, police their streets, mend their sick, or operate their courts, jails, utilities, and garbage plants. The reason is simple. A city's tax jurisdiction ends at its borders. As long as it grows within these borders, generating more tax-paying sources and increasing its revenues, it can remain solvent. But when more of its good taxpayers leave and a poorer population enters, revenues decrease, and costs simultaneously rise. This forces the city to borrow more, which in turn adds to its maintenance costs. Taxes are raised to meet these maintenance costs, further accelerating the exodus of its paying customers. But an urban society in which there is freedom of movement and which sees thirty-five million people moving annually from house to house, city to suburb, and state to state, including millions of poor people in search of a better education and life for their children, cannot put up a "No Entry" sign as many suburbs have done. The metropolis must remain a free port open to all and must be equipped to educate the nation's poor as well as pay the soaring costs of city life. It cannot do this, however, under theories devised for a nineteenth-century economy. The United States has successfully weathered the shift from an agricultural to an industrial society but has not coped with the urban revolution that came in its wake.

FINANCING CITY GOVERNMENT

The cities need federal support for what have become federal responsibilities. Poverty is a national problem. Migration is of interstate origin. The Negro problem which entailed federal intervention in 1861 should be no less a federal concern a century later.

Congress, the courts, and the President acknowledge the existence of a federal welfare responsibility, but the laws and the federal appropriations do not. The tendency in Washington is to place increased fiscal burden on the cities by originating new, and doubtlessly needed, programs such as welfare and old age assistance, housing, urban renewal, and the war on poverty. But most of these programs require contributions from the cities which they are in no position to make. Meanwhile, the federal government ignores the growing costs of public education, street maintenance, garbage removal, policing, and the soaring wages of city personnel, although these burdens are also the by-products of the shift to an urban society.

Among the reasons for federal reluctance to assume this housekeeping burden is that the central city no longer wields the political power it did fifty years ago. With the shift to the suburbs of the more politically vocal citizenry, the cities are losing important support for both congressional and state urban legislation. Moreover, while 70 per cent of the people today live on only 1 per cent of the land, many Senators represent people who live across the wide, less populated, stretches of the nation. The Senators from Montana or Idaho are not likely to lose sleep over Boston's 11 per cent tax on real estate or be inclined to pump extra money into Philadelphia, Newark, Cleveland, or Detroit because they have especially difficult problems caused by the influx of the Negro poor. So too, the seniority system often puts control of legislation in the hands of Congressmen whose prime concerns are not in the cities.

One result of this is that while the city's social problems and its educational needs, pensions, and payrolls are rising, its springs of revenue have been drying up. A generation ago, municipalities were

collecting more taxes than the national and state governments
combined. Their take, 52 per cent of the total in 1932, had dropped
to 7.3 per cent by 1962. In 1902, the combined net revenues of federal,
state, and local governments were less than $1.4 billion, but by 1964
they exceeded $158 billion, of which the federal share was then
more than two thirds. On a per capita basis, local debt between 1946
and 1964 rose from $13.6 billion to $68.4 billion, while federal debt
increased from $269 billion to only $312 billion. In other words, on
a per capita basis, local debt in that period rose from $97 to $357,
while federal debt actually decreased by about $300.

Although federal revenue has been steadily increasing, it has not
been effectively used to solve the problems of the cities. It is recognized
that the deteriorating schools of cities have been an important cause
of poverty and of the flight to suburbia, but there is still no sign of
real aid to city school systems. Up to 1965, only about $1.3 billion
of federal funds were available annually for education of all kinds in
rural, urban, and suburban areas, and the big cities got only a small
fraction of this small appropriation.

Direct federal aid to cities for housing and community development
was only $400 million in 1963 compared to $7.7 billion spent by
the Department of Agriculture. Yet the nation is now about 70 per
cent urban.

In short, a real renewal of our central cities calls not simply for the
demolition and rebuilding of a few bits of urban real estate but for the
demolition of outmoded concepts and for the rebuilding of fiscal
formulas so that they make sense for an urban society. This means a
direct assumption by the federal government of a major share of the
growing costs of education and other urban operations. It means that
the federal government may have to levy those taxes which neither
cities nor states can effectively levy without inviting a taxpayer exodus.

REVISING FEDERAL HOUSING PROGRAMS

Our thinking on the housing problems of cities is no more enlightened
or more current than our programs to finance city government. We
have overemphasized the importance of federal housing programs as
the redeemers of cities and, at the same time, have accepted existing
programs that are often obsolete and irrelevant to the situations
of many cities. They are a mixed bag of tricks accumulated over the last
three decades, some of them having been ushered in because of the

energy of a particular pressure group, others because some bright lad in the Department of Housing and Urban Development or a Senator's office thought up a new politically palatable appendage to current legislation. There is a reluctance to discard what has been won, a fear of introducing anything that is bold and new, and a tendency to try to suit everybody in the effort to gain approval of an appropriation. There is little disposition to concede that a particular idea has seen its day, and if a good program happens to be offered by the wrong man from the wrong party, it becomes taboo to the party in power.

One of the consequences of this situation is that the cities tailor their programs to the categories of federal aid available, irrespective of their particular needs or circumstances. The federal programs may be irrelevant or unsuited to the situation of a city, but money is money and has an inexorable magnetic power. I can best illustrate what is happening by a case study I recently made for the city of Philadelphia.

Philadelphia, like all older cities, has a mixed inventory of housing. Unlike cities such as New York and Chicago, but similar to most other cities, it has a large supply of one-family dwellings. The main types of housing available to its moderate- and low-income families are as follows:

1. New three-bedroom houses that can be bought on terms for about $12,000
2. Good, relatively new, houses in Levittown or its equivalent which can be bought on terms for about $10,000
3. Public housing built at a cost of about $22,000 per unit
4. A good supply of older row houses in move-in condition which could be bought at prices of $2,000 to $5,000.

The significant aspects of this situation are the inordinately high cost of public housing, the reasonable cost of new and relatively new housing, and the amazingly low cost of good, older housing.

If houses in move-in condition can be purchased for $2,000 to $5,000, as I found to be the case, it is manifest that the houses should be made available for ownership by low-income families and that an appropriate federal program should make this possible. With a down payment of $100 and a 5 per cent twenty-year mortgage, a $3,000 house would entail a monthly cost of $40.89. A $4,000 house with a $200 down payment would cost $60.27.

This finding flies in the face of everything congressional committees have declared; it flies in the face of HUD policy and even the policy of Philadelphia officialdom. It opens a new opportunity for the poor which federal programs do not offer them. If my findings in Philadelphia are applicable to other cities, it should effect a revolution in housing policy.

How can I explain the phenomenon? It can best be explained as follows: Houses are not relatively homogeneous commodities like packaged bread or bananas. Unlike the relatively stable price of an item of food, available to all in any store, the price of a home is influenced by location, which can affect its value far more than the amount of the cubage or the cost of the brick and mortar. However justified, the fact is that middle-class families move from neighborhoods when the schools become predominantly Negro, and when they do, the housing market may become glutted, bringing a sharp drop in prices.

It is simple economics that the price of a house in Philadelphia or in Watts is determined not by the replacement value but by the capacity of a family to pay for it. If the potential buyer earns only $3,000 a year and can afford no more than $60 a month in carrying charges, the net profit on the house would be about $300 or $400 a year, and that house should be worth no more than $3,000 to $4,000. If the only bidders for the houses are Negroes and Puerto Ricans who have lower incomes, this will be reflected in even lower house prices.

The second reason for the depressed prices is the lack of an institutional mortgage market for this type of property. This absence prevents people with little cash from buying houses. When they do buy them, it is from a professional who purchases the houses for cash and resells them at twice the price with a nominal down payment.

A third reason for the depressed price level is the unpopularity of this type of investment among people with capital looking for rental property as an investment. Compensation is inadequate if one considers the problems of management. An owner in a section rented to minorities is often labeled a slumlord; he is hated and subjected to an excessive amount of cavil from the city officials, whose crusades make good copy. If the property is vacant, it is more apt to be vandalized, making it difficult to insure, and, in turn, impossible to mortgage.

THE CASE FOR HOME OWNERSHIP

Unquestionably, slums, bad neighborhoods, lack of social services, and poor and segregated schools exist, but public housing and rent subsidies are not the only answers. The Administration should have the curiosity to inquire into new programs, such as the possibility of home ownership, and the courage to concede the irrelevance of other existing programs. Theories, however, die hard, particularly when engraved into official policy. That there is a nation-wide gap everywhere and at all times between what the low-income family can pay for shelter and what private enterprise offers is one theory which has shown great survival power. It is true for new housing, good housing in suburbs, and housing in the better sections of cities. It is true also where a housing shortage exists, as in New York City. But, because of the exodus to the suburbs of many white families since the census of 1960, I suspect that it may not be true today in many other cities. Baltimore and St. Louis are two examples.

A second theory is that Negro families pay more for their housing than whites and get less for their money. This, too, is true in some cases. It is true where Negroes are in desperate need and either can afford or are forced to pay premium prices for houses. It is not true in sections substantially vacated by white families, where the supply exceeds the effective demand.

A third theory that has gained immortality is that no poor family should ever be helped to buy a house; both risk and expense are too great. This theory was first propounded by the public housing group in the thirties and was valid when families put their life's savings into ownership, bought subject to short-term mortgages, and paid high interest and bonuses for second mortgages. This is not comparable to most current transactions in which the risk extends to a nominal down payment but where there is a potential profit to be made if the house value rises. I suggest that we created a good part of our middle-class in the 1930's and 1940's by inducing them to go into mortgage debt at the right time. It might not be a bad idea to give the Negro family a similar opportunity today.

Home ownership is not a panacea for poverty or race friction, but it does free the family from dependency upon a landlord and gives the poorer family something it can call its own—some pride in possession and a better stake in the community. And the fact is that a majority of American families prefer it and a large proportion of Negroes already own their homes. In Philadelphia some 35,000 Negro families became home owners between 1950 and 1960. I noticed that, where ownership existed, the blocks had been improved and the general neighborhood advanced in status and condition. If the carrying costs of ownership are equal to or less than rental, as they would be in Philadelphia, the risk is no greater to the mortgage holder than it would be to the owner, and the stake risked by the family is nominal.

PHILADELPHIA EXPERIENCE

Instead of initiating a home ownerhip program, however, the Philadelphia Housing Authority, with the blessing of the Housing Assistance Administration, proceeded to a program under which many of the same houses that could have been bought for a few thousand dollars and resold, without major improvements, to poor families were substantially altered and rented to these families under the public housing program. Instead of houses for sale at $2,000 to $5,000, the total cost of each house rose to more than $12,300, thus making tenancy the only alternative for low-income families.

I sought the reason for the $12,300 cost of houses and found it in some twenty-six pages of Housing Authority specifications. A good oil heater, for example, had to be replaced by a gas heater; all wallpaper had to be removed irrespective of its condition; unless walls were crack free, new plastering was mandatory; drywall was unacceptable; roofing had to be renewed and existing shingle roofs reshingled, even if recently redone; all wood trim had to be of one type or style; kitchen and bathroom floors had to be covered with asphalt tile free of irregularities, even when there was good vinyl. In short, each house had to be gutted, regardless of its condition. The result was a permanently subsidized, permanently supervised, and permanently dependent tenantry.

In recommending ownership, I do not dispute the need for other programs such as the building of new housing on vacant lots or the substantial rehabilitation and rental by the city's housing authority of vandalized and deteriorated housing. This type of housing is costly and will have to be subsidized. But I deplore the tendency to spend hundreds of millions of dollars simply because there happens to be a federal program that provides the money.

NEEDED: CURRENT LOCAL PROFILES

It might be contended that Philadelphia is a special situation. It seems incumbent on HUD to determine whether it is or not. It seems likely, however, that other cities (Baltimore and St. Louis, for example, but not such cities as New York, Chicago, Detroit, and San Francisco) which have had a similar flight of white families may also have experienced a collapse in the prices of good houses that now make it possible for the Negro and other poor families to purchase them.

There can be no sound debate in Congress on housing without a fresh study of current local situations. And by a study I do not mean a Senate hearing of experts before TV cameras. Nor will the applications under the Model Cities Program reveal the situation, for the tendency will be to get the maximum federal subsidies possible under the legislation regardless of specific need. It is essential that each city be profiled in the context of its own environment and its own current requirements, and HUD should authorize these profiles without delay. When the studies are completed, they can provide the pieces in the jigsaw that will disclose the true situation in the nation as a whole.

The federal officials who are making policy at HUD are men of integrity, but they should be curious and courageous enough to re-examine the housing situation as it currently exists. When and if that step is taken, an entirely new program may be indicated. I believe, when the new facts are known, that Congress, too, may have the courage to ignore politics and rise to the occasion.

3.

Racial Issues in Urban America
Thomas F. Pettigrew

Frank Lloyd Wright, when asked once to suggest a solution to the physical problems of a major American city, gestured grandly toward its grimy hills and exclaimed, "Abandon it! Abandon it!"

Many current observers of the same scene are also tempted, in moments of despair, to advise abandonment. In addition to problems of clogged traffic, deteriorating schools, slum housing, rising crime rates, an eroding tax base, and water and air pollution, the increasingly serious racial issues in our cities surely encourage pessimism. The cities, however, have become too essential in our complex society to allow the luxury of Wright's solution. Following Catherine Bauer Wurster's lead, we must, instead, continue the long-term struggle to make urban existence more livable. A substantial portion of our attention must be given over to resolution of the racial issues.

Proposed solutions to the physical difficulties of the cities often revolve around metropolitan planning and cooperation. Standing alone, the inner city simply does not have the resources, financial and otherwise, to mount a sustained attack on such vast problems as traffic, slums, and pollution. This point applies as well to urban America's racial issues. Indeed, the future of race relations in America is directly dependent upon the success of metropolitan cooperation.

THE NEGRO AND THE CITY

In this century the Negro has become an urbanite. Three out of every four Negro Americans today reside in cities, while only one in four did so as recently as 1910.[1] This shift represents a process of massive migration involving many millions of uprooted people. The dimensions and character of this historical process provide the larger perspective within which we must view current racial issues in urban America

Significant Negro migration to the city began during World War I. European hostilities simultaneously provided large war orders for American industry and stemmed the vast tide of immigrant labor, thereby opening up new employment opportunities for those Negroes willing to migrate. Labor recruiters encouraged the process, and young Negroes in vast numbers began what one demographer describes

---

[1] These and other data cited in this section are taken from two excellent review articles, both of which are recommended to the interested reader: Karl E. Taeuber and Alma F. Taeuber, "The Negro Population in the United States," in John P. Davis, ed., *The American Negro Reference Book* (Englewood Cliffs, N.J.: Prentice-Hall, 1966), pp. 96–160; and C. Horace Hamilton, "The Negro Leaves the South," *Demography*, Vol. 1 (1964), pp. 273–295.

as "the greatest and most significant sociological event of our country's recent history."[2]

Not all of this human surge, however, was stimulated by the attractive pull of new jobs; there were significant "push" factors as well. The high birth rate among rural southerners, the mechanization of southern agriculture, the boll weevil, government programs limiting agricultural production, and, finally, the shift of cotton cultivation to the Southwest and West—during the past half-century these factors literally almost starved the Negro off the southern farm.

The migration increased to enormous proportions in the 1920's. The pace slowed during the depression years, but accelerated rapidly again with America's entry into World War II and continued during the 1950's. Between 1950 and 1960, over a million and a half Negro southerners broke their home ties and left the region. More than a half million went to the Northeast, a like number to the Midwest, and over a third of a million to the West. Thus, Negro migration has involved not only a movement from farm to southern city but also a movement out of the South into nonsouthern cities. This wider distribution of Negro Americans throughout the nation has made absurd the time-honored segregationist claim that race relations are a southern problem and should be left exclusively to the South to solve. Now that virtually as many Negroes live outside the ex-Confederacy as in it, race relations are clearly a national concern.

It is a national concern, however, with a strongly urban cast. Today the Negro American is more urban than the white American and is especially concentrated in our largest metropolitan centers. Twenty metropolitan areas, only half of them in the South, contain 40 per cent of the nation's Negroes. Our five largest cities dramatically illustrate the point. Between 1940 and 1960, the central-city nonwhite proportion of the population more than doubled in New York City and Philadelphia and approximately tripled in Chicago, Los Angeles, and Detroit. Today more Negroes live in the New York metropolitan area than in any single southern state, about as many Negroes live in metropolitan Chicago as in the entire state of Mississippi, and more Negroes live in metropolitan Philadelphia than in the entire states of Arkansas and Kentucky combined.

[2] Hamilton, "The Negro Leaves the South," p. 294. Thus, the five deep South states—South Carolina, Georgia, Alabama, Mississippi, and Louisiana—lost 400,000 Negroes through out-migration from 1910 to 1920.

Dramatic as these data are, they systematically understate the mass movement of the Negro American over the past two generations by showing merely the net result of those moving to cities minus those few who move back to rural America. There is, in addition, considerable movement back and forth between cities that does not appear in these figures but which accounts for an increasing proportion of in-migrants. Consequently, if the old stereotype of the Negro sharecropper is outdated, so, too, is the only slightly less dated stereotype of the urban Negro as a raw migrant fresh from the hinterland. The typical pattern is for the Negro to come to a northern city not from the farm but from a southern city. These Negroes tend to be the better-educated Negro southerners, though their educational level is still below that of the typical Negro northerner.[3] In addition, many Negroes migrate from one northern city to another, and these intercity migrants are often skilled and well educated.

The raw-migrant stereotype particularly neglects the growing number of Negroes who were born and raised in cities and have never exprienced rural living. In many cities, natural increase already accounts for a larger component of Negro population growth than in-migration. The urban-born Negro American, especially in the North, is truly the newest "new Negro." He is young, somewhat better educated and skilled, far more militant, and less religious than his parents. He has grown up with great aspirations through a time of promised change and has seen those aspirations largely thwarted. The emergence and growth of this new and unsatisfied Negro segment are the demographic ingredients in the racial dynamite that exists in metropolitan America today.

In the immediate future, American race relations will fuse even more intimately with the city. In 1964, Negro Americans numbered 21 million people and constituted 10.6 per cent of the nation's population; by 1984—to select a fateful year—they will probably number between 30 and 33 million people and constitute about 12 per cent of the nation's population. Most of this expansion will be absorbed by our largest metropolitan centers in the North and West, followed by continued growth of metropolitan centers in the South. The demographer C. Horace Hamilton predicts: "Ultimately, if present migration trends continue, from 75 to 85 per cent of the Negro population will

---

[3] This process leads to the unusual phenomenon of depressing the median Negro educational levels of both the place of origin and the place of destination.

live outside of the South."[4] At any rate, this expansion will mean
Negro majorities in many central cities. Cleveland, Detroit, Baltimore,
and Philadelphia in the North, and Richmond, Atlanta, New Orleans,
and Memphis in the South may soon join Washington and Newark,
where Negro majorities already exist.

Another important projection is the age profile of the Negro
population. With a median age in the early twenties, Negroes constitute
a young group, and the unusually high Negro birth rates from 1948
on, rates that did not level off until 1957, mean that twelve- to
twenty-one-year-old Negroes will be especially numerous from 1969
to 1978. Since riots are often sparked by this age segment, the potential
for urban racial disturbances will remain ominously high for some
years to come. The young Negro age profile also demonstrates the
urgent need for expanded civic services and opportunities, for more
public schools, recreational facilities, welfare programs, housing,
and for a larger labor market. The need far exceeds present plans
for expansion in most of our major urban areas largely because of
costs. Yet these are the social costs incurred by any rapidly growing
and migrating group, costs which the central city alone cannot and
should not be expected to bear. Federal funding at an order of magnitude
not yet envisioned will be absolutely essential. Equally important, this
funding must require metropolitan involvement in order to possess
any hope of success.

From a national perspective, the Negro's move to the city should not
be viewed exclusively in cost terms, for this movement contains many
positive features. It has prevented an uneconomic piling up of
near-peasant Negroes in the South's depressed agricultural areas.
The South, it is true, loses its investment in young migrants who go
North, but at the same time the nonsouthern metropolis adds to
its young, productive labor force. In addition, the shift from farm to
city has been more responsible for Negro gains in income, education,
health, and housing during the past twenty-five years than has the
concurrent reduction in racial discrimination.[5] Finally, urbanization

[4] Hamilton, "The Negro Leaves the South," p. 294. Rates of Negro out-migration
from the South in the sixties have declined from those of the fifties. Nevertheless,
percentages of nonwhites in southern metropolitan areas of less than a half million have
started to decline, in direct contradiction with metropolitan areas of all sizes in the rest
of the nation. Leo Schnore and Harry Sharp, "Racial Changes in Metropolitan Areas,
1950–1960," *Social Forces,* Vol. 41 (1963), pp. 247–253.
[5] Thomas F. Pettigrew, *A Profile of the Negro American* (Princeton, N.J.: Van
Nostrand, 1964), pp. 180–181.

has created a more sophisticated people capable of effective protest, a people more cognizant of what discrimination over the years has denied them and more eager to benefit from the full privileges of American citizenship.

These national advantages would probably outweigh the local disadvantages were it not for the enforced segregation of Negroes into central-city ghettos. Concentrated into blighted and underserviced areas, all of the problems of rapid growth are multiplied for both the Negro and the city. It is this embedded pattern of racial separation that provides the backdrop for the four key racial issues confronting urban America today: law enforcement, housing, employment, and education.

LAW ENFORCEMENT

No one can view urban race relations today without becoming concerned about the administration of justice in general and police-Negro relations in particular. The administration of justice is marred by racial discrimination even in the courts of some of our leading cities. Witness the dramatic racial differences uncovered by Marvin Wolfgang in his examination of criminal homicide in Philadelphia from 1948 through 1952.[6] Among defendants receiving a court trial, 81 per cent of the Negroes were found guilty as opposed to 62 per cent of the whites; for each level of charge, Negroes received more severe sentences, despite the fact that they were more often provoked by their victims and were less likely to possess a previous police record. These data are consistent with other studies on arrests, commitment, parole, and execution conducted throughout the United States.[7]

POLICE-NEGRO RELATIONS

Equally disturbing are the routine relations between police and Negroes in the cities. Strained to begin with, the Negro's interactions with the police are rapidly deteriorating in many of our major cities and in some, such as Los Angeles and Springfield, Massachusetts, have broken down completely. Charges of "police brutality" are made repeatedly, with the term "brutality" referring to police use of racially derogatory terms as well as physical abuse. Negroes are also understandably suspicious when all-white police review boards

---

[6] Marvin E. Wolfgang, *Patterns in Criminal Homicide* (Philadelphia: University of Pennsylvania Press, 1958), pp. 299–307.
[7] Pettigrew, *A Profile of the Negro American,* Chapter 6.

exonerate their fellow officers from all charges lodged against them
by Negroes.

It is not surprising, then, that serious race riots can be predicted by
studying the "police variable"; considerable research confirms this
point. Allen Grimshaw has contrasted the generally poor response
of local police to the nation's major race riots in this century with
the typically efficient response of military intervention. He believes the
key difference is that the police are often seen by Negroes as biased
representatives of the white world, while federal forces are viewed
as racially neutral arbiters.[8] Two major studies of the Detroit race
riot of 1943 clearly document harsh police treatment of Negroes.[9]
The Detroit police, virtually all white, arrested hundreds of Negroes
but few whites and killed seventeen Negroes but no whites. In
general, cities with relatively large Negro representation on their police
force have had fewer race riots in this century than comparable
cities.[10]

Police incidents triggered the 1965–1967 riots in New York City,
Los Angeles, Chicago, Cleveland, and Detroit, and the resulting hostilities
were especially directed at the police. The 1965 Watts riot in Los
Angeles is particularly instructive in this regard. Two years earlier,
a comparative study of police-Negro relations in Los Angeles,
San Francisco, and Oakland conducted by the California Advisory
Committee to the United States Commission on Civil Rights had
noted the typical "storm warnings" before the riot in Los Angeles.
Just as had been described by observers of the 1943 Detroit riot,[11]
the committee discovered in Los Angeles hostile officials, increasing
Negro distrust of the police, mounting charges of "police brutality,"
virtually no communication between the force and the Negro community,
flagrant police use of racially offensive language, and largely segregated
assignments for the few Negroes on the force.[12] It did not require a

[8] Military units are also far more interracial than most police forces. For the general
point see: Allen D. Grimshaw, "Actions of the Police and the Military in American
Race Riots," *Phylon*, Vol. 24 (1963), pp. 271–289. See also Allen D. Grimshaw, "Urban
Racial Violence in the United States: Changing Ecological Considerations," *American
Journal of Sociology*, Vol. 66 (1960), pp. 109–119.
[9] Alfred M. Lee and Norman D. Humphrey, *Race Riot* (New York: Dryden Press, 1943)
and Robert Shogan and Tom Craig, *The Detroit Race Riot* (Philadelphia: Chilton, 1964).
[10] Stanley Lieberson and Arnold R. Silverman, "Precipitants and Conditions of Race
Riots." *American Sociological Review*, Vol. 30 (1965), pp. 887–898.
[11] Lee and Humphrey, *Race Riot*, pp. 114–116.
[12] California Advisory Committee to the United States Commission on Civil Rights,
Police–Minority Group Relations in Los Angeles and the San Francisco Bay Area

prophet to foresee a future police-Negro clash of major proportions in Los Angeles.

The position of the police is not enviable. They must carry out unpopular duties in a hostile ghetto as agents of the white world. They are a conspicuous and available symbol of hated white authority. Conversely, many urban police see themselves as lonely and unappreciated guardians of law and order, increasingly alienated from the larger society, white as well as black.[13] The former glamor of policework has tarnished, pay and promotion opportunities remain relatively poor, competing employment opportunities have expanded, and even the Supreme Court of the United States seems to many of the police to have become procriminal and antipolice. In short, the urban police sense a serious loss of occupational status, while at the same time they view the status of Negroes as rapidly rising.

The ultimate encroachment upon police status is the pressure to hire Negroes on the force. Much like the medieval guilds (especially as they survive today in the building trade unions), our Eastern and Midwestern police forces have served as traditional enclaves of ethnic employment. Ingroup ties have bound the force together, and the ethnic Gemeinschaft has formed the basis for high morale and respect from the wider society. The existence of such kinship and social bonds explains much of the resistance to hiring Negro officers. Even though the efficacy of a racially mixed force is now widely recognized, most cities still have extremely small Negro representation; Negroes comprise only about 3 per cent of the policemen of Detroit, and Los Angeles and even less in such cities as San Francisco, Oakland, Berkeley, and Boston.[14]

Difficult as the assignment of the urban police admittedly is, and no matter how much they may be deserving of sympathy for the squeezed position in which they find themselves, two facts inescapably remain: increasingly tense relations between Negroes and the police are the most accurate storm warnings of impending race riot, and those cities

---

(Washington, D.C.: U.S. Government Printing Office, August 1963); hereafter this is cited as California Advisory Committee, *Police–Minority Group Relations.*
[13] James Q. Wilson, "Police Morale, Reform, and Citizen Respect: The Chicago Case" (unpublished paper, Dept. of Government, Harvard University). Wilson notes that thorough police reform and professionalization during recent years in Chicago have not significantly altered the force's morale and sense of isolation.
[14] Shogan and Craig, *The Detroit Race Riot,* p. 136; and California Advisory Committee to the U.S. Commission on Civil Rights, *op. cit.,* p. 34. The Philadelphia force is notable in this regard, for more than 20 per cent of its members are Negro.

with significant numbers of Negroes on their police forces have had
fewer such upheavals. We cannot, therefore, accept the police force's
threatened point of view.

Furthermore, the police by their own actions often exacerbate an
already-tense situation. Research by William Kephart in Philadelphia
reveals the direct link between personal bigotry and harsh treatment
of Negroes.[15] More than half the city's district patrolmen found it
"necessary" to be more strict with Negro than white offenders. These
same men also harbored the most unfavorable attitudes toward Negro
policemen: they more often objected to riding with a Negro patrolman,
resented taking orders from a "well-qualified" Negro sergeant or
captain, felt there were too many Negroes on the force, and preferred
that Negro policemen not be assigned to their districts.

The ever-present danger in the area of law enforcement is that a set
of self-fulfilling prophecies will spiral among both police and Negroes.
The police anticipate resistance when dealing with Negroes, and
Negroes anticipate mishandling by the police. Each side expects
trouble from the other and acts accordingly. The reciprocal expectations, then, actually elicit the provocative behavior each side predicts
and fears.

REMEDIAL ACTION

This increasingly dangerous spiral of distrust is easier to prevent than
it is to alter once established, but three short-run remedies are often
mentioned: police training, complaint procedures, and Negro
recruitment. Police training, both recruit and in-service, often includes
"human relations" content, but its effectiveness varies directly with
the informal communications and norms about race sanctioned within
the force. If police review boards rarely regard Negro complaints
seriously, if the force is slow to hire Negro officers, if the chief publicly
denounces civil rights protests, then no race relations training ever
devised will alter the actual daily practices of the patrolman. Police
forces are structured hierarchically; only if those in charge desire
changes in this area and direct their subordinates accordingly can
special police training in minority relations prove useful.

Citizens' complaints against the police constitute a critical focal
point. Police review boards and other internal arrangements for
handling such complaints have generally failed to gain public con-

---

[15] W. M. Kephart, *Racial Factors and Urban Law Enforcement* (Philadelphia: University
of Pennsylvania Press, 1957).

fidence, precipitating demands in many localities for civilian review. Although the police uniformly and heatedly reject such demands, seeing civilian review as yet another blow to their status and authority, the goal of public confidence in complaint review procedures can and must be met. For example, San Mateo County, California, has evolved a formal procedure that does not include a civilian review board but has nevertheless gained wide community favor.[16] A review board combining high-ranking police officials and respected white and Negro citizens is also a possibility.

The most important remedy is substantial representation of Negroes on urban police forces. Token desegregation and restricted assignments for Negro officers conspicuously communicate to the public that the force is racially biased. In defense, police officials complain that few Negroes apply and many who do cannot meet the eligibility standards. They provide two reasons for this paucity of qualified candidates. First, Negroes who meet police standards can find higher-paid work elsewhere. Second, Negroes are thought to shun police work "because such employment isolates them from the Negro community."[17] Yet sufficient motivation on the part of a police force can overcome these obstacles. As in other occupational realms today, remedial training and extensive on-the-job experience could enable many promising Negro applicants to meet regular standards. This would be especially true once word spread throughout the Negro community that the force was sincerely seeking and preparing Negroes for equal-status employment. The second problem, isolation from the Negro community, is in part a function of the token numbers of Negro policemen involved so far. Once a force reaches a significant per-centage—20 to 25 per cent, for instance, rather than today's typical figure of 3 per cent—the Negro community would have less reason to suspect the Negro officer of being a tool of a white institution.

The White House Conference "To Fulfill These Rights," held in June 1966, suggested more extensive ways to improve "police-community relations." It called upon the federal government to establish "assistance programs in the areas of recruitment, testing,

---

[16] California Advisory Committee, *Police–Minority Group Relations,* pp. 29–31. The procedure basically involves the calling in by the police of interested civil rights organizations to observe the investigation of incidents which potentially could lead to complaints against the police.

[17] *Ibid.,* pp. 34–35.

selection, training, organization and pay" of the police.[18] Rapid
expansion of the current experimental program directed by the Office
of Law Enforcement Assistance of the U.S. Department of Justice
was suggested. The conference report also recommended college
scholarships for ambitious police officers and establishment by the
federal government of a National Police Cadet Training Corps for
high school graduates.[19] States were urged to hire qualified minority
group members for state highway patrols, set minimum police
standards through uniform state examinations and licensing, and
provide in-service training programs and college educations for police
officers. Finally, the report requested local governments to upgrade
their police, institute adequate complaint procedures, define clearly the
role the police are expected to play in the community, and establish
a community relations unit within the force.

These suggestions for action are important and urgent, but the
long-term solution nevertheless depends in large part upon changes in
other areas of urban life. As long as Negroes are discriminated against
in education and jobs and are segregated into blighted ghettos, profound
Negro resentment will be stirred, and problems of law enforcement
will persist.

HOUSING

"Since the Supreme Court decision on desegregation of schools,"
wrote Catherine Bauer Wurster in 1955, "the frontier for race relations
has been shifting more and more to the housing field. . . . Residential
segregation vs. nonsegregation is certain to be a lively political issue,
nationally and locally, for some time to come."[20]

During the ensuing years, residential segregation has intensified as a
"lively political issue." The housing trends of recent years readily
explain this heightened concern. Of the nation's total metropolitan
population, about 80 per cent of the Negroes reside in the central cities

---

[18] White House Conference "To Fulfill These Rights," *Council's Report and Recommendations to the Conference* (Washington, D.C.: U.S. Government Printing Office, June 1–2, 1966), pp. 90–94.
[19] One important consideration underlying the idea of such a training corps is that many otherwise qualified high school graduates who now wish to embark upon a police career cannot meet the usual age requirement of twenty-one years. The corps, therefore, would be for graduates of high school during the years of nineteen to twenty-one.
[20] Catherine Bauer, "The Pattern of Urban and Economic Development: Social Implications," *The Annals,* Vol. 305 (1956), pp. 60–69.

contrasted with only about half the whites.[21] The concentration of
Negroes in the central city is found in every region of the country,
though it is strongest in the East and Midwest. Moreover, the trends in
every region point to still larger percentages of Negroes and smaller
percentages of whites residing in the central cities of the future. Apart
from the previously discussed in-migration of Negroes, natural increase
will heighten the present situation; while Negroes of childbearing age
reside chiefly in the central city, comparably young white adults are
disproportionately found in the newly developed suburbs.[22]

Even these striking comparisons between suburban rings and
central cities grossly understate the Negro's concentration, for within
both suburbs and central cities the Negro is still further segregated
into particular neighborhoods. For the median city in the United States
in 1960, the Taeubers found that 88 per cent of all Negro households
would have to move from their present Negro block to a predominantly
white block before racially random residential patterns would exist.
In some cities the separation could hardly become more complete: based
on the same test, Miami, Fort Lauderdale, and Orlando, Florida, and
Odessa, Texas, all had a 98 per cent index of racial segregation. Even
the least segregated city, San Jose, California, had an index of 60 per
cent. Within this narrow range, northeastern (particularly New
England) and western cities tended to have the lowest indices,
midwestern cities somewhat higher ones, and southern cities the highest
of all. From 1940 to 1950, housing segregation increased throughout
the nation; but from 1950 to 1960, it continued to rise in the South
while decreasing slightly in other regions.[23]

In addition, the relatively few Negroes who do maintain suburban
homes are also generally segregated. For example, the Negro population
in the suburban ring of metropolitan Chicago increased from 44,000

[21] Taeuber and Taeuber, in Davis, *The American Negro Reference Book*, pp. 131–136.
[22] The meaning of such trends has been calculated for metropolitan Philadelphia by
George Schermer. He notes that a yearly outflow of 8,000 Negro households to white
areas would be required just to keep Negro areas from expanding further. To reverse
the trend and spread the Negro population evenly throughout metropolitan Philadelphia
by the year 2000 would require at a minimum the entry of 9,700 Negro households
annually into presently white areas and the reciprocal movement of 3,700 white households into presently Negro areas. The absence of such shifts and the continued growth of
central cities means that these minimal estimates will progressively increase. Quoted in
Eunice and George Grier, "Equality and Beyond: Housing Segregation in the Great
Society," in Talcott Parsons and Kenneth B. Clark, eds., *The Negro American* (Boston
Houghton Mifflin, 1966), p. 535.
[23] Karl E. Taeuber and Alma F. Taeuber, *Negroes in Cities* (Chicago: Aldine, 1965).

to 78,000 between 1950 and 1960. Yet the Taeubers have demonstrated that 83 per cent of this apparent improvement occurred either in heavily "Negro suburbs" or in industrial suburbs with Negro ghettos of their own.[24]

Indeed, there is an especially devastating aspect to the separation of Negroes. Index comparisons reveal that Negro Americans are far more segregated residentially than those in low-status occupations or minority nationality groups, a fact which cannot be explained by the Negro's relative poverty. "Economic factors," state the Taeubers flatly, "cannot account for more than a small portion of observed levels of racial residential segregation."[25] Consequently, they conclude, "Improving the economic status of Negroes is unlikely by itself to alter prevailing patterns of racial residential segregation."[26] Several interrelated factors are more important than poverty: federal housing policies, blatant racial discrimination, the tight supply of low-income housing, suburban zoning barriers, and binding ties within the Negro community.

FEDERAL POLICIES

The housing policy of the federal government, from the National Housing Act of 1935 until 1950, strove diligently and effectively to establish racial segregation in the more than eleven million units constructed during this critical period. From 1950 to 1962, federal housing policy was officially neutral but in practice still segregationist. Finally, President Kennedy's limited antidiscrimination executive order in 1962 set an important precedent and ushered in the present federal housing policy that is best described as ineffectively integrationist. These three decades of federal mismanagement must now be counteracted. Perhaps, what the law giveth, the law can take away.

Our present plight has come about in a number of ways. The Federal Housing Administration's mortgage insurance program and the Veterans Administration's loan guarantee program both encouraged suburban home ownership with more liberal terms, but they generally discriminated economically and racially against Negroes. "If a neighborhood is to retain stability," asserted the FHA manual for years, "it is necessary that properties shall be continued to be occupied by

[24] Taeuber and Taeuber, in Davis, *The American Negro Reference Book,* pp. 132–136. Other analyses indicate that Chicago is typical in the extent of its suburban segregation; see Taeuber and Taeuber, *Negroes in Cities,* pp. 55–62.
[25] *Ibid.,* p. 2.
[26] *Ibid.,* p. 95.

the same social and racial classes."[27] Indeed, Eunice and George Grier
cite two cases in which the FHA actually drove developers who insisted
upon racially open policies out of business.[28] As these efforts
encouraged whites to leave the central city, public housing developments
concurrently helped to seal the Negroes in. Large and often unattractive
projects were constructed within the central city and were segregated
by design.[29]

The *coup de grâce* came with the initiation of urban renewal. In city
after city, this program has been utilized to clear slums and convert
the land to heavier tax-bearing uses, typically removing low-income
Negroes in the process to make way for upper-income whites. The
caustic slogan "Negro removal" has been well justified.[30] Further erosion
of low-income housing has come from federally financed highways
that frequently affect Negro neighborhoods disproportionately in their
search for inexpensive routes.[31]

The racial results of these various federal efforts have been well
described by the Griers: "if the FHA, VA, and public housing programs
have helped produce metropolitan areas which increasingly resemble
black bullseyes and white outer rings, urban renewal has too often

---

[27] Quoted by Charles Abrams, "The Housing Problem and the Negro," in Parsons and Clark, *The Negro American*, p. 523.
[28] Eunice and George Grier, *Privately Developed Interracial Housing* (Berkeley: University of California Press, 1960), Chapter 8.
[29] In those relatively few public housing projects which have achieved full racial integration, striking gains in positive racial attitudes have occurred among both the Negro and white tenants. See Morton Deutsch and Mary Collins, *Interracial Housing: A Psychological Evaluation of a Social Experiment* (Minneapolis: University of Minnesota Press, 1951); Marie Jahoda and Patricia West, "Race Relations in Public Housing," *Journal of Social Issues*, Vol. 7 (1951), pp. 132–139; D. M. Wilner, Rosabelle Walkley, and S. W. Cook, *Human Relations in Interracial Housing: A Study of the Contact Hypothesis* (Minneapolis: University of Minnesota Press, 1955); and Ernest Works, "The Prejudice-Interaction Hypothesis from the Point of View of the Negro Minority Group," *American Journal of Sociology*, Vol. 67 (1961), pp. 47–52.
[30] Writes Abrams: "In the United States, from 69 to 72 per cent of those who have been displaced from their homes by urban renewal projects have been Negroes, while only a tiny fraction of the new houses built on the sites have been open to them. . . . In Stockton, California, a renewal project not only leveled a whole Negro neighborhood but destroyed 32 Negro churches in the process." Abrams, in Parsons and Clark, *The Negro American*, p. 514.
[31] Even in St. Paul, Minnesota, which is 97 per cent white, freeway displacement struck Negroes hardest by eliminating the housing for 311 Negro households. This number represented 72 per cent of all of the displacement and 14 per cent of the city's Negro housing. Furthermore, only 35 per cent of those displaced Negro householders who sought housing outside of the ghetto obtained it, while all of the displaced white householders who sought such housing obtained it. F. James Davis, "The Effects of a Freeway Displacement on Racial Housing Segregation in a Northern City," *Phylon*, Vol. 26 (1965), pp. 209–215.

created small white or largely white areas in the center of the bullseyes—simultaneously causing the black ghettos to expand outward even further."[32] This federally influenced pattern is now widely recognized, with a summary indictment rendered by the 1966 White House Conference "To Fulfill These Rights":

Housing policy—both governmental and private—has traditionally ignored the needs of the nonwhite and the economically disadvantaged . . . . The slums and ghettos have grown larger, overcrowding has been intensified, and the alienation of the ghetto dweller has become a national crisis. Too often, public housing and urban renewal programs have aggravated rather than ameliorated the degree of segregation and congestion.[33]

Nevertheless, relatively few of the roughly sixteen hundred urban renewal projects now under way in about eight hundred communities throughout the nation promise positive remedies, in part because they are typically confined within city boundaries and thus are antimetropolitan in their effects.

RACIAL DISCRIMINATION

Attention to the impact of government programs, however, should not blind us to an even more important factor in creating residential separatism: blatant racial discrimination. In all American cities today there exist two essentially separate housing markets, one for whites, another for Negroes. The prejudicial attitudes which lurk behind this pattern of exclusion are widespread, well known, and pervasive. Suffice it here to note that roughly two-to-one majorities favoring residential segregation have characterized the results of referenda in Akron, Detroit, Seattle, and the state of California; and opinion surveys reveal a surprising resistance to housing integration even among many college-educated respondents who at least pay lip service to desegregation in other respects.

This blatant discrimination has set the scene for ghetto race riots by fostering overcrowding, inferior facilities, and inflated rents. Negroes are squeezed into Watts under conditions four times as congested as those in the rest of Los Angeles;[34] in Atlanta, Negroes comprise over a third of the population but claim only one sixth of the city's developed

[32] Eunice and George Grier, "Equality and Beyond," in Parsons and Clark, *The Negro American*, p. 533.
[33] White House Conference "To Fulfill These Rights," pp. 57, 69.
[34] Abrams, in Parsons and Clark, *The Negro American*, p. 513.

residential land;[35] and for the nation as a whole during the 1950's, the number of overcrowded units among nonwhites increased by a million and a third while it declined among whites by one fifth of a million.[36]

Overcrowding such as this reflects the inferior housing available in the separate Negro market. Differences in housing quality are especially conspicuous in the South, but they are still marked in northern metropolitan areas. In 1960, the Negro-owned housing units of an average northern city were three times more likely to be substandard than white-owned units, and Negro-rented units were over twice as likely to be substandard as white-rented units.[37] In Boston, for example, ten of thirteen predominantly Negro census tracts in 1960 were among the city's worst areas in housing quality, and eleven had more than 95 per cent of their units built before 1940.[38] Put briefly, the predominantly Negro areas of the nation's cities are characterized by overcrowded old buildings of sharply inferior quality.

Income differentials, of course, contribute to housing differentials, but discrimination augments economics to create this great disparity. The median monthly rents paid by white and Negro residents in northern metropolitan areas are *not* significantly different ($77 for whites and $73 for Negroes), but the differences in quality are enormous.[39] A rigorous analysis of Chicago in 1956 concluded that nonwhites had to pay roughly $15 per month more than whites to secure comparable housing.[40] Given their considerably smaller incomes, most Negroes must therefore devote a much larger share of their resourecs to shelter; in 1960, about a third of all metropolitan Negro tenants spent above 35 per cent of their annual income in gross rent compared to less than a fifth of white metropolitan tenants who did so.[41]

[35] Constance Baker Motley, "The Legal Status of the Negro in the United States," in Davis, *The American Negro Reference Book,* p. 501.
[36] Joseph H. Douglass, "The Urban Negro Family," in Davis, *The American Negro Reference Book,* p. 345. The shifting base between "Negroes" and "nonwhites" throughout the chapter is made necessary by the lack of comparable data on many indices, but the distortion thus generated is minimal and insignificant since Negroes constituted in 1960 over 90 per cent of the nation's "nonwhites."
[37] Taeuber and Taeuber, in Davis, *The American Negro Reference Book,* p. 140.
[38] Thomas F. Pettigrew, "Metropolitan Boston's Race Problem in Perspective," in Joint Center for Urban Studies of M.I.T. and Harvard, *Social Structure and Human Problems in the Boston Metropolitan Area* (Cambridge, Mass.: Joint Center for Urban Studies of M.I.T. and Harvard, 1965), p. 39.
[39] Taeuber and Taeuber, in Davis, *The American Negro Reference Book,* pp. 139–140.
[40] Beverly Duncan and Philip M. Hauser, *Housing a Metropolis—Chicago* (New York: Free Press, 1960).
[41] Taeuber and Taeuber, in Davis, *The American Negro Reference Book,* p. 140.

Negroes have made definite gains in housing quality in recent years. Thus, in the entire nation from 1950 to 1960, the percentage of nonwhites living in adequate, standard housing doubled,[42] and Negro home ownership rose from 35 per cent to 38 per cent.[43] These gains, however, have not kept pace with comparable white advances (white home ownership rose from 57 per cent to 64 per cent), and they have not eradicated the dual housing market. The Negro gains are largely a function of farm-to-city migration and the acquisition of older homes left behind in the central city by suburban-bound whites, rather than of a genuine relaxation of discrimination.[44]

Efforts to end housing discrimination have been feeble and ineffective. By mid-1965, sixteen states and the District of Columbia, together covering almost half of the population, had barred discrimination in a major portion of their private housing supply.[45] In addition, over five hundred private fair housing committees are operating throughout the country, most of them strategically located in metropolitan suburbs. Yet neither the laws nor the committees have made substantial progress. In general, both state laws and citizens' committees apply a case-by-case approach, relying upon individual complaints or contacts; the problem has such deep roots, however, that only direct and patterned confrontation with the housing industry as a whole offers any hope for substantial improvement.[46]

THE HOUSING SHORTAGE

In addition to fashioning new housing policies on the federal level and halting discrimination, vigorous, positive remedial actions which greatly swell the available supply of low- and middle-income housing are essential if the segregationist trend in our metropolitan centers is to

[42] Marian P. Yankauer and M. B. Sunderhauf, "Housing: Equal Opportunity to Choose Where One Shall Live," *Journal of Negro Education, 1963 Yearbook,* Vol. 32:4 (1963), pp. 402–414.

[43] Douglass, in Davis, *The American Negro Reference Book,* p. 345.

[44] Research on this phenomenon in Toledo leads McKee to predict a growing opposition to urban renewal and highway construction dislocations by these more numerous Negro home owners. James B. McKee, "Changing Patterns of Race and Housing: A Toledo Study," *Social Forces,* Vol. 41 (1963), pp. 253–260.

[45] Eunice and George Grier, "Equality and Beyond," *op. cit.,* p. 544.

[46] For documentation of the ineffectiveness of complaint procedures in antidiscrimination legislation, see Leon Mayhew, "Law and Equal Opportunity: Anti-Discrimination Law in Massachusetts" (unpublished Ph.D. dissertation, Harvard University, 1964). For documentation of blatant discrimination even in a small city (Schenectady, New York), which has a tiny Negro population and operates under a relatively well administered state antidiscrimination statute, see Norman A. Mercer, "Discrimination in Rental Housing: A Study of Resistance of Landlords to Non-White Tenants," *Phylon,* Vol. 23 (1962), pp. 47–54.

be stemmed, much less reversed. The White House Conference "To Fulfill These Rights" summarized the situation as follows:

More than one million new houses per year are required to take care of the housing needs of the expanding population. To replace existing stock at the rate of just one percent annually would require another half million houses. In addition, there are more than 10 million substandard houses in stock now and millions of others are too old or in too poor condition to last until they are replaced at the prevailing annual rate of one or two percent. A production rate of two million units annually is a conservative estimate of requirements. The present rate of production is only about 1.4 million, and practically all of this new stock is priced beyond the reach of families below the median income level. At least half, preferably more, of the new stock should be made available to low and moderate income families. . . . As far as the production of housing in the lower cost brackets is concerned the economy has been in paralysis for years. At present it is being strangled to death. . . . Now, when the housing industry needs priming, is a particularly propitious time to offer incentives for builders to supply housing for low and moderate income families.[47]

One indication of this short supply of modest-income shelter is the backed-up demand for public housing.[48] In Massachusetts, for example, there are 42,000 units of publicly assisted housing. These limited facilities have an annual turnover of only 6,000 units, while 25,000 families remain on the waiting list and are joined by an additional 15,000 eligible applicants each year.[49]

Not only is modest-income housing scarce, but poor Negroes are largely restricted to that part of the market which lies within the ghetto. Typically, this ghetto market is located close to the central business district and is characterized by high rates of social disorganization. The fringes of the ghetto farthest from the disorganization are generally inhabited by upper-status Negroes who can afford better housing and have acquired homes in formerly white neighborhoods.[50]

SUBURBAN ZONING BARRIERS

Further essentials for distributing Negroes throughout the metropolitan area and allowing greater residential choice include alterations in suburban zoning and a willingness among Negroes to venture into formerly all-white suburbs. Replacing unenforceable restrictive

---

[47] White House Conference "To Fulfill These Rights," *op. cit.,* pp. 62–63.
[48] Public housing accounts for about 1 per cent of the nation's housing. *Ibid.,* p. 58.
[49] Special Commission on Low-Income Housing, *Decent Housing For All* (Boston, March 1965).
[50] Leo F. Schnore, "Social Class Segregation among Non-Whites in Metropolitan Centers," *Demography,* Vol. 2 (1965), pp. 126–133.

convenants with more evasive zoning regulations, many suburbs have become, in Charles Abrams' words, the "new Mason-Dixon lines of America." Sometimes these zoning devices are nakedly direct: when a union tried to build houses for its Negro members in Milpitas, California, the area was immediately rezoned for industrial use; when a private developer attempted to construct integrated housing in Deerfield, Illinois, the town condemned the land for a park.[51] Sometimes zoning ordinances and building codes are rigorously enforced for Negroes but not for whites. "State governments have clothed these suburban jurisdictions," as the White House Conference "To Fulfill These Rights" concludes, "with the power to zone the use of the land and to control the issuance of building permits in such a manner that only housing for the affluent can be built there."[52] In short, what federal policies, direct discrimination, economics, and the scarcity of modest-income housing have left undone, the white suburb's zoning methods have completed.

Bernard Frieden places suburban zoning in a broader context by pointing out that restrictive policies, such as required size of lot and minimum dwelling cost, result in part from local tax pressures.[53] Like the central city's efforts to upgrade revenues through urban renewal, the suburb is eager to attract residents who will contribute to local taxes more than they will require in social services. The Negro, reason too many suburban officials, is a problem for "downtown." Clearly such an attitude cannot be appeased much longer if the racial dynamite in our cities is to be deactivated.

Frieden also notes that the suburb's restrictive zoning practices nourish racial fears and prejudices. Indeed, the public has thoroughly adapted to the long-established practices and patterns of the dual housing markets. White Americans frequently accept the sales promotion of the real estate industry and are easily frightened into thinking that their security is dependent upon separation from Negro Americans. For their part, many middle-class Negroes have so accommodated to exclusion that few challenge the existing patterns even when law and other circumstances favor change. This was shown in a study of Boston's middle-income Negroes.[54] Despite numerous incentives and

[51] Abrams, in Parsons and Clark, *The Negro American,* p. 516.
[52] White House Conference "To Fulfill These Rights," p. 58.
[53] Bernard J. Frieden, "Toward Equality of Urban Opportunity," *Journal of the American Institute of Planners,* Vol. 31:4 (1965), pp. 320–330.
[54] Lewis G. Watts, Howard E. Freeman, Helen Hughes, Robert Morris, and Thomas

favorable circumstances, only 9 of 250 families (less than 4 per cent) moved to interracial areas during a critical sixteen-month period.[55] For that matter, less than 20 per cent of these prosperous Negro Bostonians made any realistic effort to investigate suburban housing.

HOUSING STRATEGIES

Detailed strategies for achieving residential integration in urban America can evolve only over time, but it is absolutely essential that we begin now. The goal is not, as some maintain, to eliminate the ghetto, but to convert it from an isolated racial prison to an ethnic area of choice. This effort, to be successful, must be metropolitan, that is, projected for an entire metropolitan area; it must be systemic, carefully intermeshed with other components of the urban structural system, such as mass transit, education, and employment; and it must be interactive, fostering optimal interracial contact. Admittedly, these are rigorous specifications, but a plethora of concrete ideas which appear promising is now available.

On the metropolitan level, the White House Conference "To Fulfill These Rights" urged that public housing authorities assume responsibility for entire metropolitan areas. It also called for area-wide "land banks," and state-initiated housing development corporations modeled after industrial development groups, which would promote the spread of modest-income housing throughout the metropolis.[56] Frieden suggests a number of ways suburban zoning practices might be countered: court challenges to exclusionary controls; legislation reallocating zoning authority only to large municipalities and counties; and extra state and federal aid to communities with low-income families, in order to reverse the present economic incentive to exclude the poor.[57]

The ultimate weapon, of course, would be to cut off state and federal funds to communities which resist inclusive residential policies. A bolder use of Title VI of the 1964 Civil Rights Act in northern as well as southern situations is necessary.[58] Short of this, however, considerable

---

F. Pettigrew, *The Middle-Income Negro Family Faces Urban Renewal* (Boston: Massachusetts Department of Commerce and Development, 1965), p. 79.
[55] Helen Hughes and Lewis G. Watts, "Portrait of the Self-Integrator," *Journal of Social Issues,* Vol. 20 (1964), pp. 103–115.
[56] White House Conference "To Fulfill These Rights."
[57] Frieden, *op. cit.* A recent Pennsylvania court decision against the four-acre-per-home zoning requirement of Easttown township may prove a landmark challenge to suburban restrictions. Neil Ulman, "States Move to Trim Local Zoning Autonomy as Criticisms Increase," *Wall Street Journal,* August 15, 1966, pp. 1, 12.
[58] Title VI of the 1964 Civil Rights Act requires the cutoff of federal funds to any program which racially discriminates. The title did not exclude so-called *de facto,* as

progress could still be made if future federal urban grants: (1) were kept almost exclusively metropolitan in character, so that they required formal cooperation between suburbs and central city; (2) provided not only housing aid but a coordinated package for the whole urban system; and (3) gave bonus points and incentive funds for previous metropolitan cooperation. Several current HUD programs which require metropolitan planning commission review of a community's proposal are forerunners of this new approach to federal funding.

Packaged metropolitan federal grants of this type logically encourage a systemic approach. Thus, the imaginative proposal for "model cities," so gingerly handled by Congress, is a far more systemic attack than the typical bulldozer demolition accomplished by urban renewal. If the model cities program actively required metropolitan involvement, it could truly serve as a model for the new and needed federal approach to urban grants.

Systemic planning also calls for a careful assessment of the social needs of each metropolitan system. While the White House Conference's recommendation of two million new modest-income housing units a year for the entire nation is sufficient as a gross specification, each particular area has its own unique mix of low-, medium-, and high-income housing requirements based upon its income profile and projected labor force expansion. Programs must be tailored to suit these individual conditions.

A final aspect of a systemic approach is consideration of available resources and an attempt to put them to productive use. In the housing field, a number of techniques could be used to help develop adequate low-income shelter out of current substandard stock: state involvement in local housing code enforcement; strengthened judicial powers, including court-administered withholding of rent to force basic repairs and use of a court housing investigator analogous to the probation officer; state guarantee of rehabilitation-loan funds; and new procedures for the disposition of buildings abandoned because of stricter code enforcement.[59] Related possibilities include the allocation of federal funds to support long-overdue research in low-cost housing and the

---

opposed to *de jure,* segregation, nor did it directly include it. The legal question as to its application to *de facto* segregation arises in part because this condition was specifically excluded by Congress in a number of other titles of the act.
[59] Special Commission on Low-Income Housing, *op. cit.*

establishment of a massive National Housing Corporation that would combine public and private interests in the manner of the Communications Satellite Corporation.[60]

Together with metropolitan and systemic concerns, any remedy for Negro housing must also foster positive Negro-white interaction. A prerequisite is the elimination of racial discrimination and the dual housing markets that now exist. While the 1968 federal civil rights law marked a vital step toward open-housing legislation, realistic enforcement of the measure is still needed. In the meantime, significant progress could be made by converting state antidiscrimination commissions and private fair-housing groups from case-by-case, complaint-based efforts to patterned action. Nondiscriminatory practices should also be made a requirement in state licensing of real estate agents.

Direct action to achieve interracial contact is also possible. A precedent-setting example is the sparsely supported federal rent supplement program. Heretofore, American public housing has segregated the poor, Negroes and others, from the rest of society in a latter-day version of the poorhouse. Such segregation virtually guarantees the evolution of deviant norms and values by seriously limiting contact with other Americans. Rent supplements mark an important break with these past mistakes by promoting vitally needed equal-status contact between advantaged and disadvantaged. To be effective, however, funding must be substantially increased (the current appropriation is less than 1 per cent of the necessary amount), and the veto power that local jurisdictions now have over implementation of the program in their communities must be eliminated. The rent supplement concept also suggests similar measures for subsidizing home ownership among the poor. A few observers argue that, in the American tradition of giving land to homesteaders, low-income families should be given housing without cost providing they maintain it. Others stress the need for subsidized incentives and technical assistance in a variety of cooperative efforts.[61]

[60] A thorough upgrading of America's badly outdated home-building methods was a lifelong goal of Catherine Bauer Wurster; it was a major theme of her classic volume *Modern Housing* (Boston: Houghton Mifflin, 1934). The National Housing Corporation could establish revolving funds to purchase, for resale or rental on a desegregated basis, strategically located existing structures as they become available. James Tobin, "On Improving the Economic Status of the Negro," in Parsons and Clark, *The Negro American*, p. 461.
[61] Below-market interest programs (such as for 221(d)(3) housing) for nonprofit

Whatever course is pursued, it must be kept in mind that mere contact between persons of different races and classes does not necessarily generate tolerance. In fact, contact may actually lead to conflict and intolerance, the conditions of the contact being crucial. Social psychologists have studied this problem in a variety of situations, including public housing, and have generally concluded that prejudice is alleviated when the two groups possess equal status in the situation, seek common goals, depend cooperatively upon each other, and interact with the positive support of authorities, custom, or law.[62] Careful planning can nurture the creation of these conditions in the public housing of the future.

The issue of race in housing poses a formidable problem for urban America; the metropolitan-wide programs to counter it must necessarily be varied and complex. The White House Conference stated confidently: "The dimensions of this program are staggering—but they are no larger than America's space ventures, the demands for defense, or the tremendous growth of the nation's economy. Americans are conditioned to thinking big. They can think big enough to cope with this problem as well."[63] The Griers remind us of the stakes: "The choice is not merely between segregation and desegregation, but between wholesale destruction of property and human values and the continued growth and security of American society itself."[64]

EMPLOYMENT

The Negro's employment status in urban America is as grim as his housing. Though there have been improvements in the past twenty-six years, the upgrading of Negro employment has not kept pace with the upgrading created by automation, nor has it significantly narrowed the gap with white employment. At the rate of nonwhite gains from 1950 to 1960, nonwhites would not attain equal proportional representation throughout the nation among clerical workers until

groups are the most noteworthy examples of this approach, though these efforts as yet constitute a bare fraction of the low-cost housing needed. Among the more interesting cooperating groups are the Foundation for Cooperative Housing in Stamford, Conn., Action Housing, Inc., in Pittsburgh, Community Resources Corporation in New York City, and the Housing Development Corporation in Washington, D.C.
[62] Allport reviews many of these studies: G. W. Allport, *The Nature of Prejudice* (Cambridge, Mass.: Addison-Wesley, 1954), Chapter 16. The key studies on contact effects between Negro and white Americans in public housing are listed in footnote 29.
[63] White House Conference "To Fulfill These Rights," p. 58.
[64] Eunice and George Grier, in Parsons and Clark, *The Negro American*, p. 550.

1992, among skilled workers until 2005, among professionals until 2017, among sales workers until 2114, and among business managers and proprietors until 2730.[65] These data do not reflect discrimination only in the South. The structure of Boston's labor force, for example, presents a similar pattern.[66] Boston Negroes are concentrated in low-skilled jobs and a few specific white-collar positions but are virtually excluded from the jobs in between, ranging from firemen to accountants.

Even more profoundly troubling is the concurrent picture of Negro unemployment; rates for Negro adults and youths have both remained roughly twice those of white unemployment since the Korean War. The tight labor market of 1966, with its total unemployment rate reduced to below 4 per cent, still witnessed a Negro adult rate of roughly 7 per cent. Among youths, recent rates soar as high as 25–30 per cent for out-of-school Negroes aged sixteen to nineteen and at least 19 per cent for the larger sixteen to twenty-one age group.[67] Rashi Fein sums up the problem: "What is recession for the white (say, an unemployment rate of 6 per cent) is prosperity for the non-white. . . . Therefore, perhaps, it is appropriate to say that whites fluctuate between prosperity and recession but Negroes fluctuate between depression and great depression."[68]

The statistics from which this picture is drawn actually underestimate the desperate economic crisis of the Negro ghetto, for several reasons. First, many Negroes listed as job holders are seriously underemployed; they less often work full time and throughout the year, and less frequently hold positions commensurate with their education. Witness the Negro downgrading, for example, among high school graduates: well over half the nonwhite men with a high school education in 1960 worked as low-skilled operatives, service workers, or laborers compared

[65] N. D. Glenn, "Some Changes in the Relative Status of American Non-Whites, 1940 to 1960," *Phylon,* Vol. 24 (1963), pp. 109–122. See also Eli Ginzberg and Dale L. Hiestand, "Employment Patterns of Negro Men and Women," in Davis, *The American Negro Reference Book,* pp. 234–235.

[66] Thus, in 1960 two thirds of metropolitan Boston's employed nonwhites were below the skilled craftsmen level; 28 per cent of the area's 2,038 employed Negro professionals were women who served either as nurses, teachers, or social workers; and the census reported only 18 Negro accountants in the area, 4 Negro firemen, and no Negro metal molders, locomotive engineers, or railroad brakemen and switchmen. Pettigrew, "Metropolitan Boston's Race Problem in Perspective," pp. 45–48.

[67] White House Conference "To Fulfill These Rights," pp. 5–6.

[68] Rashi Fein, "An Economic and Social Profile of the Negro American," in Parsons and Clark, *The Negro American,* pp. 114–115.

to only a quarter of the similarly educated white males, and almost two thirds of the nonwhite females with this education in 1960 were in such occupations compared to less than a quarter of the white females.[69]

Second, Negroes often do not earn as much as whites in comparable jobs.[70] As a result, the median family income of nonwhites has remained only slightly over half that of white families since World War II, despite more members of the nonwhite family in the labor force.[71] Indeed, nonwhite families with an employed head of household have a lower median family income than white families with an unemployed head.[72]

A third factor intensifying the statistics is Negro withdrawal from the labor force. A disproportionately large share of working-age Negroes give up the search for a job, and unemployment statistics enumerate only those who are still actively seeking work. Economists estimate that if those who have despaired of finding employment and those who involuntarily work only part-time were considered, the Negro unemployment rate would approximate 12 per cent even during a tight labor market year such as 1966.[73] A fourth statistical artifact involves the imprecise concept of "nonwhite." Japanese- and Chinese-Americans constitute less than a tenth of this statistical category, but their unusually secure over-all economic position tends to improve the nonwhite statistics beyond the actual conditions of Negroes alone.[74]

Finally, recent economic and social data reveal an ominous trend that is masked by the aggregate statistics: some Negroes are making significant gains, while many others are slipping further behind the increasing prosperity of the most affluent country on earth.[75] Those

---

[69] Ginzberg and Hiestand, in Davis, *The American Negro Reference Book*, p. 242.
[70] *Ibid.*, p. 231. Among males in 1960, for example, the median income of nonwhite professionals was only 69 per cent that of white professionals; among salesmen, 57 per cent; among craftsmen, 66 per cent; and among operatives, 71 per cent. The only reversal to this pattern, interestingly, is among private household workers, where for both sexes nonwhites earn slightly more than whites.
[71] Andrew Brimmer, "The Negro in the National Economy," in Davis, *The American Negro Reference Book*, pp. 258–260.
[72] Daniel Patrick Moynihan, "Employment, Income, and the Negro Family," in Parsons and Clark, *The Negro American*, pp. 148–149.
[73] White House Conference "To Fulfill These Rights," p. 6.
[74] Moynihan, in Parsons and Clark, *The Negro American*, p. 143. Moynihan points out that in 1960 there were only 192,000 nonwhite managers, officials, and proprietors; over a fourth of these were Asian Americans.
[75] Brimmer, in Davis, *The American Negro Reference Book*, pp. 266–271, provides the economic confirmation for this income differentiation. The bottom two fifths of nonwhite families in terms of income accounted for 15.0 per cent of total nonwhite income in 1947, but only 13.5 per cent in 1960; the top two fifths garnered 69.3

Negroes less scarred by past deprivations are in a position to take advantage of current racial adjustments, and it is to these more fortunate people that fingers point when "racial progress" is proudly cited. These are the Negro Americans who by 1984 will be not just desegregated but truly integrated into "the affluent society."[76]

THE OTHER NEGRO AMERICA

There is, however, another Negro America that is less fortunate. Now constituting at least two thirds of all Negroes, this group has not been significantly touched by present racial adjustments. Its hopes were raised in the 1950's,[77] but now it cannot even rationalize personal failure entirely in racial terms, for *Ebony* bulges each month with evidence that the affluent Negro America is making rapid strides. Basic progress in improving the economic position of Negroes depends upon reaching the other Negro America.

Although blatant racial discrimination is an obvious cause of the other Negro America's economic plight, it is not the sole one. Relative to whites, Negroes more often reside in the South, have received fewer years and a poorer quality of education, and form a younger segment of the labor force, all characteristics apart from race which contribute to economic marginality. Moreover, the central cities of the North and West, where Negroes are concentrated in increasing numbers, are actually losing manufacturing jobs.[78] Implicit in these factors are forms of indirect economic discrimination. For instance, the inability of most Negroes to move to the suburbs puts them at a disadvantage in following the manufacturing jobs from central city to outer ring. Likewise, educational discrimination indirectly fosters economic discrimination.

Nevertheless, direct and obvious job discrimination by both employers and unions remains the major barrier, for the economic position of the other Negro America still lags dangerously behind the rest of the

---

per cent of total nonwhite income in 1947 and 70.1 per cent in 1960. These figures reveal a sharper income differentiation than among whites, for in 1960 the bottom two fifths of white families acquired 17.4 per cent and the top two fifths 64.7 per cent of total white income.

[76] Progress for "the affluent Negro America" is, of course, not inconsequential. Successful middle-class Negroes offer needed achievement models for the Negro community; they can effectively obliterate racial barriers by being "the first of the race" in previously all-white situations; they help eliminate the Negro stigma by providing a constant contradiction between class and caste; and they furnish the great majority of protest leaders. But middle-class Negroes remain only a minority of the group.

[77] Pettigrew, *A Profile of the Negro American*, pp. 184–185.

[78] Moynihan, in Parsons and Clark, *The Negro American*, p. 142.

country even after these indirect factors are taken into account. Attacks upon blatant discrimination in employment also offer far more hope for short-term effects than the slower, though ultimately necessary, alterations in these indirect contributors.[79]

The urgency for both short-term and long-term remedial action becomes clear when we survey the consequences of the dire poverty of the other Negro America. At the national level, the gross national product would be lifted annually by 5 billion dollars if Negro unemployment were lowered to the 1966 white rate; an additional GNP gain of 22 billion dollars would result if the Negro labor force's productivity equaled that of the white; and gains beyond this annual 27 billion dollars would result if Negroes obtained jobs commensurate with their abilities and training.[80] Some further investment would be necessary, of course, to achieve these GNP increments.

More important, however, are the social consequences of the other Negro America's poverty. The statistics themselves suggest the dire results of the unemployment pattern, particularly among the young. Early unemployment means that Negro youths are less likely to secure the on-the-job training necessary for the more stable, skilled work, thus condemning them to low-skilled, low-paying, low-seniority jobs, and predisposing them as adults to join the devastated ranks of the hard-core unemployed. It is these factors which account for much of the grossly higher rate of unemployment of Negro adults.[81] Youth joblessness also swells the ranks of those riot-aged ghetto residents with little to lose from mass destruction. Significantly, the total unemployment rates in such strife-torn urban areas as Watts often run as high as 40 per cent.

A more subtle consequence has been noted by Daniel Patrick Moynihan, who has documented the close and positive relationship over the years between the unemployment rate of nonwhite men, the percentage of nonwhite married women separated from their husbands, and the number of new cases opened under the Aid to Families of

[79] Fein, in Parsons and Clark, *The Negro American*, pp. 112, 119–121.
[80] White House Conference "To Fulfill These Rights," p. 6. Twenty-seven billion dollars represents roughly 3 per cent of the total GNP, approximately the real gain annually during the 1960's. The degree of investment requirement is difficult to estimate but would probably not be substantial relative to the long-term gain.
[81] They do not account for all of the higher rate, however. Negro unemployment rates remain higher at each level on the occupational scale. Ginzberg and Hiestand, in Davis, *The American Negro Reference Book*, pp. 234–235.

Dependent Children Program.[82] Widespread family disorganization in the other Negro America, particularly father absence, is unquestionably one of the bitter fruits of economic discrimination. Those urban taxpayers who cry out against rapidly rising welfare budgets but continue to foster employment discrimination against Negroes have only themselves to blame.

Moynihan's data bear another ominous message. The close associations between unemployment and family characteristics break down after 1962. While nonwhite male unemployment decreased in 1963 and 1964, the percentage of separated nonwhite women and new AFDC cases continued to rise. Although this dissociation of trends could indicate merely a transitional lag before improvements take hold, Moynihan raises the disturbing possibility that we are too late for short-term solutions. Has "the impact of economic disadvantage on the Negro community . . . gone on so long that genuine structural damage has occurred, so that a reversal in the course of economic events will no longer produce the expected response in social areas?"[83] Is the crisis "beginning to create conditions which tend to reinforce the cycle that produced it in the first instance?"[84]

ECONOMIC REMEDIES

Just as in the case of the housing problem, a successful attack on this economic situation must be metropolitan, systemic, and interactive. Fortunately, a range of serious proposals that meet these three criteria have been made.

Metropolitan job councils, "to plan, coordinate, and implement local programs to increase jobs," are required.[85] These councils should combine business, labor, and government interests and be made responsible for an area's array of programs. The U.S. Department of Labor could supply each council with the basic information for initiating a labor market effort in its area tailored to Negro needs. The councils could also serve as the local authority for administering future federal and state programs "to guarantee the availability of jobs to able workers who cannot be placed in, or promptly trained for, regular employment."[86]

---

[82] Moynihan, in Parsons and Clark, *The Negro American,* pp. 147–158.
[83] *Ibid.,* p. 155.
[84] *Ibid.,* p. 147.
[85] White House Conference "To Fulfill These Rights," p. 11.
[86] *Ibid.,* p. 19.

These job-creating projects will be necessary even when the economy otherwise achieves nearly full *recorded* employment. They must not take on a "make-work" character, however, for as such they would lose much of their psychological value. Our metropolitan areas desperately need public facilities and personnel to staff service institutions. If sufficient financing were available, employment with dignity and genuine training potential could be established throughout urban America for para-professionals and special service workers, such as teacher aides and police aides.

While urging the necessity of this government-financed employment, the critical importance to the Negro of a tight labor market must not be overlooked. James Tobin argues forcefully that only with long-continued full employment can other programs to alleviate the Negro's economic crisis be successful.[87] Tobin further maintains that we already know how to sustain a tight labor market, although "creeping inflation" would be one cost. More conservative economists counter that inflation defeats the goal since economically marginal citizens supposedly suffer most from rising prices. As far as the Negro is concerned, however, the historical evidence supports Tobin's analysis. The only times in this century the Negro has made significant gains relative to whites in employment and constant-dollar income have been during periods of war. The tight labor markets brought on by war made racial discrimination too expensive a luxury.

Tobin urges the creation of nearly full employment without war.[88] A tight labor market, he argues, would mean not only more jobs but more skilled jobs for longer hours and better pay. Not only would it soak up Negro unemployment at roughly twice the rate of white unemployment, but it would return to the labor force many Negroes who had despaired of securing work. A continued tight labor market would attract surplus rural population to higher-paying urban jobs; it would force employers to be more realistic about job requirements, to fashion these requirements to fit the available supply, and to render more on-the-job training; it would prevent the sharp cyclical fluctuations which prevent many Negroes from achieving experience

[87] Tobin, in Parsons and Clark, *The Negro American*, pp. 451–471.
[88] Tobin points out that Negro economic progress is extremely sensitive to general economic growth. If nation-wide per capita personal income is stationary, nonwhite median family income declines by about 0.5 per cent annually, while a per capita income increment of 5 per cent leads to nearly a 7.5 per cent nonwhite family gain. *Ibid.*, p. 452.

and seniority; and it would subvert policies of racial discrimination.

If it can do all of this, why do we not maintain a tight labor market as a matter of national economic policy? Tobin answers:

> The vast comfortable white middle class who are never touched by unemployment prefer to safeguard the purchasing power of their life insurance and pension rights than to expand opportunities for the disadvantaged and unemployed. . . . We are paying much too high a social price for avoiding creeping inflation and for protecting our gold stock and "the dollar." But it will not be easy to alter these national priorities. The interests of the unemployed, the poor, and the Negroes are under-represented in the comfortable consensus which supports and confines current policy.[89]

Together with a tight labor market, broader and more effective legal action is necessary. Title VII of the 1964 Civil Rights Act, the discrimination-in-employment title, looks good on paper, but an understaffed enforcement agency without enthusiastic administration support has not as yet achieved significant gains. Part of the problem is the largely case-by-case, complaint basis of enforcement. As with housing legislation, this nonstrategic, nonpatterned method has repeatedly failed in the many states that have relied upon it.[90]

The federal government as an employer has set a notable example of what can be accomplished through planning in the hiring and upgrading of Negro personnel.[91] Title VII will not achieve a similar result generally unless a number of changes are made. Its coverage must be expanded to include employees of state and local governments, private membership clubs, educational institutions, and employers and unions with eight or more employees or members. The Equal Employment Opportunity Commission (EEOC) must be authorized to issue "cease and desist orders," to command payment of back pay to persons suffering financial loss through denial of equal employment opportunity, and to initiate more patterned and strategic actions without complaint. Government contracting authority should be utilized to write new training program requirements into appropriate government contracts. Technical assistance for training and for affirmative desegregation programs must be furnished by EEOC to employers,

[89] *Ibid.*, p. 458–459.
[90] Leon Mayhew, "Law and Equal Opportunity: Anti-Discrimination Law in Massachusetts" (unpublished Ph.D. dissertation, Harvard University, 1964).
[91] John Hope II and Edward E. Shelton, "The Negro in the Federal Government," *Journal of Negro Education, 1963 Yearbook*, Vol. 32:4 (1963), pp. 367–374.

labor unions, private groups, and governmental staffs. Finally, a sharply increased operating budget must be appropriated by Congress for the commission so that it can realistically enforce Title VII.[92]

The necessity of patterned antidiscrimination enforcement points up again the systemic nature of racial issues in urban America. Gunnar Myrdal emphasized a generation ago the vicious circle formed by discrimination in housing, employment, and education;[93] successful remedies must break this circle at strategic points such as special employment, training, and counseling programs for youth. Steps toward a more systemic approach include federalizing the public employment service, expanding the Manpower Retraining Act and the educational potential of the armed forces, designing mass transit networks so that Negro workers have better access to centers of metropolitan employment, and, finally, a major overhauling of welfare programs.

Federalizing the public employment service is long overdue.[94] Although the service is operated by the states, it is totally financed by federal funds. All too often, state agencies have discriminated in their job referrals and have operated parochially, virtually ignoring the national aspects of the problem. Now that a variety of federal training functions have been assigned to them, it is imperative that this weak link be federalized, strengthened, and coordinated with the proposed metropolitan job councils.

Retraining programs should be expanded. First, the Manpower Retraining Act should be revised to lower its entrance requirements (it has largely rejected those applicants who need it most) and to furnish relocation funds so that the retrained can move to where the jobs are. Also the most vital federal source of job training for Negroes, the armed forces, should be more directly exploited. Except in wartime, the armed forces, like the manpower retraining program, exclude those Negroes who need the training and integrated experience the most. Lower entrance standards in peacetime are indicated, though the training expenditure per inductee will necessarily rise.[95] A start in

[92] Many of these items were recommended by the White House Conference "To Fulfill These Rights," p. 25.
[93] Gunnar Myrdal, *An American Dilemma* (New York: Harper, 1944).
[94] White House Conference "To Fulfill These Rights," p. 27.
[95] Discussion of the social psychological advantages of armed forces training is contained in: Pettigrew, *A Profile of the Negro American*, pp. 175–76. On the necessity of dealing expensively with the hard-core problem individuals, see T. F. Pettigrew, "Complexity and Change in American Racial Patterns: A Social Psychological View," in Parsons and Clark, *The Negro American*, pp. 345–347.

this direction has recently been made in Project One-Hundred Thousand.

Since Negro workers are more dependent upon mass transit than white workers, the new designs for urban transportation systems assume special importance. Present urban transit systems usually contribute an additional barrier between the ghetto dweller and the across-town job. Until recently in the Watts area, for instance, many workers had to travel for two hours, transfer several times, and pay fifty cents each way to commute to jobs or to visit employment agency offices.[96] With industry gaining admittance to the suburbs faster than Negroes, improved transit routing is essential.

Finally, there is widespread agreement that present welfare programs have failed, that they foster dependence and act as disincentives for employment. Developing a new approach, however, is a matter of sharp debate. Although some reactionaries suggest virtual abandonment, more concerned critics point out specific deficiencies and suggest plausible modifications. Tobin, for example, emphasizes two particularly negative aspects of the present approach to welfare, the means test and the exclusion of families with an able-bodied employed male in the house.[97] "In a society which prizes incentives for work and thrift," he comments wryly, "these are surprising regulations."[98] The means test in effect taxes earnings at a rate of 100 per cent, and it discourages saving by limiting property holdings. The exclusion of families with an employed male denies assistance to more than half the poverty-stricken children of the nation.[99] It also encourages father absence.

A new approach must offer the incentives for work, saving, and family stability now lacking. It must also be simpler to administer, avoid the indignities of present procedures, and discontinue the exclusion of significant segments of the poor. Such criteria strongly suggest a system of basic income allowances similar to what has unfortunately been tagged "a negative income tax." All Americans would file an annual income tax statement, but those falling below stated poverty levels would receive graduated funds from the government. Tobin has demonstrated that such an equitable system could easily be designed to encourage employment and thrift by taxing the income of welfare recipients at fair rates rather than the present 100 per cent.[100]

[96] White House Conference "To Fulfill These Rights," p. 27.
[97] Tobin, in Parsons and Clark, *The Negro American*, pp. 462–469.
[98] Ibid., p. 463.
[99] White House Conference "To Fulfill These Rights," p. 30.
[100] Tobin, in Parsons and Clark, *The Negro American*, pp. 462–469. Moynihan and

In addition to metropolitan and systemic criteria, consideration of positive interracial contacts on the job must be a part of effective employment remedies. The other Negro America desperately requires jobs, but it also requires experience and involvement in the mainstream of American life. The social psychological specifications are again essential: equal status, common goals, intergroup dependence, and support of authorities.

Employment will offer, in the immediate future, more opportunities for favorable interracial contact than housing, education, or any other area of activity. That this is so is an essentially negative comment about other realms of American society.[101]

EDUCATION

The chief thrust of the Negro American revolution has centered on education. Like other Americans, Negro parents regard education as the key to a better future for their children.

"But is racial integration of schools really essential to fulfilling this promise?" ask some educators. "Isn't the basic problem a matter of upgrading Negro educational standards and couldn't this be achieved most efficiently by pouring extra resources into ghetto schools for compensatory education?" Such is the reasoning behind the one-and-a-half-billion-dollar-a-year Title I of the 1965 Elementary and Secondary Education Act that funds compensatory programs for children from low-income families without integration requirements.

THE NEED FOR INTEGRATION

A considerable amount of research and educational experience, however, deny the efficacy of this comforting approach, which reinforces present educational structures and further segregates rich from poor, white from Negro. These comforting, *status quo* features are precisely why it has so completely failed in its paternalistic mission of Negro uplift; quality education is impossible without racial balance. Beyond the critical political, legal, and moral justifications for racially balanced schools, there are three vital educational reasons why school integration must be the national goal: the amelioration of racial

---

others have argued for another type of transfer of payments plan, namely a family allowance. But general application of such an allowance would be highly inefficient, since more than half of the funds would go to families that are not poor.

[101] Pettigrew, "Complexity and Change in American Racial Patterns: A Social Psychological View," in Parsons and Clark, *The Negro American*, pp. 350–352.

prejudice, preparation for the interracial world of the future, and enhanced academic achievement.

The amelioration of racial prejudice through educational desegregation is not a special-case argument for Negro students. Considerable research indicates the early formation of stereotyped racial attitudes by both Negro and white children.[102] Racial awareness typically dawns in the third and fourth years of life and takes root by the fifth year. By about the eighth year, the racial attitudes of American children generally assume an adult form; whole "races" are no longer perceived as all bad or all good but in a more differentiated light. Negroes, white children may now concede, are good after all at entertainment and athletics. Such attitude development can be modified by favorable everyday contact in which both Negro and white children learn that members of the other group are just people, with as wide a range of personal qualities as members of their own group. As one of the nine Negro children who desegregated Little Rock's Central High School in 1957 observed after a few months of her celebrated ordeal, "Now I know that there are some stupid white kids, too!"

The preparation of today's students for tomorrow's interracial world is a second educational reason for integrated schools. Catherine Bauer Wurster recognized this function clearly in 1955 and questioned the neighborhood school concept before it became widely criticized as a major barrier to interracial education:

Where the neighborhood social pattern is highly standardized, is it always a sound ideal for schools to conform to the same pattern? Clearly there are some difficult issues here, with conflicting values to be resolved. But if schools are supposed to train children to live successfully in a highly variegated world, this is a very real problem for the educational system.[103]

Research psychology has established as a firm principle that alteration of salient environmental features associated with original learning

---

[102] K. B. Clark, *Prejudice and Your Child* (2nd ed.; Boston: Beacon Press, 1963); K. B. Clark and Mamie P. Clark, "Racial Identification and Preference in Negro Children," in T. M. Newcomb and E. L. Hartley, eds., *Readings in Social Psychology* (1st ed.; New York: Holt, 1947), pp. 169–178; Mary E. Goodman, *Race Awareness in Young Children* (Cambridge, Mass.: Addison-Wesley, 1952); Catherine Landreth and Barbara C. Johnson, "Young Children's Responses to a Picture and Inset Test Designed to Reveal Reactions to Persons of Different Skin Color," *Child Development,* Vol. 24 (1953), pp. 63–80; J. K. Morland, "Racial Recognition by Nursery School Children in Lynchburg, Virginia," *Social Forces,* Vol. 37 (1958), pp. 132–137; H. W. Stevenson and E. C. Stewart, "A Developmental Study of Racial Awareness in Young Children," *Child Development,* Vol. 29 (1958), pp. 399–409; and Helen G. Trager and Marian R. Yarrow, *They Live What They Learn* (New York: Harpers, 1952).
[103] Bauer, "The Pattern of Urban and Economic Development," p. 24.

results in diminished retention and performance.[104] The extension of
this learning principle to the problem of racially balanced schools
becomes evident when we recall the changes under way in Negro
employment. Slowly but definitely, and with a quickened pace likely
in the near future, there is a proliferation of interracial work situations.
In the armed forces and in offices, retail stores, and factories with
government contracts, members of both races perform side by side,
although most of them have been educated in nonintegrated schools.
The different racial composition of learning and performance situations
is a "salient alteration." Note once again that this is not a special-case
argument for Negroes. Both whites and Negroes feel awkward and
ill at ease in interracial situations in which they have had little prior
experience. As interracial contacts become the rule rather than
the exception in America, schools will have to provide similarly
interracial learning settings in order to give these advances full effect.

Finally, school integration greatly affects the academic achievement
of Negro children. At the outset, an important distinction becomes
necessary: it is integrated, not merely desegregated, schools which are
essential. A desegregated school is merely one with a reasonable
number of both Negro and white students. Desegregation is a prerequisite for integration, but it is a minimal goal since it guarantees neither
an effective learning environment nor a positive interracial setting.
Integration, by contrast, requires true interracial acceptance and a
situation described by social psychology's four contact conditions—
equal status, common goals, group interdependence, and authority
sanction.

Two extensive investigations, one performed under controlled
laboratory settings, the other in the classroom itself, underline the
crucial relationship between integration and achievement. An elaborate
series of laboratory experiments by Irwin Katz on Negro performance
in biracial situations has led to the isolation of four central factors.[105]

---

[104] A more extended treatment of this point is provided in: T. F. Pettigrew and
Patricia Pajonis, "Social Psychological Considerations of Racially-Balanced Schools,"
an appendix to: Massachusetts State Board of Education, *Because It is Right—
Educationally: Report of the Advisory Committee on Racial Imbalance and Education*
(Boston: Massachusetts State Board of Education, April 1965), pp. 87–108.
[105] Irwin Katz, "Review of Evidence Relating to Effects of Desegregation on the
Intellectual Performance of Negroes," *American Psychologist*, Vol. 19 (June 1964),
pp. 381–399. Much of the Katz model for Negro performance in interracial situations
is appropriate to the performance of lower-class children in general in middle-class
situations. See, for example, David L. Rosenhan, "Effects of Social Class and Race

Three are on the negative side of the ledger: lowered probability of
success, social threat, and failure threat. Where there is a marked
discrepancy in the educational standards of Negro and white schools,
or where Negro children have already acquired strong feelings of
inferiority, minority group arrivals in biracial classes are likely to
have a low expectancy of academic success. This expectancy is often
realistic, given the situation, but it has the self-fulfilling effect of
lowering achievement motivation. Social threat is involved in any
biracial situation involving Negroes because of the prestige and
dominance of whites in American society. Rejection of Negro students
in these circumstances often elicits emotional responses that are
detrimental to intellectual functioning. Failure threat arises when
academic defeat means disapproval by "significant others"—parents,
teachers, perhaps even peers in school. Low expectancy of success
under failure threat may also elicit emotional responses detrimental
to performance. On the positive side, Katz notes that acceptance
of Negroes by white classmates and adults has a social facilitation
effect upon their ability to learn, apparently because it reassures the
the Negro child that he is fully expected to be as talented and
important in the classroom as anyone else. This anticipation, that
skillful performance will win general approval rather than rejection
for "not knowing his place," endows scholastic success in the biracial
situation with high incentive value for the Negro youngster.

From these findings, we should not expect Negro children to perform
markedly better in desegregated schools, where Katz's negative factors
prevail. On the contrary, we should predict that those Negro children
in truly integrated schools would tend to do best while those in
newly desegregated schools would do no better or even worse than
similar children in predominantly Negro schools. A mammoth U.S.
Office of Education classroom survey of equal educational opportunities
handsomely bears out these predictions.[106]
Analyses relevant to Katz's work were performed on the test scores
of children in the sixth, ninth, and twelfth grades in the metropolitan
Midwest and Northeast.[107] In eleven out of twelve comparisons on

on Responsiveness to Approval and Disapproval," *Journal of Personality and Social
Psychology,* Vol. 4 (1966), pp. 253–259.
[106] James S. Coleman, *Equality of Educational Opportuniy* (U.S. Department of
Health, Education, and Welfare Document OE-38001 [Washington, D.C., 1966]).
[107] *Ibid.,* pp. 330–333. The class composition was determined for the previous year
because the data were collected in October, too early in the school term for the new

reading comprehension and mathematical achievement, the mean scores of Negro students from classes that were more than half white were somewhat higher than other groups of Negro students. However, these same desegregated Negro students had considerably greater variability in both their reading and mathematical scores than the other groups of Negroes, showing Katz's positive and negative factors at work. Further analyses of these data by the U.S. Commission on Civil Rights reveal the expected difference between integrated and desegregated schools. Those racially mixed schools whose Negroes score well, when compared with similar schools whose Negroes score poorly, are characterized by greater cross-racial acceptance and less racial tension. Their students were much more likely to report close friends among members of the other race than students in the merely desegrated schools.[108]

With cross-racial acceptance, schools become truly integrated and generate subtle but critically beneficial changes in their students. For example, the equal educational opportunities survey found that a sense of controlling the environment is an unusually significant correlate of Negro academic achievement: those Negro children who considered themselves masters of their own fate tended to score high, those who did not tended to score low. Negroes in predominantly white schools more often evidenced this sense of environmental control.[109]

The major conclusion of this massive national survey throws into serious doubt the premises of Title I of the 1965 Elementary and Secondary Education Act. As in the concentration and separation of low-income Americans accomplished by public housing, this title encourages doing something special for poor children *apart* from advantaged children. Yet if we take the equal educational opportunities survey seriously, such a separatist strategy actually denies the disadvantaged child the major educational resource he needs— equal-status contact with advantaged children.

All three of these educational reasons for integration—ameliorating racial prejudice, preparing for the interracial world of the future, and enhancing academic achievement—carry special force at the

---

situation to have critical effects. Nonetheless, it is safe to assume that for the majority of the respondents the racial classroom composition of the new class is essentially the same as that of the previous year.

[108] U.S. Commission on Civil Rights, *Racial Isolation in the Public Schools* (Washington, D.C.: U.S. Government Printing Office, 1967).

[109] Coleman, *Equality of Educational Opportunity*, pp. 319–325.

elementary school level. In its detailed analysis of this point, the Office of Education study found that children who began their desegregated experience in the first three grades proved consistently more receptive to Negroes, both as classmates and as close friends, than other white children.[110] Likewise, the survey noted that reading comprehension scores of Negro children tended not only to be somewhat higher for those students in predominantly white schools but higher still for those who began their desegregated experience in the first three grades.[111]

Because racial isolation is cumulative, tending to feed upon itself, early biracial experience is also an essential preparation for interracial adulthood. This point is dramatically demonstrated in a report from the U.S. Commission on Civil Rights.[112] Louisville, Kentucky, has six high schools, all of which by 1962 had enrolled at least a few Negroes under an open-choice system. One of the high schools, Central, had been designated for Negroes before Louisville ended *de jure* school segregation, and it remained virtually all Negro in 1962. The commission checked on whether the racial compositions of the junior high schools were related to the selection by Negro children of *de facto* segregated Central High School and found the relationship to be very close: "The inference is strong that Negro high school students prefer biracial education only if they have experienced it before. If a Negro has not received his formative education in biracial schools, the chances are that he will not choose to enter in his more mature school years."[113]

The special value of elementary school integration complicates educational issues, for it is precisely the elementary school that is the most segregated in our cities and the most difficult to desegregate. The Office of Education study estimates that, in the fall of 1965, 65 per cent of Negro pupils in the first grade were in extremely segregated schools (90 to 100 per cent Negro) compared to 48 per cent of Negro pupils in the twelfth grade. Similarly, 87 per cent of Negro first-graders and 66 per cent of Negro twelfth-graders were in schools with 50 per cent or more Negroes. White students, however, are even

---

[110] *Ibid.,* p. 333. Later desegregation still has benefits, however, since those white students who had never attended school with Negroes were the least receptive.
[111] *Ibid.,* pp. 331–332. According to a footnote in the report on page 331, this trend was not a function of different family backgrounds.
[112] U.S. Commission on Civil Rights, *Civil Rights U.S.A.: Public Schools, Southern States, 1962* (Washington, D. C.: U.S. Government Printing Office, 1963), p. 55.
[113] *Ibid.,* p. 31.

more segregated. In 1965 approximately 80 per cent of all white
first-graders and twelfth-graders attended public schools with 90 to
100 per cent white student bodies.[114]

Although housing segregation and the dominant pattern of Negro
isolation within the central city are primary causes of educational
segregation, the nation's schools cannot tolerate the inevitably slow
rate of change in these fields. In American race relations, time is
the ingredient in shortest supply. The historic mission of American
public education to provide unity and opportunity in a multigroup
society can no longer be delayed.

KEY FACTORS IN INTEGRATING EDUCATION

Integrating the schools has raised a major procedural issue, because
of the varying motives involved and the widely dissimilar approaches
suggested. Before adopting any approach, however, the planner must
have thoroughly explored four key factors common to them all: the
definition of "racial balance," political pressures, the focus of responsibility, and the concept of "neighborhood schools."

Racial balance may be defined in two ways. One method pegs the
definition to the nonwhite percentage of the area's over-all school
population. Thus, if 12 per cent of a system's students are nonwhite,
each school in the system should approach a nonwhite student
composition of 12 per cent. There are at least two criticisms of this
definition: often it is impractical to achieve in scattered schools over
a large area, and it treats the individual school as a simple reflection
of the community, rather than as an institution with its own dynamics
and requirements.

A second type of definition attempts to meet these criticisms by using
a relatively fixed gauge. On the basis of several social psychological
considerations, an ideally balanced school is one with a student body
composed of roughly 20 to 45 per cent nonwhites.[115] This range
is approximate, of course, but it is not arbitrary. At one end, a figure
substantially less than 20 per cent—as in token desegregation—isolates
the Negro students, makes them appear individually conspicuous,
and encourages bigots in the hope of eventually excluding them
altogether. At the other end, a Negro majority arouses the recurrent
white fear of being "swamped" and enhances the danger of the school's

---

[114] Coleman, *Equality of Educational Opportunity*, pp. 3-7.
[115] Pettigrew and Pajonis, "Social Psychological Considerations of Racially-Balanced
Schools," p. 100.

becoming virtually all Negro. A 20 to 45 per cent Negro representation, however, assures maximal contact and participation of at least a few Negroes in all phases of the school's activities, from athletics to the honor society. It also has the advantage of approximating the racial balance thought desirable by a majority of white parents.[116]

The disadvantage of the fixed definition is that uniracial schools will necessarily result when a city has fewer than 20 per cent or greater than 45 per cent nonwhite children. If a metropolitan perspective is taken, however, this disadvantage is eliminated. Although no workable definition of racial integration can fit such central cities as Washington, Richmond, and Philadelphia, the defined upper limit of 45 per cent can be achieved by diluting these Negro cores in a metropolitan ring of white suburbs. In every metropolitan area in the country, such a solution would be effective.

A second basic factor involved in integrating the schools is politics. The school system, especially the school board, typically becomes the target of at least three conflicting sets of political pressures: the integrationist demands of committed Negro and white liberals; the resistant demands of committed segregationists; and the fears of the less committed, usually more powerful, upper-status whites.

Many urban systems, hoping these pressures would ease, have stalled for time, but this strategy has generally proved fatal. Integrationist pressures, in particular, are not likely to lessen significantly. Though it may occasionally take such separatist detours as the "black power" ideology, the current Negro American revolution is likely to expand further in terms of size, intensity, and the scope of its demands.[117] This poses a dilemma for school officials. On the one hand, refusal to deal with Negro demands for integrated education usually leads to severe community crisis, as in Boston and Chicago. On the other hand, changes made in direct response to insistent Negro protest often act to encourage further Negro pressure and to intensify white fears and resistance. This dilemma can be avoided by staying ahead of the issue, thereby averting crisis demands. As a matter of recent record, those urban systems which have chosen to act affirmatively before becoming the object of political cross-pressures have fared best.

In addition, we should not overlook the practical, "off-the-hook" function that federal desegregation pressures can provide. Federal court

[116] American Institute of Public Opinion, Press Release of May 22, 1965.
[117] Pettigrew, *A Profile of the Negro American,* Chapter 8.

orders and threats to withdraw federal monies furnish many embattled school boards, North and South, with the acceptable excuse they need to desegregate. Indeed, one large northern school board has allowed a *de facto* segregation suit to remain in the federal courts long after it could have been dismissed for this specific purpose.

The focus of intergovernmental responsibility is a third key factor. The unique feature of American public education, local school district autonomy, is often its greatest weakness. Racial integration is a prime example of a program that frequently needs external support, political as well as economic. Recent federal legislation has certainly recognized this fact, yet extensive outside aid further complicates already complex and delicate relationships between federal, state, metropolitan, and local district authorities.

Nevertheless, alleviation of the serious problems, racial and otherwise, which threaten the viability of urban public education today requires a wider focus of responsibility than now prevails; as in housing and employment, the central city cannot go it alone. State departments of education will have to be upgraded and granted more authority. State and federal funds must be increased dramatically, even becoming dominant portions of many local district budgets, so that expenditures per child may be equalized across the nation. In particular, the "white noose around the Negro's neck"—the suburbs—will have to cooperate in joint city-suburb ventures. The sources of resistance to such cooperation are predictable, but school district boundaries are neither God given nor locally fixed. They are the creation of the states, which have a constitutional duty to provide equal protection of the law to all their citizens. Direct legal analogies to the reapportionment decisions of the Supreme Court are promising and may furnish the basis for judicial relief as the metropolitan educational crisis grows still more acute.

Resistance to educational change often begins at the individual school level and involves the fourth key factor, the neighborhood school. Based on the earlier rural model of the local school, the neighborhood school idea was launched as the appropriate model for cities at the turn of this century. Progressives hoped to counter what they regarded as the evil influences of the big city by establishing "multiple communities," an array of small, self-contained towns within the city, each with its own churches, school, and business area. In a sense, the immigrant ghettos with their own language, newspaper, shops,

and church furnished concrete examples of what the progressive
planners had in mind, but they also exposed the concept's weakness:
such neighborhoods ran the danger of not preparing their youth to
enter successfully what Catherine Bauer Wurster called the "highly
variegated world." While public schools provided immigrant children
with their chief mainstream influence, teaching them English and the
customs and expectations of the new land, they usually brought
together children from diverse backgrounds and many neighborhoods.
The big city schools were the chief agent for assimilating millions of
immigrants in part because they did not adhere to the progressives'
neighborhood concept.

Yet the concept won wide acceptance in educational circles, because
it seemed to offer a personalized solution to the impersonal threats
of the metropolis, and in time it became a sacrosanct shibboleth.
This faith (which is not supported by any sound research) has persisted
in spite of the steady trend toward increasingly larger urban schools,
a trend that has destroyed any direct correspondence between school
attendance areas and actual neighborhoods. Today the concept is
flowering as a convenient, emotional, and traditional defense against
urban desegregation. Such groups as New York City's Parents and
Taxpayers League correctly sense that if they can maintain both
housing discrimination and neighborhood schools, they can forestall
racial desegregation indefinitely.

IMPLEMENTING SCHOOL INTEGRATION

The most fundamental issue with which we are concerned here
is how to implement racial integration throughout urban America.
Initially, we must make a clear distinction between small-ghetto and
large-ghetto situations, for what is possible and useful in the former
may well be counterproductive in the latter.

The small-ghetto situation generally involves a city with less than
a seventh of its public school population Negro. Its high schools and
even its junior high schools are naturally desegregated, and with good
faith it can correct elementary school segregation within its borders
by utilizing some appropriate combination of the following within-
district methods: district-wide redrawing of school lines to maximize
racial balance (positive gerrymandering), pairing predominantly white
and Negro schools along the borders of the ghetto (the Princeton
plan), and careful placement of new, larger schools outside the ghetto
(the rebuilding plan). If there is a need to desegregate at the junior

or senior high levels, two other devices are often sufficient: alteration of "feeder" arrangements from elementary grades to junior highs and from junior highs to senior highs in order to maximize racial balance, and conversion of more schools into district-wide specialized institutions. In the typical small-ghetto situation controversy is minimal because a solution can be devised that does not require widespread subsidized transportataion of students.

Much more difficult problems of implementation occur in the large-ghetto situation. For the city system with a substantial and growing percentage of Negro students, small-ghetto devices are generally no more than Band-aid remedies. Thus, pairing schools along the ghetto's borders would have to be repeated every few years as the ghetto expanded. A new school built outside the ghetto last year may become a predominantly Negro school within the next year. In Boston, whose public school system is only 26 per cent nonwhite, a sophisticated redistricting plan for elementary schools was subjected to computer-assisted analysis. The ultimate limit of redistricting was tested with the rules that children in grades one through three would not be assigned more than a half mile from their homes and children in grades four through six not more than three quarters of a mile. Yet the proportion of Boston's nonwhite elementary students attending predominantly nonwhite schools would be reduced only from 78 per cent to 66 per cent, a minor change.[118] Clearly, for Boston—not to mention the really enormous ghetto cities of New York, Philadelphia, Washington, Chicago, and Los Angeles—more sweeping measures are required.

The criteria for these sweeping measures are necessarily demanding. Larger educational complexes drawing from wide attendance areas will be essential. In order to ensure the optimal stable racial mix, these attendance areas will generally have to include both central-city and suburban territory. The sites for these facilities must be convenient to the mass transit network but must also be on racially neutral "turf," in order to avoid immediate public labeling of the school as "white" or "Negro."

There are nonracial criteria as well. Public schools in our largest cities have surrendered their former pre-eminence as innovative educational leaders to Berkeley, California, Newton and Brookline,

---

[118] Joint Center for Urban Studies of M.I.T. and Harvard, "Changes in School Attendance Districts as a Means of Alleviating Racial Imbalance in the Boston Public Schools" (unpublished report, August 1966), pp. 1–2.

Massachusetts, and a host of other small communities. Thus, the plans for the future should accent and facilitate innovation. Indeed, future public schools must possess facilities which could rarely be duplicated by private schools if they are to compete effectively for the children of advantaged parents. Such arrangements, of course, will cost considerable money; an inescapable final criterion is significant federal support of capital costs.

METROPOLITAN SCHOOL PARKS

There are several possible designs that would meet these important criteria; the metropolitan school park, serving both inner-city and suburban students, is illustrative and deserves closer study. Each park would be located on neutral turf in an inner-ring suburb or just inside the central-city boundary and would be so placed that the same spoke of the mass transit system could bring outer-ring surburban children into the park and inner-city children out to it. The attendance area of each park would ideally cut out a metropolitan pie-slice containing part of the 15,000 to 18,000 public school students.

From high-rise structures to multiple-unit campuses, a variety of designs have been suggested. The most widely discussed would involve eighty to a hundred acres of land as a minimum and no fewer than fourteen or fifteen schools, serving grades from kindergarten through high school. One educator has visualized a campus design for 18,000 students consisting of two senior high, four junior high, and eight elementary schools.[119] If the park were to serve a very densely populated section, it might be burdened by an even larger student body; in this case it would be best to reduce the number of grades included in order to retain the advantages of covering a reasonably expansive and heterogeneous attendance area. In general, however, an educational park resembles a public university, offering a variety of educational programs for a large group of students of varying abilities.

A number of school systems have considered educational parks, but they usually find the capital costs prohibitive. Moreover, many systems are currently hard-pressed for expansion funds, especially as referenda for school construction bonds continue to be defeated throughout the nation. Federal funding on a massive scale will obviously

[119] George Brain, "The Educational Park: Some Advantages and Disadvantages," in Nathan Jacobson, ed., *An Exploration of the Educational Park Concept* (New York: New York Board of Education, 1964), p. 16.

be needed, though it must be accomplished in a far more careful and strategic manner than the everybody-gets-his-cut principle of the 1965 Elementary and Secondary Education Act. As long as alternate federal funding for capital costs is available, many school systems—particularly those anxious to preserve *de facto* segregation—will not choose to join a metropolitan park plan. Future federal construction grants must exclude these alternate sources of funds and impose metropolitan, integrationist criteria. Assuming an economy not strained by war expenditures, two billion dollars a year—enough to build roughly forty parks annually—could be made available for school construction. It is imperative that urban school systems prepare now to take beneficial advantage of this opportunity, by developing plans for metropolitan school parks or something comparable.

Apart from offering racial remedies, the metropolitan park concept has a number of distinct advantages. There are considerable savings that accrue from simultaneously building many units at one location and then operating them with centralized service facilities. These savings would be used to provide better facilities than traditional schools can afford. Consequently, each child would receive far more per educational dollar in the metropolitan park.

The improved centralized facilities of the park would provide a fresh and exciting setting, encourage new educational techniques, and attract the more innovative members of the teaching profession. In addition, the park presents a rare opportunity for innovation in the physical and social structures of schools. For example, centralization would permit highly efficient concentration of electronic information storage and retrieval facilities. Such centralization of equipment need not lead inevitably to an Orwellian clutter of gadgets; with careful planning, the result can be far more flexible and individualized instruction than is now possible in scattered neighborhood schools.

Moreover, concentration would make possible some remarkable facilities, such as an Olympic-sized swimming pool and extensive theatrical equipment, which can be shared by all of the park's units. These special facilities could far surpass what is now available in all but the most affluent districts, become a source of student and community pride, and provide a competitive advantage over private schools.

Many innovations made possible by the metropolitan park go deeper than equipment. The teaching profession today is one of the most undifferentiated by rank of all professions, a characteristic that discourages a life-long career orientation to the field. While the medical profession has a graded progression of roles from intern and resident to chief of a service, teachers must either enter administration and become principals or shift to more prestigious schools in order to move up the ladder. By concentrating a large number of teachers in a relatively small area, far more role differentiation becomes possible. Thus, a teacher might progress from apprentice in a team-teaching situation to master teacher in a team, then to supervisor of master teachers. Similarly, faculty concentration allows the formation of departments across schools with rankings within departments as in universities (for example, a junior high history department consisting of all history teachers in the four or five junior highs on the campus). Concentration of faculty, when taken with concentration of students, also allows wider course offerings. Specialized classes, such as playing the lute or sevententh-century English literature, become economically possible when a specialist can teach students gathered from units throughout the park.

Finally, the metropolitan park offers unusual opportunities for an effective liaison with a local university or college. Nova, the extensive educational park near Fort Lauderdale, Florida, plans to offer college and graduate work on its campus. Even without such direct contiguity the size and quality of metropolitan park schools would facilitate a mutually beneficial coordination at all levels.

While conceding these advantages, four serious objections to the park concept can be raised. First, the park is very expensive, and major federal funding is necessary. Furthermore, mistakes in design and location could be disastrous. A park is an enormous commitment of resources and, if poorly conceived, could stand for years as a monument to poor planning. The Philadelphia Urban League, in proposing four nonmetropolitan parks within a central city whose public school student body is already 58 per cent nonwhite, has advanced just such a plan.

The second problem is phasing out existing facilities. For many urban districts this is not a problem; they already have overutilized schools with double shifts and rising enrollments, or old schools long past their usefulness. Some urban districts, however, have many new and expensive schools and would be hesitant to join a park consortium. In these districts the program's aspects must be convincingly demonstrated.

Elementary and secondary student enrollments will rise rapidly: from 48.4 million in 1964 to a projected 54.9 million in 1974 and 66 million in the fateful year 1984.[120] Beginning in the early 1970's, metropolitan parks could be opened as older facilities are retired and enrollments swiftly rise. It is also probable that the first parks would serve as attractive models of success to those districts still hesitant.

There will be special problems in localities with "planned *de facto* school segregation." These are cities which in recent years have purposely built new schools in the heart of their Negro ghettos in order to maximize racial separation. If racial progress is to be made in these cities, recent structures will have to be converted to new uses, such as much-needed community centers.

The third objection to parks is the impersonalization of such large complexes—"the Kafka problem." Indeed, much of the park's description—the latest electronic equipment, 15,000 students, a staff of 1,000—has a frightening Kafka ring, but such an inference is not necessary. In fact, imaginatively designed parks could reverse the present trend toward huge urban high schools by grouping smaller schools at each level within the park. Careful planning can establish a reasonable degree of privacy for each unit while still providing access to the shared facilities of the park.

Finally, some critics mention the park's loss of neighborhood interest and involvement, an extension of the neighborhood schools argument. This criticism assumes that most urban public schools today are neighborhood-based and that they generate considerable neighborhood involvement. Serious doubts can be raised about both assumptions: we may well be worrying about the loss of something already long gone. In any event, there is no evidence to indicate that only a neighborhood-based school can generate parental concern. Certainly, the special facilities and the university-liaison of the school park would generate community pride and interest. Widespread use of the park for adult education or community affairs would also contribute to public involvement; indeed, the special facilities of the park lend themselves to such adult use more readily than those of the typical school today.

The educational park idea is not a panacea; there can be elegantly effective and incredibly ineffective parks. Yet ample federal funding,

[120] Francis Keppel, *The Necessary Revolution in American Education* (New York: Harper & Row, 1966), p. 19.

combined with the nation's planning and architectural genius, should be able to set a new standard and direction for public schools, with racial interaction only one of many important benefits to all the nation's children. This plan and others equally imaginative demonstrate that those who say there is nothing we can do about educational segregation in our major cities are very wrong. What we must recognize now is the urgent necessity of action. America failed to offer fourteen generations of Negro Americans a first-class education and is now paying a heavy price for that failure. Will we fail the fifteenth generation, too, and pay an even greater price?

PROSPECTS FOR RACIAL CHANGE

Consensus about the seriousness of urban America's racial problems is matched by controversy over what can be done. I have attempted to demonstrate that America has barely begun to employ its vast moral, judicial, legislative, and economic resources toward the solution of racial disharmony in the interlocking realms of law enforcement, housing, employment, and education. Past efforts have either failed or led to seemingly minor improvements by being trivial and often halfhearted when great initiative and innovation are required.

The popular mass media have described in recent years a "white backlash," but the term is too variously defined and too simple to be helpful or accurate. The implication is that white attitudes toward Negroes have shifted very unfavorably. Relevant research data, however, point to a different, though equally dangerous, process which has three recognized dimensions: a mobilization of the right combined with a demobilization of the left; a rising salience of racial concerns among white Americans; and a growing resistance to the pace of change, though not generally toward the goals of the change, among white Americans—especially among the mildly prejudiced.

Roughly speaking, about 30 per cent of white Americans are reasonably solid segregationists, and another 30 per cent are reasonably solid integrationists. The shifts in survey data over time reflect the variable mood of the middle 40 per cent whose mild prejudice against Negroes is usually not nearly as salient as their desire for "law and order." When it appeared in 1964 that racial peace could be achieved by a civil rights act directed at the South, the mildly prejudiced joined the then-mobilized liberal integrationists in supporting such legislation. Now that riots and "black power" slogans threaten civic peace, the middle group has joined newly mobilized segregationists in demands to slow racial change.

How much time will be lost by this regressive trend? In American race relations, time is literally of the essence. For every year of inaction in the 1960's, two or three years will be required to make up the ground later, but make up the lost ground we must, and we will. The question is how much damage the nation must inflict upon itself before it realizes its own dream.

4.

Why New Communities?
Edward P. Eichler

When Catherine Bauer Wurster and I met in 1959, she quickly involved me in the study of urban problems, in the California Housing Commission, and in the Ford Foundation sponsored Community Development Project at Berkeley. This project was established to study the so-called New Town movement in America, which so many people seemed to herald as if it would bring an urban millennium.

Catherine and I disagreed about many of the problems and policy positions of the project, but we shared an obsession which continually influences my judgments of urban developments. We both sought the answer to the question "How can we help effectuate programs which will alleviate the sufferings of America's urban poor, especially poor Negroes, and avoid open racial conflict?" Although reason tells me that this cause may be hopeless, my guiding fiction remains that there must be a way. I cannot refrain, however, from condemning a proposed program or notion, even though it is the product of good intentions (as may be the case with New Towns) if the evidence tells me it will not work or, worse yet, will be harmful.

THE GENESIS OF THE MODERN NEW TOWN MOVEMENT

The modern New Town or New Community movement in America began in 1958 with the announcement of Eldorado Hills, a ten-thousand-acre private development north of Sacramento, California. Since then, almost every trade journal and popular magazine has painted a glowing picture of the promise of this new concept. Underlying this great interest, and, as a matter of fact, a cause of the New Towns movement itself, has been what I call the urban development critique. This critique has developed, partially, from the ambivalence Americans have always felt toward their cities and toward big cities in particular. At its inception, and throughout its great period of western settlement, this country was regarded by its citizens as the garden of the world. Even though the onset of industrialism and the growth of the cities transformed the garden of the world into a land of machine-produced plenty, mechanical agents of luxury and change have always remained somehow alien presences.[1]

Although the nation has been flooded with diatribes about

---

[1] See Leo Marx, *The Machine in the Garden* (New York and Oxford: Oxford University Press, 1964), for a penetrating discussion of the pastoral ideal in America, both in the general consciousness and American literature and how this ideal responded to the coming of the machine.

urbanization since World War II, perhaps one can date the resurgence in contemporary American thought about the defects of urban life from the time of Ebenezer Howard. Certainly, his proposal for satellites to London remains the central thesis in the plans of both British and American New Towns devotees.

THE REGIONAL MESS AND THE URBAN DEVELOPMENT CRITIQUE
___

The contributors to the urban development critique recoil in horror and outrage at what they assume are the effects of urbanization run wild. Each has his crusade, and where one leaves off, another begins in a bewildering bombardment which seems to leave no region of America unsinged. In their descriptions, language often abounds in science fiction images of devastation and monstrous growths. Lewis Mumford attacks the city itself and says that by failing "to divide its [the metropolis'] social chromosomes and split up into new cells, each bearing some portion of the original inheritance, the city continues to grow inorganically, indeed cancerously, by a continuous breaking down of old tissues, and an overgrowth of formless tissue."[2] Then the California architect Richard Neutra takes over, turning attention from the cities to the blighted countryside. In the analysis to which he gives the dark title *Survival Through Design,* he asks:

Must we remain victims, strangled and suffocated by our own design which has surrounded us with man-devouring metropolises, drab small towns manifesting a lack of order devastating to the soul, blighted countrysides along railroad tracks and highways, studded with petty 'mere-utility' structures, shaded by telephone poles and scented by gasoline fumes?[3]

Peter Blake, the editor of the *Architectural Forum,* summarizes these two attitudes in one of the most direct and concrete formulations of the basic response to the contemporary situation by the proponents of the development critique. In his book *God's Own Junkyard* he says,

. . . we are about to turn this beautiful inheritance [the American landscape] into the biggest slum on the face of the earth. "The mess that is man-made America," as a British magazine has called it, is a disgrace

___

[2] Lewis Mumford, *The City in History* (New York: Harcourt, Brace and World, 1961), p. 543.
[3] Richard Neutra, *Survival Through Design* (New York and Oxford: Oxford University Press, 1954), pp. 5–6.

of such vast proportions that only a concerted national effort can hope to return physical America to the community of civilized nations.[4]

According to the critique, neither city nor suburb nor countryside escapes the brutal marks of urbanization. In the established large cities, decentralization of mid-town business areas has begun. "Business wilts in the traffic congestion, property values sink, tax revenue declines, slums multiply and the need for a larger urban renewal program intensifies."[5]

While losing its economic function and viability, the city also loses its social function.

Suburban sprawl negates and frustrates the purpose of cities, which is to let more people live and work close together and so utilize and enjoy the maximum efficiency of community facilities and community enterprises, with easy access and cheap distribution.[6]

One might ask, then, if the suburbs are shouldering the social and economic functions that the city can no longer handle. William Whyte, in *The Exploding Metropolis,* says "no." He believes that waste and economic inefficiency are high even in new developments.

Where the new developments are scattered at random in the outlying areas, the costs of providing services become excruciating. There is not only the cost of running sewers and water mains and storm drains out to Happy Acres but much more road, per family served, has to be paved and maintained. . . . Sprawl also means low volume utility operation for the amount of installation involved.[7]

Aesthetic damage occurs. One learns from a brochure describing the situation in California in 1962, "California, Going, Going . . ." issued by California Tomorrow, a nonprofit educational institution, that

The character and quality of such urban sprawl is readily recognized: neon-bright strip cities along main traveled roads; housing tracts in profusion; clogged roads and billboard alleys; a chaotic mixture of supermarkets, used car lots, and pizza parlors; the asphalt plain of parking spaces; instead of parks, gray-looking fields forlornly waiting

[4] Peter Blake, *God's Own Junkyard* (New York: Holt, Rinehart and Winston, 1964), p. 8.
[5] Senator Harrison Williams, U.S. Congress, Senate Committee on Banking and Currency, 87th Congress, 1st Session, *Hearings,* S858, Housing Legislation of 1961, p. 998.
[6] "Land," *House and Home,* Vol. XVIII, No. 2 (1960), p. 114.
[7] William Whyte, *The Exploding Metropolis* (Garden City, N.Y.: Doubleday, Anchor Books, 1958), p. 122.

to be subdivided. These are the qualities of most of our new urban areas—of our *slurbs*—our sloppy, sleazy, slovenly, slipshod semi-cities.[8]

A new kind of emotional pressure is involved:

There is a certain psychic relief in open space that cannot be underestimated. It gives us visual relief from the tangled, jarring, and often monotonous sight of urban development, and a sense of orientation and community identity.[9]

What of the developments themselves? What are they like? How do their residents fare? The authors of the critique see no relief here either. John Keats describes the life offered in his best-selling book on conditions in the new suburbia, *The Crack in the Picture Window:*

. . . a housing development cannot be called a community, for that word implies a balanced society of men, women and children wherein work and pleasure are found and the needs of all the society's members are several. Housing developments offer no employment and as a general rule lack recreational areas, churches, schools or other cohesive influences.[10]

E. A. Gutkind, discussing suburbia in his book, *The Expanding Environment,* sums up all the apocalyptic horror of the urban development critique in the following statement:

The last vestiges of a community have disappeared. They are hardly anything else than an agglomeration of innumerable and isolated details, of human atoms, and rows of boxes, called houses, interspersed between the industries. It is a total victory of a laissez-faire insensibility and recklessness over organic growth and even over organized development.[11]

HOW DID IT HAPPEN?

The urban development critique lists many factors that have contributed to the present crisis of our cities. Prominent among them are rising levels of income, population growth, and the increased mobility provided by the automobile. The most fundamental factor, however, has been speculation by developers and misguided, piecemeal federal policies. The writings of those who espouse the urban critique say this

[8] Samuel E. Wood and Alfred E. Heller, *California, Going, Going . . .* , (Sacramento: California Tomorrow, 1962), p. 10.
[9] Williams, *Hearings,* p. 997.
[10] John Keats, *The Crack in the Picture Window* (Boston: Houghton Mifflin, 1957), p. XVI.
[11] E. A. Gutkind, *The Expanding Environment* (London: Freedom Press, 1953), quoted in *ibid.,* p. 176.

again and again, but, once more, the most concise formulation of the
argument appears in Peter Blake's *God's Own Junkyard*:

Suburbia got that way for two simple reasons: first, because the developers
who built it are, fundamentally, no different from manufacturers of any
other mass produced product: they standardize the product, package
it, arrange for rapid distribution and easy financing and sell it off the shelf
as fast as they can. And, second, because the Federal government,
through FHA and other agencies set up to cope with the serious housing
shortages that arose after World War II, has imposed a bureaucratic
straight jacket on the design of most new houses, on the placement of houses
on individual lots, on landscaping, on street planning, and on just about
everything else that gives suburbia its "waste-land" appearance.[12]

In short, the disastrous sprawl of the past twenty years is the product,
together, of the merchant builder and the government bureaucrat,
each in his own way responding only to the immediate needs of the
moment.

The past twenty years have been a period of pernicious individualism
and destructive chaos in urban development. Against these forces, the
critique opposes the rational mind and its ability to plan. To supporters
of the critique, it is planning, executed from a sufficiently high level
of comprehensiveness, that will build "Jerusalem in England's green
and pleasant land."

This relentless and seemingly thoroughgoing critique was bound to
influence men whose general interest in civic affairs was already high.
For owners of large parcels of land, like Janss and Irvine (developers
of Janss/Conejo and Irvine Ranch, respectively), for inheritors of
wealth accumulated through real estate ventures, like Robert Simon
(the developer of Reston), and for some who had earned their own
fortunes in a field related to real estate, like James Rouse (the developer
of Columbia), the chance to shape a new life style in suburbia was
irresistible. At the same time, men such as these were products of a
culture which grants esteem to those who make a profit. Thus, they
wished not only to "create better communities" but desired to earn
money doing it. The great aim of the community builders is to prove
that the profit motive can be coupled with an interest in civic affairs to
meet head on the deficiencies exposed by the critique of urban
development.

[12] Blake, *God's Own Junkyard*, p. 17.

The Community Development Project was one of the results of this critique. In addition, since the announcement of Eldorado Hills, a great many individuals, companies, and landholders stated their intentions to build New Towns. Therefore, during February and March 1964, under the auspices of the Community Development Project and assisted by Richard Raymond, Bay Area planning consultant, I spoke with over forty large landholders, land developers, and land seekers. Of these forty, nine later agreed to participate in the program for its entire life by engaging in periodic meetings and by permitting certain forms of investigation to be done. Initially, however, the interviews aimed neither at detailed review of company finances and structure nor at an examination of the site each had chosen but rather at general answers to the following questions:

1. Why were these companies thinking about undertaking a venture like community building (or why had they decided to do it)?
2. How large was their site and what section of it was under intensive planning?
3. Who was doing the planning, what were the planning goals, and who had set them?
4. How far did the company expect to go in actually carrying out and managing their development?
5. How did the owner see the relation between the metropolitan market and the location of his site?
6. How was the project being financed?
7. Under what sort of jurisdiction was the site being developed?
8. When would physical work start or what had already been done?
9. What other business activities were conducted by the company?

From the answers to these questions came a working definition of a community builder: an owner of a large, contiguous parcel of land (2,500 acres or more) who aims at applying the "best" known techniques of planning to develop industrial, commercial, residential, and public facilities, as well as amenities not normally found in new suburban developments. Scale, amenities, planning, control of all uses; these were the basic criteria.

It became clear to me as a result of these interviews that the community builder's project is, or will be, quite different from a New Town, if we use the term in the sense which was incorporated into law in Great Britain in 1947. There, it has meant the creation by the national government of a public corporation with the power of condemnation and with public funds not only to purchase land but to finance the town's infrastructure and even to build residences. The government can, and usually does, subsidize the housing.

Even more important than the financial and legal powers given to the public corporations are the measures taken by the British government to ensure that a New Town will have industry and that the land surrounding the New Town will not be developed. In most cases, new industrial plants cannot be located without the permission of the government. By refusing this permission in metropolitan London and in other urban areas and by exerting other forms of subtle and not so subtle persuasion, the government has considerable power to direct industrial settlement to a New Town. It may also offer direct subsidies to industry in the form of low land prices, although American experience suggests that these low prices, in and of themselves, are at best marginal considerations in industrial location decisions.

By refusing to give permission to develop the intervening land between New Towns or between a New Town and a nearby metropolis, the British government can control the size of the town and prevent competing development at its fringe. No such governmental power exists in the United States, and there is serious doubt that our Constitution would permit it. Thus, a community builder must compete with owners of surrounding land, and only the inherent attributes of his location and/or his business skill give him any special advantage.

The result, then, is that while a British New Town is a separate physical entity where people are intended to, and to a great extent do, spend most of their daily lives in the community itself, an American New Community is merely a different way of organizing private development at the urban fringe of a metropolis. Neighborhood and regional shopping centers, industrial parks, detached housing, and garden apartments are the principal facilities in areas developed around American cities since World War II. They are also the principal facilities in a New Community, although in the latter case the land is held by a single owner who intends to provide such facilities or, at least, to have a major influence over their planning and character.

Compared to the suburban development of the past twenty years,

New Communities will offer a greater variety and probably a higher quality of recreational facilities, such as lakes, parks, and golf courses, and they will set aside more open space. Otherwise, there has not been and, in my judgment, will not be much about New Communities to differentiate them from suburbia as we know it.

Some New Town devotees believe a town of 200,000 or less, whose surrounding area is protected from development, is large enough to support a reasonable variety of life style and small enough to promote civic concern, which many believe to be impossible in the metropolis or the megalopolis. Although I do not agree with either contention, the point remains moot in the United States because we are not building any towns or communities so separated from an existing metropolis. If we were to adopt policies similar to those of Great Britain, we too could build New Towns, but I see little reason to believe that the massive expenditures and the legal changes required to do this would be warranted. As I turn now to the discussion of American New Communities and their relation to the problems they were created to solve, I hope that my reasons for these statements will become apparent.

RESEARCH FINDINGS

Some of the urban problems to which the character of suburban development presumably contributes and the responses of incipient community builders to these problems were examined in the Community Development Project.

The most persistent criticism of suburbia was its homogeneity. Suburbanites, it was claimed, are predominantly young middle- and upper-income, white familes with children. New Communities or New Towns were to change this situation. Yet, almost without exception, community builders told us that they would not offer any housing at prices less than $20,000 at least in the early stages of development. (Purchase at this price would necessitate an income of about $8,000 per year.) The reason they gave was the standard real estate argument that the introduction of any large number of low-priced houses, and thereby, low-income families, at the early stage of the project would seriously damage its whole image. Community builders added their belief that, given their location at the metropolitan fringe and their hope to sell "planning," the demand by lower-income families was automatically limited. In business terms, they were saying that their product was being geared essentially to a middle- and upper-middle-income market and that, by offering houses to lower-income families whose demand was limited, they would be seriously reducing the product's essential appeal.

In the light of the criticism about the one-class nature of suburbia, a condition that was thought would be fostered by community building, we commissioned two specific research projects. One was conducted by Dr. Wallace Smith of the School of Business Administration at the University of California, Berkeley, and the other by Carl Werthman, a sociologist at the same university. Smith was asked to analyze housing in the Los Angeles metropolitan area with special emphasis on the needs of families earning less than $8,000 per year. Specifically, we sought to ascertain whether Los Angeles contained a significant unfulfilled demand by families in this income range for houses selling for less than $20,000, and whether Janss-Conejo (a New Community at the fringe of metropolitan Los Angeles) had failed to tap this demand. Los Angeles was chosen because it was the location of so many New Communities, and Janss-Conejo, because it had already been offering houses for several years.

Smith confirmed the findings of several previous reports claiming that new housing is primarily built for families earning more than the median income, but he did not draw the standard conclusion from this information: that there is a great shortage of, or unmet demand for, housing for low- and moderate-income families. Rather, he presented the following argument: "It is often suggested that low income groups are not served by the home building industry while high income households have a wide choice among new dwellings. This is a misleading impression. Correctly defined, the situation is more nearly the opposite of this commonly held view."

Smith maintained that one cannot analyze the housing market merely by asking what percentage of the new housing serves families of a given income. The housing situation should be viewed as one in which people move through a given stock of units, made up, in any short time period, primarily of the existing supply of houses plus a small number of new additions. Thus, the situation has been as follows: As income has risen, most new housing has served the needs of higher-income groups. Families with lower incomes (which also have risen) have gotten some new housing, but most have improved their condition by occupying the used housing abandoned by the more affluent. Given the logic of these trends, it follows that if income continues to rise and if, as has been the case in Los Angeles, the construction of new housing units continues to exceed the combined total of family formations and in-migration, the worst housing ultimately will be abandoned. (It is clear that not *all* lower-income families have participated in this "filtering" process.)

Smith forecasted the Los Angeles housing demand for the 1960–1970 decade on the assumption that income would increase at the same ratio as it did in the previous decade and concluded that the "great bulk" of demand for new housing would come from families earning more than $10,000.

This assumption was corroborated by men who possessed direct business experience in the area. In 1964 we interviewed six California merchant builders who historically had devoted all or most of their energies to building the least expensive housing possible under existing legal and cost conditions. Their comments were almost identical. Since 1959 or 1960, the prices of their cheapest house had risen, each year, $500 to $1,000 above previous prices. Further, the low-price models represented a decreasing portion of their total sales. A representative example came from one builder who had sold most of his houses in 1959 in the $13,000 to $15,000 range. By 1964, his least expensive house was $18,000.

Part of this general price increase, the builders explained, was attributable to rising costs, principally the cost of land and site improvements. The balance was owing to improvements in the housing itself and to space and quality changes that had been necessitated by shifts in buyer preferences. "We cannot sell a minimum house," said one builder, "because people demand more features like shake roofs and built-in appliances."

All the builders agreed that the families who could not afford new houses were buying used houses or renting houses or apartments. An increasing percentage of the new house buyers were moving within a radius of five to fifteen miles of their former homes, thus leaving them empty for lower-income families.

These assertions suggest that builders no longer can compete with the used house market by offering a minimum new house but must provide more space and quality. Most families see a used house to be a better buy than a new minimum house. This situation is no doubt influenced by the way jobs are distributed. Most employment opportunities in

California for blue-collar and clerical workers are near the supply of used housing. A sizable percentage of employment in the fringe areas, where there is land for new housing, is in the higher-paying job categories.

None of this should be taken to mean that there is *no* demand in a New Community for houses selling for less than $20,000. Thus, we still wanted to make some judgment on the validity of the community builders' fear that trying to tap such a market would have serious adverse repercussions upon higher-income buyers. We therefore began our second research project. We asked Carl Werthman, a University of California sociologist, to conduct a series of "depth interviews" of residents in two California New Communities, Foster City and Janss-Conejo. Werthman and his associates addressed themselves essentially to two questions:

1. Do buyers in new communities interpret "planning," especially the amenities, in the same way the planners and community builders do?
2. What effect would the inclusion of lower-priced homes have on the demand for houses selling for more than $20,000?

Werthman concluded that, to a great extent, the answer to both these questions was the same. "Planning" to these residents was a guarantee against the introduction of "undesirable" elements close to one's house and immediate surroundings. Not surprisingly, the most undesirable of these elements was the lower-priced home sold to the lower-income person. Sixty-nine per cent of the residents in Foster City, where the least expensive homes sold from $23,000 to $26,000, said they would oppose including a neighborhood of $20,000 homes even if they were separated from other neighborhoods by a lagoon and a row of apartments. We concluded from the interviews that people feared the introduction of low-income families partly because they thought this was synonymous with the introduction of Negroes. When pushed, respondents indicated that middle-class Negroes were more acceptable than lower-class residents of any race. However, it was also clear that these residents in general found it difficult to accept the idea that Negro and lower-income are not synonymous.

Most residents of both communities emphasized declining community appearance as one adverse result of nearby lower-priced homes. As one Foster City owner put it:

I think the people in this community are going to take pride in their homes
because they are middle class. If this were in the class of say $9,000 or
below, it would be different. In your $9,000 income or lower, the poor
guy is worked to death and he ain't got time to get out in the yard. It's
not that they care less, it's simply that the next door neighbor doesn't
give a damn and pretty soon he's convinced he don't give a damn either. Yet
you'll get a few out of the bunch that will take care, but in the long run
it will all go down.

Thus, to the buyers in these New Communities, "planning" means
protection from "negative knowns and unknowns." The most important
known is the introduction of lower-income families, but other knowns
might include industrial plants, offices, and stores too close to the
homes themselves. Obviously, all the unknowns cannot be enumerated,
but the residents indicated their belief that "planning" would ensure
that they, too, did not encroach on nearby vacant land.

The assurances against these negative knowns and unknowns come in
two ways: The first is by the existence of a detailed plan, approved by
a governing authority, which represents a commitment on the part of
the developer who is seen as having not only the will but the ability to
carry out the plan. The other relies simply on the reputation of a
developer himself. The Janss Corporation never presented a very
detailed plan to its prospective buyers, but the Janss family is highly
respected and well known. T. Jack Foster & Co., on the other hand,
is not particularly well known in the Bay Area but presented a very
detailed plan and engaged in an extensive public relations campaign
to assure people that the plan would be carried out.

In both Foster City and Janss-Conejo, the sales literature put heavy
emphasis on recreation and community facilities. Werthman found,
however, that few residents expected to make great use of the major
recreational facilities. This did not mean that these facilities played no
role in the purchase decision, but that the role was not so much
anticipation of use but, as one respondent put it, "To add to the general
atmosphere."

The findings of Smith and Werthman suggest that the marketing
strategy of community builders has considerable merit insofar as price
range is concerned. However, the rather minimal interest that buyers
display in the community facilities and their rather narrow definition
of the benefits of "planning" suggest that when a developer owns a large
parcel of land at the metropolitan fringe and uses "the best known

planning techniques," he may not necessarily be establishing much of an advantage in the market place. This conclusion led us to question the validity of community building as an investment and a business enterprise.

Throughout the early interviews and subsequent meetings with community builders, we tried to ascertain what techniques were used for projecting the market and for calculating a rate of return on invested capital. Most community builders spend considerable sums of money employing consultants to analyze the market. It is my judgment, however, that it is difficult, if not impossible, to make long run projections of housing demand either by estimating total demand or by breaking that total into categories of price range, size, and housing type. In addition, community building requires especially high commitments of capital (in the case of Columbia, more than $30 million) long before any revenues can be obtained by sales or leases. An unpredictable market and high initial capital outlays are the classic characteristics of a high-risk investment. By all reasonable business standards, a high-risk investment should offer the possibility of a high rate of return. Yet, we did not find a single community builder who had developed a technique for calculating this rate based on a single set of assumptions as to sales rates, sales prices, interest rates, or other costs. As a result, none could try to measure the impact of any changes in such assumptions on rate of return.

For these reasons, we commissioned Dr. Sherman Maisel, then of the School of Business Administration at the University of California, Berkeley (now a Governor of the Federal Reserve Board), and Ted Dienstfrey to develop a computer model, based on the standard system of discounting cash flows, which could be used to calculate the rate of return.

Because community building is such a new type of enterprise, we could not get very reliable estimates of the dimension of costs, sales rates, or sales prices. However, using what information we did have, we calculated that a prototype New Community would achieve an annual rate of return of 7.4 per cent on invested capital. To arrive at this figure, we assumed that 75 per cent of the total capital cost would be financed at 6 per cent interest. These terms would correspond to the figure suggested in proposed federal legislation to provide FHA insured loans for the land and the site improvements in a New Community. If, however, we had been able to drop the interest rate to 4 per cent to correspond to the approximate cost of government borrowing rather than the cost of issuing insurance, the rate of return would have risen from 7.4 per cent to 11.2 per cent.

We may, of course, have overestimated costs or underestimated sales prices, which would project a lower rate of return than that which would actually occur. However, to balance this we did use an optimistic annual sales rate of over 2,000 units starting with the fourth year after land purchase. To date, no New Community has achieved an annual sale rate of 1,000 units.

It is obvious that rates of return between 7 and 11 per cent on invested capital are hardly what one would expect from high-risk ventures.

THE PROBLEMS AND GOVERNMENT AID

As mentioned earlier, the urban critique cited a long list of problems which were to be solved or alleviated by New Communities. Our findings about the market suggest that New Communities will not alleviate separation by class, race, and income and, in fact, may exacerbate this trend.

Other problems with which New Communities were expected to deal were fiscal inequity, high costs resulting from low density, the loss of a sense of community, the dominance of the automobile as a means of transportation, and air and water pollution. Yet, we found no reason to believe that New Communities would bring about change in these areas. If class and income separation continues, and if local services continue to be financed by property taxes or any other locally based revenue system, naturally, fiscal inequity will continue. The density in New Communities, about 3.2 families per acre, is lower than that of many suburban areas developed under fragmented ownership. There is no evidence that a sense of community is created by these projects except when the community builder fails to fulfill his commitments and therefore arouses the ire of his residents. To assume that the installation of a regional shopping center, a lake, a golf course, a bridle path, some open space, and perhaps, a general purpose building will suddenly give middle-class Americans a new sense of civic pride, seems to me romantic in the extreme. With the exception of Columbia, which now plans to install a separate bus system with its own right of way, no New Community proposes to provide any transportation system other than the automobile. I cannot think of any reason why a

New Community would decrease air and water pollution in the metropolis as a whole. Of course, by keeping out any heavy industry, even where there might be a demand, it might prevent pollution in its particular area, but this would only reroute the polluting industry to some other part of the region.

For three successive years, the administration has requested Congress to pass a two-part New Communities program. The first part would provide FHA insurance and FNMA funds for up to 75 per cent of the cost of land and site development. The presumption here has been that while New Communities are considered virtuous, financial aid is required to stimulate their initiation and to make it difficult for developers to abandon virtue under later financial pressures. The second part proposed direct federal loans to state or metropolitan governments for the purchase of land and the installation of basic improvements. Presumably, the land would then be sold to private enterprise for actual construction, much as is the case with urban renewal.

Neither part of the program has ever gained any great support either from private industry or state governments. Yet, because of the administration's persistence and the absence of any organized opposition (although big-city mayors have been dubious about the whole affair), a modified version of the insurance scheme was passed by the 1966 Congress. I can find little justification for this legislation because, as I have tried to illustrate, New Communities, aided or unaided by government, will not materially affect our major problems. If anyone gains, it will be either the landowner, the developer, or the middle- and upper-middle-income residents who are likely to become the principal residents of a New Community. In addition, the program would be extremely difficult to administer and financially very risky. It seems to me that government aid for New Communities has all the wrong characteristics for a public venture. It requires a great deal of money, it involves high financial risk, it is fraught with administrative difficulties, and, worst of all, its potential benefits are minimal, and those that do occur will accrue to people in our society who are least in need of help.

There is one type of governmental involvement in New Communities which might have some merit, but it bears no relation to the problems which current proponents of legislation are trying to solve. It is conceivable that significant technological advances could be made in the study and development of community infrastructure. It is difficult to experiment with such technology without sufficient scale and a guaranteed market. The federal government, however, could provide funds to a publicly chartered corporation whose avowed purpose would be the construction of a New Community with innovations in sewer and water systems, transportation, power, and communication. Governmental funding would be necessary to such a program, even assuming the active cooperation of industry, since experimentation necessarily means risk with the likelihood of financial loss greater than the likelihood of profit.

SOME REFLECTIONS

As I arrived at these conclusions, I began to wonder why so many people have made such a great fuss about New Towns and New Communities. Almost every national publication has done one or more major articles about the glowing prospects this new phenomenon offered. I am sure this editorial proliferation has been caused, partially, by the nature of communications in America, but I would suggest that much of its nonsensical nature has been inspired by the characteristics of most people who call themselves city planners or urban critics.

Until very recently, education in architecture and city planning schools and the writings of most observers of the urban scene were both simplistic and anti-intellectual. One manifestation of this is the lack of precision in the use of words and phrases employed to criticize urban life and urban development in America. Critics use terms like "inefficient land use," "sprawl," "balance," "human scale," "community," and "explosion." But when one asks for definitions, one usually receives either a blank stare or the comment that "everyone knows what this means, and everyone knows that these are problems." I wonder, however, if "inefficient land use" refers to the total amount of land used for development, the type of land developed, or the density of development? At what scale are we to judge "balance": the municipality, the neighborhood, the block, the metropolis, the state, or the nation? "Sense of community" can be defined as shared interests. In many cases this means common fear. Many small towns in the United States, particularly in the South, are characterized by great distrust of outsiders and of ethnic or racial minorities. Is it this sense of community which urban critics cherish and hope for in New Towns or New Communities? I suggest that we need a number of master's or doctoral theses on almost

all phrases and words which find their way into city planning literature.
Obviously, I am asserting that, all too often, urban commentary is
fraught with oversimplification. We need much more hard thought
about why and how people and institutions function. This should not be
taken as a belief that urban analyses or urban problem solving can be
made easily into a science. Recently there has arisen considerable
interest in the incorporation of computers and mathematics into what
is called "systems analysis" or "regional science." These new techniques
have potential value, as they may increase our ability to understand
the complexities of urban life, but such techniques are in their infancy
and the data upon which they must depend are extremely unreliable.
The claim that the space age industries and the computer technologists
now possess the ability to produce nirvana is simply another manifestation of our addiction to proclaiming solutions to problems we have as
yet been unable to define.

Another way of characterizing the style of city planners and urban
critics is to say that they are Messianic. Their feeling seems to be that
they know what the problems are and know how to solve them but
Philistine politicians and entrepreneurs will not give them the power.
An example of this can be found in Victor Gruen's book *The Heart of
Our Cities.* Like a great many architects and city planners, he thinks
urban ills can and should be solved by a new type of professional man,
"the environmental architect." As Gruen puts it:

> The shaping of the human environment cannot be achieved by the assembly
> line technique. There is an urgent need for the training of a new type of
> professional man. Lacking a better term, I will call him the environmental
> architect. He won't need a special title, a special license, or membership
> in one or another of the professional organizations. But he will have
> to possess, through a combination of aptitude and training, and as a result
> of restless seeking for deeper insight into the nature of man, the
> kind of understanding and convictions that will allow him to view problems
> and to find their solutions from a high vantage point (not to be confused,
> however, with an ivory tower).[13]

To me, this is a deeply offensive notion. I do not believe that any
amount of professional training somehow equips a small group of men
to make decisions about something as complex as urban development,
which might affect so many millions of people. This is not to say that

---

[13] Victor Gruen, *The Heart of Our Cities* (New York: Simon and Schuster, 1964),
p. 342.

there is not a role for the profession of city planning, but we should realize that the definition of that role is still evolving. In determining the relationship of the city planner to the populace, we might consider the more deeply established relationship of lawyer to client. Here, a body of knowledge and a set of techniques have been developed which permit the lawyer to give valuable advice to his client. He can suggest goals and illustrate the effect of alternate forms of behavior upon these goals. The practicing lawyer is not afraid to acknowledge his uncertainty, and, in the last analysis, he respects the principle that the client sets his own final goal.

For the city planner the client may be a businessman, a government agency, or an elected official. If the city planner, knowing the limitations of his skill and knowledge, sees his role as improving the ability of his client to define his goals and to discriminate among tactics and strategies to reach these goals, he can play a responsible and meaningful role.

As an individual, he can be a crusader, but then he is no longer acting in his professional capacity but simply as a citizen who wishes to urge his fellow citizens and elected officials to adopt what he believes to be appropriate courses of action. Even if he understands this, the city planner should be aware of how often predictions, particularly those of demographers, have turned out to be false.

It is very common for city planners to seek ways "to preserve the integrity of the plan." I think we should not seek adoption of precise plans which will constrain future behavior. In fact, our goals should be the opposite: to adopt policies and install physical facilities which will keep open the maximum number of options for future actors, whether they be architects, developers, consumers, or politicians. We might accept the view expressed by George Kennan, who concluded his book *Russia and the West Under Lenin and Stalin* as follows:

> One of our purposes should be to stress the necessity of an American outlook which accepts the obligations of maturity and consents to operate in a world of relative and unstable values.
> The picture, then, which I hope I have presented is that of an international life in which not only is there nothing final in point of time, nothing not vulnerable to the law of change, but also nothing absolute in life itself: a life in which there is no friendship without some element of antagonism; no enmity without some rudimentary community of interest; no benevolent intervention, which is not also in part an injury; no act of recalcitrance,

no seeming evil from which—as Shakespeare put it—some "soul of goodness" may not be distilled.

A world in which these things are true is, of course, not the best of all conceivable worlds; but it is a tolerable one, and it is worth living in. . . . I am content to dismiss you, as Bismarck once did some of the more curious and impatient of his former associates, with the words: "Let us leave a few problems for our children to solve, otherwise they might get so bored."[14]

In a century of economic uncertainty and war, I am not worried that we shall solve so many problems that our children will be bored. Much progress has been made, but much remains to be done. The horrors of war did not end in 1946, nor were racial problems solved in 1865. Observing this, some of our brightest college students rail at the hypocrisy and complacency of their parents and their substitute parents, college teachers. We may not share their style, but what justification do we have to tell them to accept ours?

New Towns, New Communities, or whatever you want to call them, stem from the outworn notions and ideologies of Ebenezer Howard and nineteenth-century England. They are not evil, but they are not really very interesting. As an intellectual or social concept, they commit what is to America's activist youth the worst sin of all: They are irrelevant. I know very little about what "urban form" is more desirable than another. Like Kennan, I limit my goal: to pass on to succeeding generations a world, and an urban society, more or less intact, and free of most constraints. To seek to do much more would be evidence of both arrogance and shortsightedness, qualities which we Americans have already displayed far too often.

---

14 George Kennan, *Russia and the West Under Lenin and Stalin* (Boston: Atlantic-Little Brown, 1960), pp. 397–398.

5.

Latin American Urbanization: Plan or Process?[1]
Lowdon Wingo, Jr.

BACKGROUND

Contemporary literature on Latin American economic development abounds with expressions of anxiety over the rapidly growing problem of urbanization.[2] Fed by a seemingly inexhaustible flood of migrants from the *campos,* the growth of Latin American cities has outpaced public services, housing, and jobs. The result, it is argued, is the deterioration of urban environment and the extension of the special hopelessness and misery of urban destitution. Ultimately, if this contention is borne out, the political and social unrest produced by these conditions can destroy the social stability essential to rapid economic development and so bring the national economy to a standstill.

Analysts contend that the rapid growth of urban population creates demands for public services which put pressure on the scarce investment resources available for the development of the nation.[3] By long-used calculations, the economic planners show that such social investments are unprofitable since they are characterized by very high capital-output ratios. Nonetheless, the political potential of these populations makes it difficult for politicians to ignore their demands. The end result, then, is a deceleration of economic development as investment resources are diverted from their most profitable use.

In addition, urban growth in Latin American countries is especially rapid in the largest urban centers. These tend to outdistance their competitors, resulting in the"primate city" phenomenon, with one great metropolitan region overshadowing the other cities and dominating the life of the nation.[4] Beyond a certain point, social scientists believe, severe diseconomies of urban scale occur,[5] with a higher capital-output

[1] Reference will be made throughout this paper to two terms familiar to people with a professional interest in economic development: "overhead" and "infrastructure." "Overhead" will refer to those generalized services and the institutions producing them which broadly support the direct production and consumption of goods and services, such as water supply, public safety, and transportation. "Infrastructure" refers to the large-scale capital facilities necessary to the production of many overhead services, such as streets, electric generating plants, or school buildings.
[2] Philip Hauser, ed., *Urbanization in Latin America,* Proceedings of a Seminar Jointly Sponsored by the Bureau of Social Affairs of the United Nations, the Economic Commission for Latin America, and UNESCO . . . on Urbanization Problems in Latin America, Santiago, Chile, July 6–18, 1959 (New York: International Documents Service, 1961), pp. 58–61.
[3] *Ibid.,* pp. 60–61.
[4] "Geographic Distribution of the Population of Latin America and Regional Development Priorities," *Economic Bulletin for Latin America,* Vol. 8:1 (March 1963), pp. 51–62.
[5] E.g., Catherine Bauer Wurster, "Urban Living Conditions, Overhead Costs, and the

ratio for metropolitan services than for small-city services. The voracious overhead investment demands of large cities amplify the threat to the scarce investment resources of the nation. Furthermore, the great cities attract the lion's share of the nation's productive resources, impoverishing the provincial hinterland and impairing its capacity to share in or contribute to national economic growth. This parasitism diverts investment from potentially more profitable areas in the hinterlands into less profitable but more familiar investment in the major city and acts as a brake on development.[6]

In essence, these arguments state that uncontrolled urbanization acts as a negative feedback on economic development. By implication, then, there must be a rate and type of urbanization which would maximize some specified index of development. The achievement of this rate of development through governmental leadership is the announced objective of urbanization policies.

The following discussion will explore the construction of the link between urbanization and economic development and make some tentative statements about institutional innovations which can lead to a more appropriate decision process, minimizing the social costs of rapid urbanization. The testing ground will be Latin America. Accordingly, there will be some limits to the generality of my propositions caused by the unique features of Latin America's urbanization and economic development experience.

PRIMACY: AN ECONOMIC AND DEMOGRAPHIC PHENOMENON

For the purposes of this discussion, urbanization is considered to be a phenomenon of labor and capital mobility in which resources become distributed and concentrated at points over the national landscape. In this sense, urbanization is closely associated with regional development; a regional development program without specialized attention to urban sector requirements is unthinkable.[7] Regional development, however,

---

Development Pattern," in Roy Turner, ed., *India's Urban Future* (Berkeley and Los Angeles: University of California Press, 1962), pp. 281–287.

[6] Hoselitz has developed the thesis in detail. See Bert Hoselitz, "Generative and Parasitic Cities," *Economic Development and Cultural Change*, Vol. 3 (1955), pp. 276–294.

[7] "Moreover, a regional development policy is not conceivable without an urban development programme which constitutes a common element of national and regional policy and planning," in "Problems of Regional Economic Planning and Development in Europe and the United States," *Economic Bulletin for Europe*, Vol. 17:2 (November 1965), p. 11.

focuses on natural resources, input-output relations, and accessibility, while urbanization policy is concerned with the web of external relations among economic activities which gives the city its uniquely productive environment.

The rural-to-urban population shift which accompanies economic development parallels the growth of per capita income and the shift of labor out of farming and related work into manufacturing and service activites. In Latin America, as elsewhere, the level of per capita income is inversely proportional to the amount of the labor force engaged in agriculture. Therefore, an upward shift in per capita income can be expected to accompany shifts of labor from agriculture to nonagricultural activities, from rural areas to urban areas. In support of this proposition, the rank correlation coefficient between per capita income for 1955–1964 and proportion of the population in urban places in nineteen Latin American countries in 1960 is 0.904.[8] A higher per capita income also reflects the shift of labor resources from low to high productivity sectors, for, in spite of large degrees of urban underemployment in Latin America, there is reason to believe that the rural-urban shift would have to be much greater to increase rural labor productivity, a proposition that I will examine more fully later.

Other conditions are changing during this transition. An increasingly versatile, disciplined labor force, constantly improving market accessibility and proliferating public and private services are providing a hospitable economic climate for new enterprise by making urbanization and agglomeration economics possible.

Capital stocks increase rapidly in the cities. New manufacturing plants locate—and old ones expand—in the urban economic environment, while infrastructure investment in services to the growing industries likewise concentrates social capital in these areas. The size of the labor force permits specialization, while the concentration of national markets increases the demand for it.

[8] The rank correlation coefficient measures the degree to which the ranking of one set of variables is consistent with the ranking of another. If the ranks of the values of the two sets of variables were perfectly consistent, their rank correlation coefficient would have a value of +1.000; if the rankings of the two sets of variables ran consistently in opposite directions, their coefficient would have a value of −1.000; if there was no consistent relationship among the ranks, the correlation coefficient would reveal a value of 0.000. In the correlation reported here, the per capita income data were drawn from *The Economist*, September 25–October 10, 1965, p. xiv, and the population data from *Economic Bulletin for Latin America*, Vol. 8:1 (March 1963), p. 58.

Finally, a demographic transformation takes place. The rapid decline of death rates in the early stages brings about a rapid increase in population, which tends to persist until birth rates are brought down through the incompletely understood impact of urbanization on fertility. In the end, ideally, low birth and death rates would yield a slow but steady growth of the population.

These, then, are some of the long-range dimensions of the transformation central to urbanization induced by economic development. Historically, these processes took place at a measured pace: forty years after the 1917 revolution, less than half of the people of the Soviet Union lived in urban centers.[9] Now, however, efforts toward economic development in many parts of the world are accelerating and guiding this transition. Nowhere is this being done more earnestly than in Latin America, which is now in the explosive stage of its demographic development. Here one can find countries whose populations are growing at the rate of almost 4 per cent per annum with urban pupulations increasing at an annual rate of more than 6 per cent. Still, if the rates of urban and rural change experienced by these countries during 1950–1960 persist into the future, only Venezuela would join Uruguay before the end of the century in having 80 per cent of its population in urban areas. Thus, even with its extraordinary rates of urbanization, the transition from a rural to an urban society in Latin America will take a matter of generations, not decades.

Analysis of the 1950–1960 population estimates reveals that it is not easy to generalize about the urbanization experiences of Latin American countries.[10] Considering factors such as total growth rate, rural and urban growth rates, rural-urban composition, over-all demographic mobility, urban in-migration rates, and rural out-migration rates, only the four most highly urbanized countries—Uruguay, Argentina, Chile, and Cuba—were found to be similar. Another less distinct grouping consisted of the least advanced countries: Haiti, Panama, El Salvador, Bolivia, and Paraguay. The third group consisted of the remaining rapidly urbanizing countries, but the internal relations of this group were complex and not always easy to interpret. There is over-all evidence, however, that rates of population

[9] P. G. Podyachikh, "The Calculation of Future Population with Allowance for Planned Migration," a paper prepared for the World Population Conference, 1965, Meeting No. B-5.
[10] Lowdon Wingo, Jr., "Recent Patterns of Urbanization among Latin American Countries," *Urban Affairs Quarterly,* Vol. 3:1 (March 1967), pp. 81–109.

growth are associated in a complex way with the per cent of total population residing in urban areas.[11]

The effective mechanisms of urbanization become visible only at the subnational level, where we can open up the macroeconomic processes and observe how they evolve as the internal organization of the country is transformed. Urbanization can then be perceived in terms of cities playing more or less specialized roles in the national economy. Cities can be seen first in their relationships to an economic hinterland, and then, more generally, to the system of urban settlements. In the first role the city is the focal point for the development of a surrounding region;[12] in the second it acts as a functional part of the entire urban system. Typically, regions within a country become specialized and advance or recede economically in proportion to their ability to exploit their particular advantages in the competition for national or international markets.[13] Each country has its own leading and lagging regions, and, in each case, the region's cities play special roles in the reallocation of human and investment resources as regional roles change.

The characteristic form of the relationships of city to region centers on a relatively highly developed metropolitan core which dominates the resource area around it. This core, usually the national capital, holds a high concentration of the nation's consumer markets, its institutions of control, and a massive industrial establishment which looks to the peripheral region for its resource inputs. The core region is generally the pacemaker for the development of the peripheral regions.[14]

We can now add a final dimension to this model, that of the system of cities itself. The urban sector is often described by the frequency

---

[11] *Ibid.,* p. 104.
[12] See F. Perroux, "Consideraciones en torno a la noción de polo de crecimiento," *Cuadernos de la Sociedad Venezolana de Planificación,* Vol. 2:3-4 (June–July 1963, Caracas).
[13] The development of regions tied to international markets, such as Chile's Norte Grande, will respond to, say, international metals markets more sensitively than to conditions of the national economy. Because of their powerful role as generators of foreign exchange, they can frequently extract concessions from the rest of the economy which "protect" them from some of the negative consequences of development. In Chile, for example, part of the copper tax is earmarked for public sector development in the copper provinces. Legislation passed in 1966 requires Chile's greatest mining operator, Anaconda Copper Co., to set aside 5 per cent of its gross profits for the construction of workers' housing and new towns. See "The Perilous Prosperity of Anaconda," *Fortune,* Vol. 73:5 (May 1966), p. 236.
[14] For a discussion of this role in the history of the United States, see Harvey Perloff and Lowdon Wingo, Jr., "Natural Resource Endowment and Regional Economic Growth," in Joseph J. Spengler, ed., *Natural Resources and Economic Growth* (Washington: Resources for the Future, 1961), pp. 191–212.

distribution of its city sizes, a special form of which is the much abused but still interesting rank-size relation.[15] The rank-size arrays for most Latin American countries are characterized by a high degree of population concentration in the largest city, or "primacy," as geographers have called it. These *primate* cities typically contain 10–20 per cent or more of the country's total population or a third or more of its urban population. They are followed in rank by cities which are substantially smaller in size.[16] This phenomenon is illustrated by Chile's population figures. In 1960, its primate city, Santiago, had a population of two million, whereas Valparaiso, Chile's second largest city, had only 250,000. This concentration has increased steadily since 1907, when the twenty Chilean cities following Santiago in size contained 61 per cent of the populations which would have been predicted by the rank-size rule.[17] By 1960 they contained only 30 per cent, documenting the long-run weakening of subsidiary urban areas as Santiago gained in size and significance. Similar primate city configurations exist in other Latin American countries such as Peru and even Colombia, which recently has begun to diverge from its balanced city situation.

The only qualification to these trends of increasing concentration is furnished by Ecuador and Brazil. In these countries, two cities vie for the role of principal metropolis, but in both cases, cities of succeeding ranks are so far down the size scale that a case of "shared" primacy may be said to exist. Increasing population concentration seems to be the rule for the developing countries in Latin America.

Subnational economic development is moving with these trends. Employment surveys in several countries have indicated that unemployment rates in the metropolitan area are not substantially different from those in the smaller cities.[18] This suggests that employment

15 The "rank-size" rule is an analytical construct asserting, in general terms, that the size of the nth city is a function of n and the size of the largest city. Large countries and highly industrialized ones have a function which is roughly log linear, but in smaller or less developed countries, the relationship is highly irregular. The frequency distribution of city sizes is simply the number of cities distributed among an arbitrarily chosen set of size classes.

16 See discussion and tables in "Geographic Distribution of the Population of Latin America and Regional Development Priorities," *Economic Bulletin for Latin America*, Vol. 8:1 (March 1963), pp. 59–60.

17 According to the rank-size rule, the nth city should have a population $1/n$ times that of Santiago. Hence, the next twenty cities should have a total population equal to $(1/2 + 1/3 + 1/4 + \ldots + 1/20 + 1/21)$ times that of Santiago.

18 For example, see Universidad de Chile, Instituto de Economía Ocupación y

opportunities are at least as concentrated in the great cities as is population, and the higher labor participation rates among migrants substantiate the fact.[19] In Chile 50 per cent of new plant and equipment investment has been taking place in Santiago,[20] and among Chilean cities half of the manufacturing employment that exceeds the national growth rate of manufacturing is found in Santiago. It is likely that similar situations can be found in virtually all of the Latin American republics. Primacy, then, is not a purely demographic phenomenon; it is also an economic one that more and more dominates the urbanization picture in Latin America.

The reason for primacy is not obvious, and the most we can do at this stage is to suggest some of the significant factors at work. The foremost of these is the propensity of developing countries to employ up-to-date technologies not only for the production of new goods and services but also to replace the artisan and household technologies rising from their own unique historic conditions. These technologies carry with them organizational and institutional requirements and cannot function efficiently without the economic advantages normally met in the large cities of the industrially advanced world. A minimum urban scale, therefore, may be a precondition of the effective employment of modern productive technologies, the achievement of which may yield extensive social returns. We know that severe shortages of technical, professional, and managerial skills characterize the state of underdevelopment. The economic scale of the primate metropolis may provide the threshold conditions for mobilizing such skills productively. As these thresholds are met, more conventional industrial technologies may benefit, thus expanding employment and reinforcing centralization tendencies.

Desocupación, Gran Santiago, Valparaíso-Viña del Mar, Conjunto Provincial—Arauco, Bío-Bío, Concepción, Malleco, Ñuble (Santiago: Instituto de Economía de la Universidad de Chile, 1963), Publicación No. 61. Bruce H. Herrick, "Internal Migration, Unemployment and Economic Growth in Post-War Chile" (unpublished Ph.D. dissertation, Department of Economics and Social Science, Massachusetts Institute of Technology, May 15, 1964); hereafter cited as "Internal Migration." A revision of this document has now been published as Bruce H. Herrick, *Urban Migration and Economic Development in Chile* (Cambridge: The M.I.T. Press, 1966).
[19] Herrick "Internal Migration," p. 117.
[20] Santiago's industries produce 50.3 per cent of value added in manufacturing in Chile and account for 60.6 per cent total manufacturing employment. Guillermo Geisse Grove, "Información Basica de una Politica de Desarrollo Urbano-Regional," *Cuadernos de Economía*, No. 6, Mayo-Agosto de 1965, Pontifica Universidad Católica de Chile, Facultad de Ciencias Económicas y Sociales.

Britton Harris has pointed out that, in India, a minimum urban scale is
dictated by the technological and institutional requirements of modern
industrial activities.[21]

The high degree of economic concentration fostered by the primacy
condition is held in disrepute among Latin American urbanists, who see
it as an obstacle to the "proper" internal development of the country.
This interpretation of the facts has been prompted or at least nourished
by scholars who feel that this degree of centralization is abnormal,
hence pathological.[22] Bert Hoselitz coined the term "parasitic cities"
to describe urban areas which exploited the wealth of the economic
countryside by maintaining it in a permanent state of colonial bondage.[23]

It is quite possible that, at some point determined not so much by
the size of the city as by the stage of development of the economy, the
advantages of primacy begin to dwindle. At this point, it is also possible
that the dependence of economic, political, and social institutions on
the primacy condition may impede the country's transformation to more
effective, postprimacy arrangements. The transfer of functions to
lower-echelon cities and relative decentralization may be thwarted
simply by the lack of skilled people and organization in the
hinterland.[24] Hoselitz' parasitic condition might thus emerge when
the continued development of the primate city occurs at the expense
of the country as a whole. It is not clear, of course, that this is what
happens. If it does, it is even less clear to the policy maker when these
points of transformation are reached.

THE ECONOMIC SETTING OF URBANIZATION

The phenomenon of interest to us is the evolution of the urban system
as a corollary of economic development. Viewing the system as a
hierarchy of urban centers, we need to understand not only the nature
of its sequential transformation but the extent to which we can identify

[21] Britton Harris, "Urbanization Policy in India," *Papers and Proceedings of the Regional Science Association,* Vol. 5 (1959), p. 192. Harris, "Centralization and the Alternate Forms of Decentralization: A Key Issue," in Roy Turner, ed., *India's Urban Future* (Berkeley and Los Angeles: University of California Press, 1962), p. 268.
[22] Herrick describes the condition as "hyper-cephalism."
[23] Hoselitz, "Generative and Parasitic Cities." Hoselitz is occasionally misused by those who indiscriminately apply his concept of parasitism to all primate cities.
[24] Administrative capability is possibly the scarcest resource in the less developed countries. The Venezuelan case is discussed in Fred D. Levy, Jr., "Economic Planning in Venezuela" (unpublished Ph. D. dissertation, Yale University, 1966), pp. 187–190.

that transformation as "good" or "bad," and the degree to which it is possible to intervene to divert the process into more desired directions. One way of approaching these issues is to focus on the subnational dimension of the national economy and to identify the processes by which changes in the role of individual cities, viewed as productive establishments, come about.

In the short run, the economic capability of a city is a function of its resources. However, while the productive skills of the labor force, the existing plant and equipment, and the stock of overhead capital certainly establish the outer limits to local economic development, they do not necessarily ensure that substantial development will occur. The proximity of the local area to the sources of supply of the goods and services needed by its industries and to markets for its products can be at least as decisive as its endowment of labor, productive capital, and infrastructure. The degree to which a city may offer a favorable economic environment for particular classes of enterprise may also influence local growth. Nor can the quality of local entrepreneurship be discounted in local development. Nevertheless, the distribution of productive activity among the various parts of the country depends directly on the interregional distribution of labor, plants, equipment, and overhead capital. Changes in the spatial organization of the national economy take place through the reallocation of these resources. Redistribution of the labor force takes place through internal migration; the distribution of productive capital is altered by the establishment of new plants or by the expansion or contraction of old ones; redistribution of stocks of overhead capital takes place in large degree through public investment processes. These elements, seen in their relationship to each other at the regional level, describe urbanization processes in terms of flows of productive factors.

INTERNAL MIGRATION FLOWS

Internal migration flows are a primary factor in urbanization, yet we know too little analytically to do other than describe them. What information we possess comes from the interpretation of differential population changes reported by censuses[25] or from some sample studies

[25] For example, Universidad de Chile, Instituto de Economía, *La Migración Interna en Chile en el Período 1940–1952* (Santiago: Instituto de Economía de la Universidad de Chile, 1959). Publicación No. 20, and Horacio Nuñez Miñana, "Las Migraciones en Venezuela," *Cuadernos de la Sociedad Venezolana de Planificación,* Vol. 3:6 (May 1964).

of urban population derived from questionnaire responses of migrant and nonmigrant populations.[26] Both sources are limited, the first because it is based on assumptions about the uniformity of rates of net increase in rural and urban areas which are difficult to establish, the second because the surveys fail to distinguish recent migrants, whose responses to questions about their moves are good, from old migrants, whose responses are bound to be at least as poor as their memories.

At any rate, it would be useful to know more about several aspects of internal migration. Since our figures measure net migration over long periods of time, it is not possible to fill out an "origin-destination" or "from-to" table, especially for short periods of time: we have no annual rates by origin, or by destination. We know nothing about gross flows and their relationships to net migratory balances. We know little about lifetime migratory histories or family migration experiences that extend beyond one generation.

A number of reasonable hypotheses and analytical formats need testing. We can ask three kinds of analytical questions about internal migration: (1) microanalytic ones concerning the migration-related decisions of migrants and nonmigrants, (2) macroanalytic questions about population movements over time, and (3) impact questions dealing with the consequences of internal migration for the economy in whole or in part.

Microeconomic analysis of internal migration is concerned with who moves, from where, to where, when, and why. The emphasis is on understanding the behavior of the migrating unit in the over-all pattern. Whereas some scholars have attributed rural-urban migration to the gap between rural misery and hopelessness and the glamor or promise of the metropolis, a more satisfying hypothesis has been proposed by Theodore Schultz and Larry A. Sjaasted which says that migrants behave as though they were maximizing their "lifetime earning power."[27] Since migration is a costly process, it is better viewed as a mobility investment in a manner similar to education. Migration to nearby points is less costly than migration to more distant points; living with relatives

[26] Centro Latinoamericano de Demografía, *Encuesta sobre Inmigración en El Gran Santiago,* Informe General, Primera Parte (Santiago: Centro Latinoamericano de Demografía, 1964), and Louis J. Ducoff, "Población Migratoria en un Area Metropolitano de un País en Proceso de Desarrollo: Informe Preliminar sobre un Estudio Experimental Efectuado en El Salvador," *Journal of the Inter-American Statistical Institute,* Vol. 20 (March 1962), pp. 131–139.
[27] Larry A. Sjaasted, "The Costs and Returns of Human Migration" *Journal of Political Economy,* Vol. 70:5, Part 2 (October 1962), pp. 80–93.

while job seeking is less costly than moving to a strange town. This hypothesis has been substantiated by the studies of Bruce Herrick, who found the facts of migration in Chile consistent with those that would have been predicted by Schultz and Sjaasted.[28]

Macroeconomic analysis of internal migration has been largely dominated by Simon Rottenberg's income hypothesis.[29] He pointed out that migration seems to flow from low-income areas to higher-income areas as migrants seek to improve their economic positions. The rate of flow appears to be a function of the size of the income gap. The United States, of course, has experienced this process over a longer period of time, so the convergence of rural and urban per capita incomes which the theory would predict has occurred.[30] The lack of any widespread convergence in Latin America, however, implies that even the massive rates of rural-urban migration have not been great enough to exhaust the redundant agricultural labor force which may amount to one half of the total population. With such a large labor supply available, the marginal productivity of agricultural labor cannot rise.[31] Indeed, evidence from Venezuela, where migration from rural areas is very high, suggests that per capita income in Caracas may be ten times that in rural areas.[32] A clear and direct relationship between size of place and per capita income can therefore be asserted. One might

[28] Herrick, "Internal Migration," p. 43.
[29] Simon Rottenberg, *Notes on the Economics of Urbanization in Latin America,* a paper prepared for the Seminar on Urbanization in Latin America, July 6–18, 1959. Also, see International Labor Office, *Why Labor Leaves the Land,* Studies and Reports, New Series, No. 59 (Geneva, 1960).
[30] Harvey S. Perloff, Edgar S. Dunn, Jr., Eric E. Lampard, and Richard S. Muth, *Regions, Resources, and Economic Growth* (Baltimore: Johns Hopkins Press, 1960).
[31] Currie arrives at 75 per cent as the proportion of agricultural labor which is redundant in Colombia. Lauchlin Currie, *Accelerating Development: The Necessity and the Means* (New York: McGraw-Hill, 1966), p. 183.
[32] Distribution of income in Venezuela is shown in the table. Source: Levy, "Economic Planning in Venezuela," quoted from Carl S. Shoup, *The Fiscal System of Venezuela* (Baltimore: Johns Hopkins Press, 1959). Compare the first and last figures in column 3.

Places with Populations	1 % of all Income Earned	2 % of Total Income	3 % of National Per Capita Income*
Less than 500	38	9	23.7
500–19,999	23	19	82.6
20,000–1,000,000	22	32	145.3
Over 1,000,000 (Caracas)	17	40	235.2

* Column 2 divided by Column 1.

wonder, then, not why the migration that flows out of the rural areas is so great, but why it isn't much greater—why, indeed, anyone is left in the rural hinterlands.

The impacts of internal migration appear, first, in the changes in the socioeconomic characteristics of local populations. In this highly selective process, the character of both the agricultural and city population is changed. Rural-urban movements are dominated by young, working-age males and females, usually the better educated and probably the healthier. Therefore, migration usually results in an impoverishment of the rural labor force. Although migrant labor accumulates in urban areas at too high a rate to be immediately absorbed, causing a condition of "overurbanization,"[33] the urban economy along with the national economy still gains by the process. At the same time, however, this siphoning of high-quality human resources reinforces the conservative, traditional character of the rural economy, impeding the everywhere needed transformation of the agricultural sector.

A similar condition occurs in the flows between the provincial cities and the metropolitan capital. The more highly skilled and ambitious members of the provincial labor forces tend to move to the metropolitan center to seek their fortunes and so reduce the capacity of the provincial cities to play effective roles in the development process.[34] This development is particularly apparent in Peru, where the more educated, the skilled, and the leaders have forsaken the provincial cities for Lima, leaving those cities to the growing number of rural migrants.[35]

Internal migration also affects consumption, having a particularly strong impact on the demand for public services. Rural service levels being conventionally low in Latin American countries, the mere act of moving into the city makes the migrant demand the full array of urban services. Therefore, the migration decision not only involves private

[33] N. V. Sovani provides a detailed discussion of this phenomenon in "The Analysis of 'Over-Urbanization,' " *Economic Development and Cultural Change,* Vol. 12:2 (January 1964), pp. 113–122.

[34] Keith B. Griffen has cited the recent experience of the Peruvian *sierra* as a case in point. Keith B. Griffen, "Reflections on Latin American Development," *Oxford Economic Papers* (New Series), Vol. 18:1 (March 1966), p. 5.

[35] Reported in "Geographic Distribution of the Population of Latin America and Regional Development Priorities," *Economic Bulletin for Latin America,* Vol. 8:1 (March 1963), p. 62, based on Division of Economic Development, Department of Economic and Social Affairs, Pan American Union, *Integración Económica y Social del Perú Central* (Washington, 1962).

costs but also imposes substantial social costs on the receiving city, which must either accept the deterioration of its existing services or finance the expansion necessary to meet the increasing demand.

INDUSTRIAL LOCATION DECISIONS

The second major component of urbanization consists of the flows of investment throughout the country into new plants and equipment. One could build an interregional model considering the processes by which industries are located and the limits of national demand. This could then be used to predict the location of new enterprises. Such a model is limited by implicit institutional assumptions about who is making the location decisions and how they are being made. In Latin America, these location decisions result from the interplay of public inducements and private decisions, emphasizing profit maximization under rigid public policy constraints. The potent role of the state in economic matters is justified by the judgment that entrepreneurship is weakly motivated and uninspired in these countries; the government, it is argued, has to play at least part of the entrepreneurial role. Under these conditions, monopolies seem unavoidable, often resulting in a high degree of insensitivity to profit-making opportunities. Thus, the role of government seems unavoidable, since it alone has the informational resources on which to base objective location decisions.

The result of this type of interplay is a complex, shifting relationship between government development agencies and private investors, a relationship which has not always been completely successful in producing decisions consistent with the long-run development interests of the country. Chile possesses the oldest development corporation in Latin America, the Corporación de Fomento (CORFO). In recent years, government policies and CORFO activities have sought to bolster the economy of Chile's northernmost provinces.

During the 1950's, total employment in Arica, for example, was almost doubled and manufacturing employment virtually quadrupled largely because of the location of the whole of Chile's small automobile assembly industry in Arica. This change was brought about by means of certain free port advantages in the importation of auto parts. However, Arica is 1,000 miles from Santiago and the populous central region of the country, where the bulk of the auto market is located. Also, Chilean-made parts are expected to replace imported auto parts gradually in a few years, and the auto parts industry is centered in the

Santiago area. Judged by any standards of locational efficiency, there is little to be said for the decision.[36] Under the best of circumstances it would have been impossible to predict.

Iquique, also in the far north, was a boom town that was ruined by the collapse of the international nitrate market. Observing the miraculous growth of the Peruvian fish meal industry, CORFO made credit available at extraordinarily advantageous terms to build a fish meal industry at Iquique, which has alternatively flourished and languished because of the unforeseen capriciousness of the anchovy in Chilean waters. Another northern Chilean city, La Serena, had the good fortune to have one of its citizens elected to the presidency of the country, and the city received spectacular attention from the national government in the improvement of its public facilities to attract private investment to strengthen its economic base. Nevertheless, its gain in industrial employment during the 1952–1960 period fell 43 per cent short of the national average.

Location decisions, and hence the flows of investment funds in countries with mixed public-private investment, such as Chile, exhibit a high degree of uncertainty, caused by the lack of policy continuity from administration to administration, as well as by administrative caprice. Consistent government policies for industrial location might possibly bend the economy toward some specific objectives simply by establishing the locational parameters of economic activity. Under present circumstances, however, we must develop a more versatile framework for the analysis of flows of investment between regions and sectors.

It is hard to fault the contention that national economic development prospers from a maximum exploitation of the comparative advantages

[36] Leland Johnson says, "automobile assemblers were not free to locate their plants wherever they chose. They were legally required to build in Arica, situated on the Pacific Coast 1000 miles north of Santiago and only a few miles south of the Peruvian border. No assembler would have picked Arica of his own free will, but would obviously have picked a spot in or near Santiago—the area constituting both the primary market for automobiles and the primary source of locally fabricated components in the integration program. Assembly operations in Arica face the double handicap of requiring that national components be brought up from Santiago and the assembled units sent down again. Furthermore, Arica had little in the way of a skilled labor pool, or an industrial infrastructure upon which the automobile industry could draw. Everything had to be started from scratch. The selection of Arica for the industry was based on a mixture of political and economic considerations." *Problems of Industrialization in Chile: Some Preliminary Observations,* Memorandum RM-4794-AID, December 1965, The RAND Corporation, p. 5.

of its several regions. However, this is often not the case in Latin America. For most national industries other than raw material processors, such as fish flour mills or mineral refineries, the locational decision is undoubtedly a choice between the scale economies of the metropolitan core and the advantages of access to the sites where its material inputs are produced. New technologies are increasing the economies of scale available to producers, and these economies can be realized most easily in the metropolitan markets. All conditions, then, seem to favor the increasing centralization of economic activity in developing countries. To arrest this trend involves substantial and costly intervention in interregional investment flows. Whether it can be justified by efficiency, equity, or stability criteria is another question.

INVESTMENT IN URBAN INFRASTRUCTURE

The treatment of investment in urban infrastructure would be simple if we could accept the theory that such investment decisions are independent and controllable. Any serious examination of such investment in Latin American countries, however, must lead to a contrary conclusion. The processes by which these decisions are made are institutionalized in the public bureaucracy and in its relations with the private sector.

In the unitary governments that characterize most of Latin America, the allocation of investment among classes of urban facilities and among the various urban communities is carried out largely by agencies of the central government operating from the national capital. If such central agencies followed principles of maximizing social welfare and had access to perfect information, their investments would vary only with states of the national economy and society. This is, of course, not the case, but it does not follow that in Latin America public investment can be viewed as a discretionary variable for planners.

Consider the institutional structure from which policies influencing the character of urban development are emerging. Typically, one finds a high degree of concentration of responsibility at the national level with ineffectual local governments responsible only for the trivia of community life. National concentration of responsibility does not carry with it effective centralization of decision making, however. Powerful ministries, each highly insulated from the others and to some degree politically independent of the nation's chief executive, share these responsibilities along functional lines. Consequently, the achievement of some degree of comprehensiveness in national policies and plans, rare as it may be, carries with it no assurance that a similar degree of comprehensiveness can be achieved at less than the national level.

The typical recourse of local residents concerned with community needs is to petition the minister of the national agency concerned with their problems. When this course fails, a local deputy or senator may be entreated to represent the cause to the ministry. The crucial attribute of these processes is the indeterminacy of their outcome, when local needs are dealt with at the national level in the absence of (1) effective policy feedbacks and (2) responsibility for policy impacts. Public investment decisions are made by these same quasi-independent ministries and autonomous public agencies, each pursuing its own particular mission and allocating its resources accordingly.[37] In developing countries interagency coordination is a condition devoutly to be desired and scarcely ever achieved.

In Chile, although it is true that direct feedbacks from localities to decision makers are rarely provided for, political mechanisms have evolved within the complex bureaucratic and legislative processes surrounding the appropriation of public funds through which feedback from the urban communities can make itself felt. While it is likely that, over the long run, these processes work in a fairly predictable fashion, it is less likely that anything so clumsy can be very reliable in its welfare dimensions.

At this time, however, local decision-making capabilities are so atrophied that assertion of community wants must take its chances in the national political arena. Local revenues are limited to such sources as documentary fees; the responsibilities of local government are confined to parks, street lighting, historical monuments, and the like. Again, national political decision processes, and not national planners, do the allocating.

At this point, it is perhaps useful to restate the over-all analytical format: urbanization can be usefully viewed in terms of the subnational flows of three kinds of productive factors: labor or, more largely, population; investment in industry; and investment in urban infrastructure. These flows take place through quite distinct processes and at rates only partially interdependent.

Now it is worth taking a few moments to examine the ways in which

---

[37] Levy describes the Venezuelan agencies as "independent empires" in "Economic Planning in Venezuela," pp. 84–91.

these flows relate to each other to bring about the differential rates of urbanization at the subnational level previously discussed.

THE RELATIONSHIPS BETWEEN MIGRATION AND PUBLIC
AND PRIVATE INVESTMENT

The interdependence of infrastructure investment and investment in productive capital has been posed by Albert Hirschman.[38] He describes a cycle in which excess capacity in urban overhead systems offers economizing opportunities to industry, thereby inducing investment in new enterprise. This, in turn, taxes the capacity of the overhead systems and, when this occurs, costs of production rise. Rising costs, in turn, generate pressures to expand the capacity of existing urban infrastructure, which will again reduce production costs, inducing further investment in industry. This cycle can be repeated indefinitely until long-run increasing costs or declining demand stabilizes the process. In this process, infrastructure investment can act as a lead factor, providing a necessary, if not sufficient, condition for local productive investment. One can, however, turn the cycle around and view existing plants as the lead factor to overhead investment. This investment would be induced by the abnormally high ratio of benefits to costs resulting from the particular relationship of productive capital to infrastructure. It follows, then, that the net benefits of infrastructure investment will be substantially influenced by the relationship of plant capital to infrastructure capital.

Some strong and reasonably straightforward relations can be shown to exist between urban capital and internal migration. Most directly, populations, however structured by demographic and socioeconomic variables, establish the basic demands for the overhead services requiring capital investment. Internal migration does not merely shift demand among the various parts of the nation; it changes the very nature of that demand. A man migrating from the campos to Santiago demands many public services which were unnecessary or unavailable in the countryside. Consequently, this particular move has different demand implications than if he had moved from a provincial city to the

---

[38] Albert O. Hirschman, *The Strategy of Economic Development* (New Haven: Yale University Press, 1958), pp. 83–97. See also discussion of Hirschman model and unbalanced growth in Warren F. Ilchman and Ravindra C. Bhargava, "Balanced Thought and Economic Growth," *Economic Development and Cultural Change,* Vol. 14:4: (July 1966), and Ashok Mathur, "Balanced v. Unbalanced Growth: A Reconciliatory View," *Oxford Economic Papers* (New Series) Vol. 18:2 (July 1966), 137–157; among others.

capital. If an effective response is not made to these demands, urban overhead investment may appear only loosely linked to population movements. When overhead systems are available, however, their output is directly affected by the increased utilization of the facilities. This can result either in increased public costs necessitated by the allocation of new resources to maintain service levels or in higher user costs caused by deterioration of service.

The impact of levels of overhead services on internal migration has received a great deal of discussion but little research. It seems reasonably clear that rural populations generally appreciate the fact that urban dwellers enjoy much higher levels of public service than do *campesinos,* but it is more difficult to ascribe a specific role in the migration decision to the attractions of public services. Other attractions would certainly include the desire of families to provide education for their children[39] and the real income effect experienced by the migrants to urban areas. In Chile's case, this effect appears to be considerable.

The relationship of internal migration to the flows of investment into productive capital tends to be more easily related to conventional economic analysis. Labor and capital are conventional productive factors which should seek their most efficient employment. Thus internal migration is in large part a phenomenon of imperfectly mobile and imperfectly informed labor moving from lower to higher real income levels. While it is doubtful that labor is so highly job-oriented and mobile that differential unemployment is evened out, there is evidence in Chile, at any rate, that migration flows are sensitive to the broad opportunities for employment. On the other hand, industrial location of some classes of enterprise may be strongly influenced by the characteristics of the labor supply, especially when activities depend on high levels of technical and professional skills, which exist in the capital in greater abundance than anywhere else in the country.

It should be understood, then, that the urbanization problem exists not simply because rural people have a capricious desire to enjoy the metropolitan bright lights. While in all Latin American nations except Uruguay rural populations are growing at rates ranging from 1 to 2 per cent per annum, the agricultural sectors of these nations are in trouble. Food prices lead inflationary advances.[40] In Chile, per capita

---

[39] In the city of La Serena, the opinion was generally held by local officials that a sizable portion of its inmigration could be attributed to the desire of rural families to place their children in the city's splendid schools. Out-migration was ascribed as the transfer of the "products" of the system to the great labor market of Santiago.
[40] Of six countries with high rates of inflation during 1950–1964, five found food

agricultural output actually declined between the 1950–1954 period and the 1955–1961 period.[41] Because of this, the accumulated per capita deficit per annum between 1950 and 1960 must have amounted to around 10 per cent. At the same time, net imports of agricultural products had grown to the point that the balance-of-payments deficit of Chile from 1955 to 1961 was exceeded by the deficit in the agricultural sector alone.[42] In recent years this agricultural deficit has amounted to $100 million per year.[43] That agricultural development demands attention of the same order of magnitude as industrialization hardly needs defense.

In the last decade, population pressures have forced millions of rural dwellers to migrate from the campos to the slums and shacktowns of the Latin American cities. Nevertheless, as I have shown, rates of rural-urban migration have not been great enough to change the basic conditions of production in agriculture. The evidence suggests that the gap between urban and rural incomes has grown rather than diminished, as a result of the shift of resources away from agriculture toward the urban sectors. Agrarian reform movements persistently confront the conclusion that improvement of agricultural output will require a lower man/land ratio at a time when that ratio is still increasing.

We can adduce from recent demographic experience that migration rates from rural to urban areas would typically have to double if any dent were to be made in rural overpopulation.[44] At the same time, current rates of migration into the cities have defeated all efforts to improve the frequently appalling conditions in areas now doubling in population every ten to fifteen years. The turning point in agricultural productivity would come only when the rural population ceased to

---

prices outstripping all other sectors. Department of Statistics, Pan American Union, *Consumer Price Indexes of the American Nations, 1955–March 1965,* No. 21–22 (Washington, 1965).

[41] Chile's production from crops, livestock, hunting, and fishing increased at the rate of 1.3 per cent per annum during this period. *The Economic Development of Latin America in the Post-War Period* (New York: United Nations, 1964), p. 26, while population was increasing at the rate of 2.4 per cent per annum, *Statistical Bulletin for Latin America, March 1964,* Vol. 1:1, (New York: United Nations, 1964), p. 17.

[42] *La Economía de Chile en el Período 1950–1963,* Vol. 2 (Santiago: Institute de Economía de la Universidad de Chile, 1963), Publication No. 60, pp. 75, 174, 196.

[43] *World Business* (September 1966), p. 20.

[44] Honduras, Haiti, and El Salvador would have to increase their rural outmigration rates five- to tenfold before their rural populations would stabilize, given existing natural increase rates. In contrast, Venezuela would stabilize with an increase of a third. Wingo, "Recent Patterns of Urbanization among Latin American Countries," p. 900.

grow and began to decrease. The policy question then becomes: when will the urban sector be able to absorb the total national population increase and more? This depends, in turn, on rates of investment both in new job-creating activities and in the creation of new overhead capital.

Thus, urbanization rates depend also on the intricate interrelationship between agricultural and industrial development. Any effort to increase the rate of industrial development is likely to produce substantial increases in rural-urban migration which will, in turn, influence the scale of the problem confronted by urbanization policy. Consequently, a vital function of urbanization policy should be to make explicit the relationship between development and urbanization so that it can be considered in the development decision. The need for such an urbanization feedback in the national planning processes will increase as development efforts escalate. It cannot now be said to exist.

THE IMPLICATIONS OF URBANIZATION POLICIES

The choice of development rates and relations leads us to the next basic determination: the long-run strategy necessary to improve living conditions in the urban sector. The development of such a strategy will be encountered in all questions concerning the relative advantages of various urban scales, mixes of city sizes, regional development, and urban organization. Present rates of urban growth define, in large degree, how fast Latin American urban policy will have to run just to stand still. There is some evidence that, in recent years, most Latin American countries have fallen behind in most urban overhead services. Although the figures are subject to several interpretations, the growth of housing deficits is great indeed.[45] The deterioration of metropolitan transportation has been documented in Santiago[46] and Bogotá.[47] Although, on the whole, the provision of drinking water and electricity seems to have improved because of the availability of loans from international agencies, sewage disposal and telephone service

---

[45] By 1960 the United Nations estimated the housing deficit in Latin America at 19.5 million units, equivalent to more than 50 per cent of total households. Economic Commission for Latin America, Housing Conditions, *Policies and Programmes in Latin America, 1960–1963*, Study Tour and Workshop on National Housing Agencies and Programmes, Copenhagen, Denmark, August 30 to September 19, 1964, p. 4.
[46] Robert T. Brown and Carlos Hurtado Ruiz-Tagle, *Una Política de Transportes para Chile* (Santiago: Instituto de Economía, Universidad de Chile, 1964), Publicación No. 59.
[47] Lauchlin Currie. *Una Política Urbana para los Países en Desarrollo* (Bogotá: Ediciones TERCER MUNDO, 1965), pp. 88–102.

appear to be declining. The capacity of existing infrastructure can be extended only so far before damage is done to the productive environment and political stability of the city.

It is not enough, however, merely to maintain existing service levels as measured by physical indices. At the same time that they are physically growing, demand factors are being transformed. The changing composition and location of industry will shift emphasis among overhead services: new large factories located in the urban periphery, for example, will require scales and mixes of services different from old, smaller, centrally located establishments. Rising urban incomes and a rapidly growing middle class, spilling out in new suburbias, demand expensive property services similar to their counterparts in the United States. These transformation requirements are likely to increase with increasing rates of development.

A strategy will have to be delineated which will bring about the general improvement of the urban service environment. Although holding strategies may suffice to temporarily arrest deterioration, the requirements of longer-run improvements in urban living conditions will need to be explicitly identified. Such "social outlays" have frequently been considered expendable in the press of more urgent demands for resources. Over the longer run, however, the rising consumption aspirations of the urban population are not likely to tolerate the indefinite perseverance and capricious distribution of severely restricted urban services. Thus, the strategy of improvement will need to proceed by seeking out pockets of severe service deprivation and focusing community resources on their improvement.

Stabilize, transform, improve—these three incontrovertible parts of urbanization policy suggest that the growing demands of urban development on the resources of Latin America will increase even more rapidly than the growth of the urban sector itself. When national economic planners have viewed these demands as discretionary, events have consistently proved them wrong. Massive invasion of private land by shack builders is a clear response to the increasing lack of adequate housing caused by the pressures of urban growth. In Chile, student strikes and rioting touched off by modest increases in bus fares have, on occasion, paralyzed the capital and once brought a government to its knees. While the fare increases each time triggered the disorders, the extraordinarily low level of service offered by the transit system has been a frequent target of the protests. Less obvious, of course, are the direct political pressures generated by living conditions which work not only on the national government but on party programs.

The processes of economic development clearly confront the urban policy maker with a special dynamic deriving, first, from the manner in which labor and public and private investment get distributed in the urban systems, and, second, from the economic, social, and political transformations which accompany the development process. Understanding the drift of this dynamic is a prerequisite to diverting it into directions more consistent with society's goals. If, in the long run, the allocative processes tend to search out the best strategy, policy needs only to assure that the processes do not get distorted by unforeseen events. If not, the role of policy is to transform them so far as is necessary (and possible) to satisfy the development goals.

There are three areas in which the optimum-seeking characteristics of these allocative processes might need qualification: first, the market or quasi-market machinery by which they operate may be grossly imperfect; second, there may be consequences for the society as a whole which do not enter into the separate calculations of individuals in the labor market, entrepreneurs, or public agencies; and third, there may be long-run developmental requirements which are not well served by short-run optimization. Each of these cases suggests a different policy prescription.

In the first case, we are concerned with the limits to rational behavior of the actors. Do they have access to information about options and costs which would allow them to make an objectively "best" decision? Do they have equitable access to the allocation institutions, or, in other words, do they have equitable, if not equal, standing in the market place in terms of wealth and power? Finally, are the actors motivated optimizers? In the Chilean case, it is not difficult to identify some crucial imperfections in these allocation mechanisms.

In the allocation of productive capital, the economic environment of stagnation or rapid inflation characteristic of many developing countries is hardly conducive to rational short-run behavior. Take Chile as an example. Government regulation of the interest rates during a period of recent inflation has resulted in a negative real interest rate and rationing of credit by banking institutions, which are operating by criteria that can only be guessed at.[48] Apparently, credit has been

[48] Johnson, *Problems of Industrialization in Chile*, p. 26.

diverted from high-return, moderate-risk investment in the hinterlands to low-risk, low-return investments in the Santiago area. Even more serious is the evidence that the rural areas frequently export capital to the metropolitan core.[49] Further, it appears that, more often than not, the intervention of government in the interregional allocation of investment through ill-advised regional development programs has resulted in a social deficit, as in the history of policies employed to develop Chile's northern provinces. Finally, recent economic researchers have analyzed the weakness of entrepreneurship in Chile and found that aggressive entrepreneurial roles are played essentially by recent migrants and their successors. In summary, then, we can see that the processes allocating capital investment among parts of the country and sectors of the economy appear to be grossly imperfect. More important, however, is a growing ability among social scientists to describe and calculate the implications of these defects.

The allocation of investment to urban overhead facilities exhibits grievous imperfection. Clearly, local governments have not been effective in recognizing and responding to public needs and wants,[50] and the formal political machinery offers a poor surrogate, especially when, as in Chile, local political power structures are not interested in the welfare of the local urban community.[51] Centralized allocation of these funds at the national level with substantial political intervention at each point of decision does not make a prima facie case against the allocation processes at work, but it does not inspire confidence in their ability to channel society's resources in a manner consistent with society's best interests. Add to this the arbitrary, preferential treatment of some sections of the country, as typified by the earmarking of part of the

[49] Jorge Ahumada argued that the region containing the metropolitan core of Chile receives transfers from the other Chilean regions in substantial volume. Jorge Ahumada C., *En Vez de la Miséria* (Santiago: Editorial del Pacifico, S.A., 1964), pp. 179–180.
[50] "In most countries municipal authorities have no power to tax land. Consequently, the provision by them of more than rudimentary services requires aid from the higher levels of government, and the municipal authorities concentrate all their attention on the securing of such aid." Economic Commission for Latin America, "Rural Settlement Patterns and Social Change in Latin America: Notes for a Strategy of Rural Development," *Economic Bulletin for Latin America,* Vol. 10:1 (March 1965), p. 10.
[51] The ECLA study also points out that "Since the wealthier and more influential part of the *municipio* population lives in the *cabecera,* and since the rural neighborhoods have no effective way of making their demands heard, public services are concentrated in the *cabecera,* and any financial aid received from the higher authorities is spent there, largely on projects that will constitute lasting monuments to the administration of the time—public buildings and parks." *Ibid.*

copper tax for the benefit of public programs in the chief mineral provinces of Chile; the highly compartmentalized structure of the national government agencies engaged in one form or another of interregional public investment; and the lack of any effective feedback mechanisms to gauge the impact of public policies. Then, at least to some degree, the capriciousness of public investment process becomes very evident.

Finally, although labor allocation mechanisms seem basically rational, there are some big gaps in our knowledge about them. We know little about the amount and distribution of disguised unemployment hidden in the employment figures. Better information here would lead to a reconsideration of the effectiveness of labor allocation mechanisms and of the welfare implications of internal migration. Even if migratory behavior should be found to be basically rational, the social costs of this process might be excessive and call for some direct intervention in the allocation processes by the community.

In general, then, the imperfections in these processes are many and serious, and it would strain credulity to conclude that, left to themselves, they are likely to lead automatically to any desirable state. At the same time, goals such as income redistribution, competing with the goal of income maximization, need to be introduced. Many goals of public policy exist, and those that remain unrealized in the total pursuit of income maximization become real costs to the society.[52] Finally, many persons suggest that short-run optimal goal achievement could lead to a developmental cul-de-sac in which succeeding stages of development would be rendered more difficult to achieve. This argument is also frequently leveled against primate city organization.

STRATEGY FOR THE FUTURE

At any rate, having weighed these processes of urbanization on the scale of the perfect market and found them wanting, how should we proceed? On the one hand, we can supplant these mechanisms by

---

[52] "No nation has ever had or could have an exclusive, secular goal of economic development to which all others must be subordinated. The elites and mobilized publics of every nation, rich and poor, have many objectives for public policy: national survival, national grandeur, distributive-welfare goals, political stability, maximum public choice, maintaining a particular elite combination in power, and the 'higher life' among them. While it is true that economic development is necessary for some of these goals, it is also true that economic development is not sufficient." Ilchman and Bhargava, *op. cit.*, p. 396.

"rational planning" and even greater concentration of decision making. The problem is, of course, that the social organism is neither completely plastic nor completely passive. Given the most well-meaning innovators, one would still expect informal processes to emerge and adapt themselves to the formal decision-making machinery, indeed to capture it and distort its Platonic elegance into something jerry-built, active, and responsive, in direct or devious manner, to the interests at stake. It is not at all certain that the end results would be an improvement, judged by efficiency, distributive, or stability criteria.[53]

The appropriate strategy, then, seems to fall somewhere between the "Platonic takeover" and the indifferent acceptance of whatever the unfolding of these processes might leave us. What we are left with is a strategy of judicious, if increasing, intervention in the processes themselves through the progressive evolution of new institutions. We might as well accept the fact, however, that societal intervention in these development processes does not always recalibrate them in a realistic manner. It can, in fact, increase the divergence of events from the optimal development path. To combat this divergence, governments need guides to distinguish on-path characteristics from off-path characteristics. This leads us to some innovations that might be useful in the matter of urbanization policy in Latin America.

The United Nations and its organs have frequently pointed to the need to establish effective links between national planning and regional and local development.[54] Yet, the preoccupation of national planners with the global sectors of the economy has been accompanied by a thoroughgoing indifference to the subnational dimensions of development.[55] Almost no mechanism has been perfected to translate over-all planning into information which might be valuable to the decision makers at work rearranging the regional organization of the national economy. The difficulties of regionalizing national plan recommendations have been frequently discussed, but the conceptual and institutional

[53] Levy concludes from an examination of the institutional circumstances surrounding planning activities that, "thus, it would appear that the centrally imposed solution is no less arbitrary or demonstrably more rational than any other." Levy, "Economic Planning in Venezuela," p. 206.
[54] See "Problems of Regional Economic Planning and Development in Europe and the United States," *Economic Bulletin for Europe,* Vol. 17:2 (November 1965), p. 8.
[55] "Thus far no Latin American country has an integrated system of regional plans, but plans have been drawn up for certain regions in Argentina, Brazil, Colombia, Mexico, Peru and Venezuela." *Economic Survey of Latin America, 1964* (New York: United Nations, 1966), p. 331.

response to the problem has been, at best, tentative. The interrelationship between the broad, direction-setting and pace-setting overview of national planning and the particular processes at work locating physical capital and integrating it with other resources continues to be largely undefined. It is not enough to say that national plans should establish guidelines for regional development. Far more often than not, national plan recommendations give ambiguous information to the subnational planner or decision maker.[56] No tests for consistency between regional decisions and the national plan may exist beyond the very general conditions imposed by resource allocations. For any one region, there may be a large number of development sequences which are not inconsistent per se with the general requirements of the national planning process. The fact is that consistency characterizes only the aggregate of regional development sequences, so no one region can guide itself along paths that optimize national development.

This says something important about the subnational dimensions of national economic planning in Latin America. For the most part, one studies the national planning documents of Latin American countries in vain for some discussion of their regional implications. Urbanization is treated as an across-the-board problem which enters into the planning process only as a refinement in the projection of sectoral needs: the aggregate planning targets for water supply or housing, for example, take into consideration the projected urban populations, and these targets will be expressed in terms of the proportions of the deficits that can be met in each of the urban and rural sectors. It is possible to meet such targets without developing a single, well-serviced community in the entire country: the housing targets may be met by eliminating 100 per cent of the deficit in City A and none of it in City B, while water supply deficits are eliminated totally in City B and continue unabated in City A.

Almost nowhere in the network of planning and program development, typical of Latin American governments, does there exist a point from which the subnational implications of national policies can be analyzed and evaluated. Likewise, there is no point from which policy recommendations can be developed to guide the development of the urban

---

[56] One ought to distinguish decentralized regional planning, in which the planner has a special responsibility to the region, from centralized regional planning, where his responsibility is to the national government. I use it in the first sense here, assuming a number of regions each seeking to maximize their own welfare within the constraints of national policies.

sector. Without such a focus, discussion about urbanization policy is little more than fantasy.

Nevertheless, tentative innovations in Latin American policy making have evolved in recent years and, projected into the future, promise a growing capability to promulgate consistent programs to guide urbanization processes. Many of these innovations have ridden on the coattails of political reform in Venezuela, Peru, and Chile, and so are identified in part with peaceful popular revolutions. They represent a beginning, at least.

The concept of community development has demonstrated a substantial popular political appeal.[57] Venezuela's community development program, begun in 1960, has played a growing role in guiding the development of local public facilities and services throughout the country. Colombia's program is focused on the creation of community facilities through utilization of the skills and energy of underemployed labor in the community. Chile's program of "Participación Popular" has set about not only to organize self-help strategies for the poor but concurrently to develop a new net of community decision-making units, the "juntas de vecinos," with direct ties to a national community development agency. This would create a new national-local responsibility relationship in local development.[58] In Peru the movement is called "Cooperación Popular." It is more strongly focused on aided, self-help development of community facilities such as water systems, community centers, schools, clinics, and the like, which will directly improve the level of overhead services in the *barriadas*. Ecuador and Bolivia also have similar programs of community development.

Deliberate programs designed to strengthen the responsibility and effectiveness of local government roles in urban development have begun the difficult task of decentralizing the functions of urban service decisions. Venezuela's Foundation for Municipal Development, working within government programs, has succeeded spectacularly in helping cities take advantage of the broader responsibilities offered

[57] An excellent appraisal of community development programs in Latin America is to be found in "Popular Participation and Principles of Community Development in Relation to the Acceleration of Economic and Social Development," *Economic Bulletin for Latin America,* Vol. 9:2 (November 1964). See also Secretary General of the United Nations, *Desarrollo de la Comunidad en las Zonas Urbanas* (United Nations, New York, 1961).
[58] This is not accepted as a benevolent change by all parties. The conservative newspaper *El Mercurio*, in a series of editorial analyses June 22–25, 1966, found that the movement threatened the development effort with confusion of responsibility.

to them by the national government and in upgrading the quality of municipal administration.

The most notable innovations have taken place in regional development efforts. Venezuela's massive effort to exploit the riches of its Guayana region is particularly well known in the United States because of the participation of the Joint Center for Urban Studies of M.I.T. and Harvard. Here, a broad plan for the regional development of an extraordinarily rich base of natural resources will alter substantially the character of the Venezuelan economy in coming years. The program also offers a special lesson in urbanization policy considerations, since the growth of the urban pole of the region, Santo Tomé de Guayana, has proceeded hand in hand with industrial development.[59]

The SUDENE program for the development of northeastern Brazil, older and more extensive than the Guayana plan, has also concentrated much of its attention on the rapid improvement of the region's urban sector, justifying its emphasis on the needs of new industry for a hospitable urban economic environment.[60]

Innovations which seek a more viable national-local relationship have also taken place at the national level. Within Peru's National Planning Institute is found not only a national office of regional planning whose purpose is to organize regional development activities throughout the country but also a national office of urban planning with a strong interest in improving the quality of development in all the urban centers in Peru.

Regional development and urbanization problems have received high-priority attention from President Eduardo Frei of Chile. At his policy-making elbow he placed the National Planning Office whose well-staffed regional planning corps aims to organize broad regional development activities throughout the country, and then to relate national development planning to them. At the same time, the government overhauled the existing ministries to create a new Ministry

[59] The brochure *Guayana, Cornerstone of the Development of Venezuela* (Caracas: Corporación Venezolana de Guayana, August 1963) provides an over-all description of the program.
[60] See especially Superintendencia do Desenvolvimento do Nordeste, Presidencia da Republica, *Plano Quinquinal de Desenvolvimento para o Nordeste 1961–1965,* Vol. 2 (Recife, SUDENE-Seção de Impressão). Robock presents a general description and analysis of the SUDENE program, Stefan H. Robock, *Brazil's Developing Northeast* (Washington: The Brookings Institution, 1963), p. 66.

of Housing and Urbanism which contains quite explicitly among its divisions an office for urbanization policies.[61] Even so partial a catalogue as this should not ignore the international agencies whose consciousness of the problem is steadily growing. The Inter-American Development Bank recently embarked on a new policy of supporting comprehensive urban development programs in Latin America.[62] The Economic Commission for Latin America has begun to explore cost factors in urban development so that they may extend technical assistance on these problems.

Many things, then, concerning urbanization policy in Latin America are in motion and are producing a greater capability to manage the urban dimensions of national economic development. When taken in the context of the very rapid rates of change in the urban sectors of Latin American countries, however, all of these improvements constitute only a beginning. The rate of innovation and experimentation needs not only some acceleration but some directions. But we must begin with the basic proposition that we really know too little about the processes of urbanization to be able to make very reliable policies. The state of knowledge about causality in internal migration, industrial location, and public investment is such that the reliability of predictions of the consequences of alternative government policies is very low. In addition, we realize that useful techniques for evaluating these consequences are hard to evolve: the weighing of explicit social gains and losses of policies is a scarcely developed art.

Nevertheless, the imperatives to action are so great that action cannot be forestalled until we know enough, simply because we never know enough. Policy will have to be made while understanding is advanced. Indeed, a vital policy strategy at this point would, by its nature, build into the whole policy-making complex a strong research and analysis core focused on expanding our understanding of internal migration,

61 Juan B. Astica, "Use of Urban National Policy and Local Planning in the Process of Integral Development" (The Chilean Case), paper prepared for the conference on *The Role of the City in the Modernization of Latin America,* Cornell University, November 1965, and Dirección de Planificación del Desarrollo Urbano, Ministerio de Vivienda y Urbanismo, República de Chile, *Funciones, Organización, e Instrumentos para la Planificación del Desarrollo Urbano,* Informe Preliminar (Santiago, April 1966).
62 Banco Interamericano de Desarrollo, "EL BID y el Financiamiento de Proyectos de Carácter Municipal," documento preparado por el personal profesional del Banco para la Reunión sobre Financiamiento Municipal en Latinoamerica (Washington, January 23–26, 1966), pp. 11–12.

subnational flows of investment capital, and the causes and consequences of public investment in urban overhead.[63] It would further serve the role of monitor and interpreter of changes in these processes. Its principal policy-making function would concern the progressive elaboration of an urban policy model for the country which would help planners concerned with urbanization policies play through and evaluate various alternatives that might influence the emerging characteristics of the urban sector. The development of policies must then take into consideration the cumulative nature of research and analysis by confining itself, in the first instance, to urgent problems or to problems which have a high strategic importance. One would expect that decisions could then follow the decreasingly tentative conclusions of the researchers. Clearly, the roles both of analysis and interpretation ought to be in close touch with the source of over-all national economic development policies. They must be near regional development activities and other agencies involved in the production of urban overhead services, or their viewpoint is likely to become limited to the mission of a parent agency such as housing or industrial location.

In addition, several gradual reforms in national-local relations appear to be essential. A program of progressive delegation to local governments of those urban service decisions in which there is not an explicit national interest should be undertaken, paced by the development of an increasing administrative capability to handle such decisions competently and responsibly. By itself, such a program should take an enormous load of responsibility from the national government. Financially, direct national outlays for local services would give way to grant-in-aid programs to local government operations. One set of urbanization policies might then consist of the establishment of minimum service standards to be used as the basis for allocating national subsidies to local governments.

A related role would be that of technical assistance to improve service standards, administration, and planning in local areas, perhaps modeled along the lines of the urban extension programs in the United States. Increasingly, there would have to be a shift in emphasis away from the functional independence of national policies affecting urban development and toward comprehensiveness at the local level. Only

63 A more detailed statement of this analytical framework is set forth in *Design for a World-wide Study of Regional Development* (Washington: Resources for the Future, 1966).

through such a shift will it be possible to exploit the complementarities among programs so important for local economic activities. National policy would be seen as setting basic standards and guidelines for urban development, while effective responsibility for urban development decisions would be increasingly decentralized.

To complement these local-national relations, it is imperative to carry out institutional modifications at the national level. Agency missions need to be redirected by the imposition of policy criteria which reflect the interdependencies among government programs. Thus, the test for a successful water distribution program might shift from the "capacity added to the nation's water supply systems" to the contribution that the water resource agency has made to comprehensive local development programs. Such shifts could contribute increasing consistency between national and local development objectives.

Finally, of course, there is a great need for the massive training of people to take new roles in this unfolding policy environment. Universities, vocational schools, on-the-job training programs, wholesale retraining of existing personnel: these and more will have to be integrated as parts of the over-all transformation of urban development policies.

At this point in the development of Latin America, it seems that the principal constraints on effective regional and urban development are caused by two factors. First, policies gone awry generally reflect an incomplete understanding of the processes by which the subnational economies of these countries are being shaped. The consequences can be either unrealistic policy objectives whose social costs are extravagant or the choice of means inappropriate to the objectives. This is illustrated by the numerous cases in which overhead investment has failed to hire new industrial capital in regions which have been subject to development policies.

Second, institutional parameters surrounding urban and regional development policies in developing countries generally ensure that the best-laid plans of dedicated men miscarry. Existing organizational structures, patterns of political behavior, and the decision processes embedded in public bureaucracies and private institutions are as much dimensions of the problem of planning as are the lack of resources and the imperfections of development mechanisms. These circumstances have not been ignored by planners and policy makers, but, too frequently, they have been merely labeled as obstacles and blamed for the failure of programs. The lesson to be drawn from them is that institutional changes are the first order of business for urban and regional development, not in the sense of eliminating the roadblocks in front of clever plans, but in the sense of the directed evolution of institutions with a capability to make sensible and appropriate decisions to guide wisely unfolding subnational development. Without this, the best plans and the wisest men will be wasted, the "optimum size of cities" will continue to titillate only the academics, and regional development criteria will generate more journal articles than development programs.

This article, therefore, has been less concerned with how to influence internal migration, how to locate new plant investment, and where to put new public facilities than it has been with the processes and institutions involved, not because they are less important but because the institutional issues come first. As democracy is government not by men but by laws, so subnational development seems to me to be a process generated by institutions rather than by men, no matter how clever and well-intentioned they may be.

6.

Changing Governmental Roles in Urban Development
Norman Beckman

Evidence continues to mount that the cities of the nation are undergoing an explosion in which governments, public policy, and society itself are being atomized and scattered across the urban landscape. Although the forces of dispersal are now in ascendance, there are, at the same time, developments working for consolidation, rationalization, and integration. The situation is not simply a matter of dispersive elements being undesirable and the factors of consolidation desirable. The goal should be an equilibrium achieved within our governmental system. Perhaps a better simile of what is desired is the growth of a healthy child, who explores, experiments, and innovates but remains secure and firmly bound into a path toward maturity—the old Greek definitions of both government and city.

The late Morton Grodzins, one of the most thoughtful observers of the intergovernmental scene, concluded that

> The centrifugal force of domestic politics needs to be balanced by the centripetal force of strong presidential leadership. Simultaneous strength at center and periphery exhibits the American system at its best, if also at its noisiest. . . .[1]

Grodzins' concern was with the distribution of powers among federal, state, and local governments. I am likewise concerned with the traditional division of federal powers but, in addition, am concerned with other centrifugal and centripetal forces in the public sector affecting urban development such as the number and variety of federal aids, interagency relationships, local government patterns, the central city–suburban dialectic, the role of the states, and administrative and organizational adaptations within as well as between the levels of government.

It is chastening to the political scientist to find that the role of government in urban development is often depreciated. When *Scientific American* devoted its September 1965 issue[2] to a series of essays on cities, it included articles on their origin and evolution, on the land, transportation, and the metabolism of cities, but no articles and little space to the role of the federal, state, and local governments.

Yet, government is most important in urban development, not because it supplies the shelter, the food, or the clothing needed by urban

---

[1] Morton Grodzins, "The Federal System," in President's Commission on National Goals, *Goal for Americans* (Englewood Cliffs, N.J.: Prentice-Hall, 1960), p. 282.
[2] Later published as *Cities* (New York: Knopf, 1965).

populations—it doesn't. Government is crucial because it is the major mechanism for protecting the public interest, for refereeing or resolving conflicting interests, for achieving greater equity in social and economic opportunity, and for doing, in Lincoln's words, "for the communities of people whatever they need to have done, but cannot do so well, for themselves in their separate and individual capacities."

At the same time, we know that the interest of the general public in urban governmental issues is low. Voting participation in presidential elections is not particularly high in the United States compared to other democracies. Yet, a survey of voter reactions to governmental reorganization proposals in eighteen metropolitan areas from 1950 to 1962 revealed that less than half as many people voted in the reorganization referenda as voted for President in that period.

V. O. Key estimated that the political activists and active public in the United States constitute no more than 10 to 15 per cent of the adult population.[3] Because of these public attitudes, a wide range of discretion is permitted within which federal, state, and local governments may act. Events and popular leadership, not the electorate, form the major variables in determining public policy.

The generality of public preferences, the low intensity of the opinions of many people, the low level of political animosities of substantial sectors of the public, the tortuousness of the process of translation of disapproval of specific policies into electoral reprisal, and many other factors point to the existence of a wide latitude for the exercise of creative leadership.[4]

Thus, the roles of the scholar, the public administrator, and the politician are crucial in determining the changing role of government in urban development.

This essay has as its objective tracing three major sets of trends toward fragmentation and the countervailing forces of consolidation currently at work in our federal, state, and local governments. The first set of trends has to do with the variety, number, and specificity of federal aids and the organizational reaction to this proliferation. A second set of trends deals with the patterns of autocracy in grant administration and their countertrends. The third set of centrifugal and centripetal

[3] V. O. Key, Jr., *Public Opinion and American Democracy* (New York: Knopf, 1964), p. 546.
[4] *Ibid.*, p. 555.

forces has to do with the lack of state involvement in the cities in the past and the current offsetting factors.

Some additional future steps are then identified that would promote a reconciliation of forces at work in urban development, including areal administration, urban research, fiscal equalization, a Metropolitan Workable Program, metropolitan party organization, and other innovations drawn from experience at all levels of government during the last few years.

THE FEDERAL CORNUCOPIA:
THE VARIETY, NUMBER, AND SPECIFICITY OF FEDERAL AIDS

The tempo of federal aid for urban development is rapidly increasing— in variety, amount, and objectives. Grants-in-aid, the indispensable "glue" of our federal system, work toward equalization of tax burdens, achievement of national minimum standards, and stimulation of new activities. Each grant has, to a greater or lesser extent, different requirements for local eligibility and organization, the role of the state government, planning, interagency coordination, equalization and matching provisions, relocation services, and termination dates.

By the end of 1965, the federal government was administering more than seventy separate programs of financial aid specifically for urban development. More than three quarters of these were authorized after January 1950.

The Housing and Urban Development Act, which was enacted by Congress in 1965, included grants for basic water and sewer facilities, neighborhood facilities, advance acquisition of land, open space and urban beautification, code enforcement assistance, demolition of unsafe structures, rent supplements, and support for councils of elected officials. In addition, during that year, increased presidential and congressional attention to the nation's urban needs was confirmed by enactment of the Water Quality Act, the amendments to the Clean Air Act, the Solid Waste Disposal Act, the Public Works and Economic Development Act, expansion of the Economic Opportunity Program, extension of the Juvenile Delinquency Control Program, the Law Enforcement Assistance Act, the Higher Education Act, and the Highway Beautification Act.

In ten years, federal aid to state and local governments, the great bulk of which is ultimately administered in urban areas, has more than tripled, rising from $4 billion in 1957 to an estimated $14.5 billion in 1967.[5] Over the last few years this aid has been increasing at the fairly consistent rate of $1 billion a year. The increase has been necessitated by rising state expenditures, which have swelled 100 per cent in that decade, and by local expenditures, which rose $2.5 billion per year in the same period.

At the state level we find an increase in federal monies relative to state revenues from own sources. In 1946, $1 came from the national government for each $6.8 raised from the states' own sources. By 1964 the relationship had fallen to the point where $3 of state money was used for every $1 of funds from the national government. At the local level, the change is even more spectacular, moving from approximately $115 to $32 of local own revenue per $1 of federal funds. Combining state and local funds, this index of financial interdependence changes from 13.5 in 1946, to 5.8 in 1964, and to a projected 4.0 in 1970. Thus, as the business of all levels of government has grown, state and local governments have become much more closely entwined with the national government. It is important to observe that the major part of this change has already taken place.[6]

Although such budgetary analysis might indicate that the departments of the federal government are ceding their urban functions to state and local agencies, this is not the case. None of these government departments is willing to be read out of the rapid and continuing urbanization of the country. Thus, the Interstate and Defense Highways Commission, with 90 per cent of the mileage under its jurisdiction found outside of urban areas, will spend more than half of its funds, $4 billion in 1967, within standard metropolitan areas. Even the nation's official guardian of rural values and interest, the Department of Agriculture, is deeply involved in assisting the urbanization process. The President's 1966 Message to the Congress on Rural Poverty declared that the ultimate solution to that problem was social and economic linkage to urban communities, large and small. The *1963 Yearbook of Agriculture* stated this new view in its preface:

Our purpose is to inform all Americans about the effects of urbanization and industrialization on rural America and the need for plans and action so that people will have a proper place to live. Many of the forces of change

5 *Special Analyses: Budget of the United States,* Fiscal Year 1967, p. 134.
6 Selma J. Mushkin and Robert F. Adams, "Emerging Patterns of Federalism," *National Tax Journal,* Vol. 19:3 (September 1966), pp. 236–237.

are most apparent in the urban-rural fringe, but our interest is in functional, rather than geographic, aspects—in the interaction of rural and urban influences wherever they occur.[7]

The rapid expansion of urban-oriented federal programs has created a new communication problem. For the first time, a comparative shopping or market basket situation has been created whereby one grant program may offer more attractive terms for a local applicant than another program designed to accomplish the same purpose. This competitive situation is already abundantly evident in program areas such as parks and open space, planning, water supply, and sewage treatment. But local government officials, state administrators, and even congressional committees are having increasing difficulty in simply being aware of the availability of these programs.

A situation has been reached in which, increasingly, we need a score card to identify the players. The Office of Economic Opportunity has produced a volume resembling a good-size telephone book, titled *Catalog of Federal Programs for Individual and Community Improvement*. It became a collector's item several days after its first printing of 100,000 was made available. It has since been revised and given an even wider circulation.[8]

Cities throughout the country are showing an increasing interest in assigning "our man in Washington" to ensure that the city maximizes its opportunities for assistance in the welter of aids now available. To forestall a flood of individual representatives, the National League of Cities and the U.S. Conference of Mayors have joined together to form a Joint Council of Urban Development to provide such a Washington representative service to cities on a contract basis.

What are some of the factors that have led to the multiplicity of grant programs? First is the fragmented organization within the federal establishment. Each grant-administering agency, aided and abetted by its various attendant interest groups, is placed under the equally fragmented jurisdiction of congressional committees and subcommittees. The reforms of the Legislative Reorganization Act of 1946 consolidating a number of standing committees have been vitiated by expansion in the number of these subcommittees.[9]

[7] U. S. Department of Agriculture, *A Place to Live—The Yearbook of Agriculture, 1963* (Washington: U.S. Government Printing Office, 1965), p. ix.
[8] Office of Economic Opportunity, *Catalog of Federal Assistance Programs,* (Washington, June 1, 1967).
[9] Within the federal Establishment, organization of water activities illustrates the

Another factor leading to the proliferation of federal aids is the tendency for grants-in-aid to stay on the books once they are authorized and funded. In addition, each new grant program creates its own interest groups, is supported by them and, once enacted, helps create additional vested interests who join their governmental counterparts in a symbiotic relationship. Also, these grants quickly become built into the budgetary base of state and local governments, creating an additional resistance to change. It may take thirty years to get a program such as Medicare or aid to elementary or secondary education on the statute books. But once the issue has been fought out and Congress has acted, a new and highly stable framework of public opinion will be established that accepts the new governmental role. With the exception of poliomyelitis vaccination and veterans re-use housing, no grant program has been terminated since 1950.

THE ORGANIZATIONAL REACTION TO GRANT PROLIFERATION

A standard text in public administration defines "coordination" as "a technique for drawing together a number of conflicting skills and interests and leading them toward a common end. It is the centripetal force in administration."[10]

Arrayed against the continuing increase in fragmented, individual, usually narrowly defined and sometimes duplicating, federal grant programs, is the centripetal force of a number of new procedural and organizational developments at the federal, state, and local level. This coordinating machinery includes the use of planning requirements and assistance by federal and state agencies. It involves both strengthened planning machinery at the local level and state agencies for local affairs concerned with giving systematic and continuing consideration

---

problem. As early as 1950, the Hoover Commission found that twenty-five offices and bureaus in six departments and five independent agencies were charged with administering federal water programs. It is therefore not surprising to find that there are at least five aid programs currently available for sewage facilities. These include the sewage treatment construction grant program of the Federal Water Pollution Control Administration of the Department of the Interior, the grants and loans for basic water and sewer facilities of the Department of Housing and Urban Development, the public works funds for redevelopment areas in the Economic Development Administration of the Department of Commerce, the grants for construction of disaster-related community facilities of the Office of Emergency Planning in the Office of the President, and the grants and loans for construction of rural water and waste disposal systems available from the Farmer's Home Administration of the Department of Agriculture.

[10] John M. Pfiffner and Robert V. Presthus, *Public Administration* (New York: The Ronald Press, 1960), p. 111.

to local government needs and problems. It comprises, also, departments of city development at the municipal level with responsibility for relating planning to public and private development decisions in a meaningful local municipal development program.

METROPOLITAN PLANNING AND LOCAL POLITICIANS

In order to ensure that federal aid funds contribute to coordinated urban development goals, the national government is increasingly requiring and promoting effective planning in jurisdictionally fragmented metropolitan areas. Planning as a performance requirement under federal grant programs is now accepted as a major device for relating federal aid projects to each other and to state, local, and private development decisions. Aids to functional and comprehensive planning have become legion in number if not in reputation.

In 1960 the term "metropolitan" could seldom be found in federal law or regulation. Today, most new grant-in-aid programs and more than one third of the existing federal programs affecting urban development encourage by law, official policy statements, and definitions of eligible projects a broader jurisdiction for area-wide coordination.[11]

A few of the more outstanding examples of this new dimension in the use of federal performance requirements will suffice. The Federal-Aid Highway Act of 1962 required that, beginning in July 1965, no funds under this massive program could be approved for a project in any urban area of more than 50,000 population unless there was an established, continuing, comprehensive transportation planning program for the urban area as a whole. By December of that year, it was reported that this transportation planning was

. . . underway in all 224 urbanized areas of more than 50,000 population and in many smaller areas as well. In the majority the process is fully adequate to permit evaluation of any proposed transportation system and in most of the remainder it can provide reasonable bases of review of individual projects. The fears of some that the planning requirement of the 1965 Act would serve to delay the Federal-aid highway program have proved unfounded.[12]

11 Advisory Commission on Intergovernmental Relations, *Impact of Federal Urban Development Programs on Local Government Organization and Planning* (Washington: U.S. Government Printing Office, 1964), p. 16 (hereafter cited as Advisory Commission, *Impact*.)
12 E. H. Holmes, "Progress and Events Since the First National Conference on Highways and Urban Development," remarks at the Second National Conference on Highways and Urban Development, Williamsburg, Virginia, December 12–16, 1965, p. 5.

The requirement marked a milestone in intergovernmental affairs by: (*a*) requiring planning cooperation among the local governments in the area and the state agency affected in the planning process; (*b*) operating across the entire urbanized and urbanizing area; and (*c*) directly linking policy making to implementation machinery. Whether the functional planning operations established so quickly under the Highway Act will undermine or strengthen metropolitan comprehensive planning agencies remains to be seen.

The "701" Metropolitan Planning Program authorized by Congress in 1955 has led to the establishment of metropolitan planning agencies in about three fourths of the urban areas of the country. This two-thirds federal matching program has aided more than 400 projects for metropolitan regional planning, 77 statewide plans, and more than 1,300 projects in small urban areas. Even the Model Cities legislation requires that the municipal program developed be "consistent with comprehensive planning for the entire urban or metropolitan area."[13]

The water and sewer facilities grant program requires that four planning requirements be met: conformance to local functional plans; conformance to area-wide functional plans; conformance to area-wide comprehensive plans; and, finally, that this comprehensive planning is conceived and carried out to attain urban area goals and objectives under the policy direction of local, elected officials.[14]

Until recently, little use was made of monetary incentives to achieve effective area-wide administration, presumably on the ground that the federal government shouldn't have to pay for, but can simply require, effective area-wide performance. However, the Clean Water Program and the Economic Development Program, both authorized in 1965, provide an additional 10 per cent grant for projects officially certified as being in conformity with a comprehensive plan.[15] The Demonstration Cities and Metropolitan Development Act of 1966 authorized an additional 20 per cent for certain federally aided development projects that contribute to metropolitan-wide comprehensive planning and programming. To date, Congress has not funded this incentive program.

Planning requirements, planning funds, planning agencies, and the planning profession are on the upswing. Yet there is a pervasive attitude, held by many planners and other observers of the urban scene, that

[13] Sec. 4(c)(5) of S. 2842, 89th Cong., 2d Sess.
[14] Department of Housing and Urban Development, *Water and Sewer Facilities Planning Requirements: A Program Guide* (Washington, November 20, 1965), p. i.
[15] Until amended in 1965, the Open Space Land Program contained a similar 10 per cent incentive grant provision.

little progress has been made or is likely to be made toward implementation of sound development plans: a feeling that something is rotten in the state of the art. In a national survey, almost half the metropolitan planning agencies cite as major weaknesses that: (*a*) their powers are inadequate; (*b*) their funds and staff are too limited; and (*c*) they have insufficient public and governmental support. While more than half were satisfied that they had developed a good technical program, only 20 per cent thought that their metropolitan planning was being accepted.[16]

Ways are being sought to facilitate the implementation of these metropolitan plans. The Department of Housing and Urban Development, in awarding "701" metropolitan planning assistance grants, now requires that the chief executives and legislative bodies of the localities in the planning area review preliminary drafts of planning proposals. Review by planning councils made up of elected officials in the metropolitan area is also recommended as desirable practice. This has been facilitated by a new grant program in the Housing and Urban Development Act of 1965, which makes two-thirds matching grants available to such councils for the study of metropolitan-wide legal, governmental, and administrative problems. By 1968, approximately eighty such councils have been established.

Although many have high hopes for metropolitan councils, their effectiveness will depend in large part on whether they bring out the full expression of conflicting views and create an awareness of varying problems and interests among jurisdictions. Although they must use existing local governmental machinery to implement their decisions, they must exert regional leadership, that crucial but currently missing ingredient of the metropolitan mix, and thus must present a united front in negotiations with federal and state agencies. Otherwise, real conflicts may be neutralized or obscured, central-city problems may fail to be adequately represented, and metropolitan councils, elected or voluntary, may merely serve to protect the *status quo,* making no real contribution to regional progress.

STATE OFFICES OF LOCAL AFFAIRS

In recent years a number of states have been adapting their governmental machinery to meet the dynamic requirements of urbanization. At least seventeen states have now established state agencies for urban affairs

---

[16] U.S. Congress, Senate Committee on Government Operations, *National Survey of Metropolitan Planning,* 88th Cong., 1st Sess. (Washington: U.S. Government Printing Office, 1963), p. 23.

which give continuing attention, review, and assistance to the solution of problems of local government finance, structure, organization, and planning. Their functions include advising the governor and legislature on coordination of state programs affecting urban development, serving as a clearing house of information on common problems of local government, and providing technical assistance for local governmental units on problems of structure, financing, and improvement in management of urban services.

The organization and function of these agencies vary widely from state to state. Typically, however, they do not directly operate urban programs. In some instances, the offices were established by legislation to provide broad technical assistance services for local governments. In other cases, agencies initially responsible for supervisory control over local finance have evolved a broader program of general assistance. In essence, the others provide a number of pairs of hands devoted, on a continuing basis, to problems of state-local relations.

FEDERAL-STATE LIAISON OFFICES

Another significant organizational trend at the state level has been the creation of liaison units in a number of states to survey the increasing number and diversity of federal programs and determine where the state stands in relation to them. They seek to coordinate federal programs which involve more than one state agency, provide background for gubernatorial policy decisions, and carry out the technical work prerequisite to state participation.

The majority of these coordinating offices were created beginning in 1965, although California and Pennsylvania initiated programs earlier. Special committees or task forces were established in 1965 in New York, North Carolina, and Rhode Island. In Tennessee, Connecticut, Missouri, New Hampshire, South Carolina, Massachusetts, South Dakota, and Maine, special assistants have been named by the governors to coordinate federal development programs affecting more than one state agency, collect summary information on all federal aid programs, and keep abreast of new and changing federal programs.[17]

The National Association of Counties has recommended a similar approach at their level. It has proposed that each county appoint a County Federal Aid Coordinator (or Urban Advisor) to be responsible

[17] The Council of State Governments, *State Government News,* Vol. 8:12 (December 1965), pp. 5–6.

for coordinating all county-federal relations, developing local grant programs, establishing state, regional, and national contacts, and maintaining a follow-through on federal aid programs from the information stage through the grant approval stage.[18]

A number of states have found it desirable to establish representatives in Washington as federal-state liaison officials. California established such an office as early as 1959. It was followed by Pennsylvania in 1962, and Ohio, Oklahoma, West Virginia, Illinois, New York, Indiana, and others have taken similar steps.

CITY DEVELOPMENT AGENCIES

At the community level, about a dozen cities have established a city development department in which the city's planning function is made part of a general public works and development agency. The city of Milwaukee, in 1961, set the precedent by establishing a Department of City Development encompassing public housing, redevelopment, code enforcement, the management of city real estate, and planning. The city's planning commission, housing authority, and redevelopment authority serve in an advisory capacity to the executive director of the new agency, who in turn is responsible to the mayor. Pittsburgh, in 1965, combined the office of director of planning and that of renewal coordination into a single office, and San Francisco established the position of Coordinator of Planning, Housing, and Redevelopment to better coordinate the city's various development programs.[19]

Jerome Kaufman, of the American Society of Planning Officials, in a thoughtful analysis of this trend, observes that

> Critics of the new-type department fear that planning will become subservient to development—instead of guiding development, it may merely mop up in its wake. Others view with foreboding the eventual disappearance of the lay planning commission, an independent, often neutralizing check on government. To date, experience fails to substantiate these concerns.
>
> What is significant for planning is that more and more such reorganizations will take place in the future. As they do, planning will gradually lose its ivory tower reputation. In fact, evidence points to other moves to sew the planning function into the local government fabric, and with it the opportunity to relate Federal, State, and local private development activities in a more meaningful and purposeful way.[20]

[18] National Association of Counties (Federal Aid Advisory Service), "Guidelines for Federal Aid Programs," p. 1.
[19] Jerome L. Kaufman, "Some Planning Trends in the 'Sixties,'" *Public Management*, December 1965, pp. 310–316.
[20] *Ibid.*, p. 311.

NO PROFESSION IS AN ISLAND:
VERTICAL AUTOCRACY IN GRANT ADMINISTRATION

Working relations have almost always been satisfactory among functional specialists at each level of government. The Public Health Service works easily with the State Health Officers. Indeed, it provides the secretariat for their State and Territorial Health Officers Association. The Renewal Assistance Administration staff, both in Washington and in the field, know the directors of the larger local renewal agencies. There is good communication and even mobility of staffs between federal and state highway departments, prison systems, welfare agencies, and so on down the professional list. The growing problem is not so much interjurisdictional as interdisciplinary: one of weaving the individual physical, social, and economic efforts into a harmonious development pattern.

The Senate Subcommittee on Intergovernmental Relations in 1965 published the results of a survey of federal officials[21] responsible for administering some 109 programs of grant-in-aid assistance. Among the major findings were the following:

1. Federal administrators attach little importance to coordinating related federal programs.
2. Federal administrators are reluctant to insist upon coordination of state and local agencies using federal funds.
3. There are conflicts and hostilities between those who are politically accountable and those who administer at all levels of government with respect to the method by which federal aid programs should be carried out.
4. Special-purpose agencies have proliferated to take advantage of federal funds where "general purpose" state, county, and city government agencies were not meeting their responsibilities.

Federal agencies have generally fostered the proliferation of state, local, and county agencies by the nature of the organizational requirements which they set for eligibility in their programs. Federal interest is not in consolidation but merely in the professional execution of specific program objectives. Thus, most federal aid is available, indiscriminately, to both general-purpose and special units of local

21 U.S. Congress, Senate Committee on Government Operations, *The Federal System as Seen by Federal Aid Officials*, 89th Cong., 1st Sess., December 15, 1965.

government. At times, special-purpose units are actively endorsed, and in about one quarter of all federal programs their participation is required. For many years independent local renewal and public housing agencies were encouraged. The Office of Economic Opportunity favored autonomous public and private community action agencies, and so on.

GETTING THE FEDERAL HOUSE IN ORDER

Within the federal government, a number of trends, precedents, and proposals can be cited seeking to redress the dangers of bureaucratic free enterprise. Formal and informal agency cooperation agreements have been intitiated; under the Economic Opportunity Act, preference is being given to projects which are part of an approved community action program; the leadership potential of the Department of Housing and Urban Development is being exploited; and some innovations have been made to improve federal field administration.

INTERAGENCY COOPERATION

Working relationships among different federal agencies administering related programs and even within the larger bureaucratic holding companies have been established in a number of ways: by legislation, by presidential direction, by formal interagency agreement, and by informal agreements.

While there is no evidence of any grand scheme of urban development to which all federal programs pay obeisance, interagency working relationships of one kind or another have been established in at least some portions of every agency's activities.[22] Informal relationships are by far the most common, covering at least two thirds of the federal urban development programs. About one quarter of the programs operate under formal interagency agreements for sharing review responsibilities for plans or projects, and slightly more than one quarter have legislatively established working relationships.

Typical of the web of interagency coordination within the federal Establishment is that of the Housing Assistance Program of the Department of Housing and Urban Development. It works with the Renewal Assistance Administration on relocation timetables, the Bureau of Public Roads on site selection, the Federal Housing Administration and Veterans Administration on defaulted properties, the Department

[22] Advisory Commission, *Impact,* p. 11.

of Health, Education, and Welfare on welfare aids and housing programs, and the Bureau of Indian Affairs on their model health program.[23]

The Economic Opportunity Act created in law one of the most ambitious pieces of coordinating machinery on the Washington scene, the Economic Opportunity Council. It is made up of department and agency heads responsible for the various aspects of the Administration's whole war on poverty and is described by the President as a "domestic security council." The difficulty of achieving coordination among peers is indicated by the fact that the council met only four times in its first year of operation. In 1966 the President issued "Convenor Orders" to the secretaries of the Department of Housing and Urban Development and the Department of Agriculture to provide a focus of leadership on urban and rural concerns within the federal Establishment. These orders have been formally invoked only occasionally.

Improved interagency working relations are largely a question of building up competence in procedures and understanding of interrelationships, rather than one of overcoming resistance. It is noteworthy that the establishment of the Water Resources Council in the Executive Office of the President and the sophisticated interagency agreements in the field of water resources took almost a generation to reach its present stage of development.

PREFERENCE PROVISION

A most promising precedent for focusing federal resources on broad problem areas within a given community was established by the preference provision of the Economic Opportunity Act. The act provides[24] that preference in all federal aids be given to projects which are parts of an approved community action program. The purpose of the provision is to make more effective the mobilization of federal and community resources for eliminating poverty. It is sobering to discover that agencies are still seeking ways to implement this innovation.

DEPARTMENT LEADERSHIP

Creation of the Department of Housing and Urban Development in 1965 gave belated political and administrative recognition to the

23 See *Hearings on the Intergovernmental Cooperation Act of 1965* before the Subcommittee on Intergovernmental Relations of the Committee on Government Operations, U.S. Senate, 89th Cong., 1st Sess., pp. 68–70, for a tabulation of (1) interagency coordination within the federal government established by legislative or executive action or interagency agreement, and (2) programs where interagency coordination machinery would appear to be desirable.
24 Sec. 211 and Sec. 612 of the Economic Opportunity Act of 1964.

urbanization of the United States. In the Declaration of Purpose of the enabling bill submitted to Congress by the President, the responsibility of the Secretary was stated to be the assistance of the President "in achieving maximum coordination of the various Federal activities which have a major effect upon urban, suburban, or metropolitan development." In addition, the Secretary was empowered to exercise "leadership at the discretion of the President in coordinating Federal activities affecting housing and urban development." In considering the department proposal, however, the Senate Committee on Government Operations was not satisfied that these responsibilities, plus certain clearinghouse duties, would sufficiently achieve the coordination of broad national policies that the administration of national programs required. One of the few provisions added by the Congress in establishing the department was the creation of the position of Director of Urban Coordination, who would be concerned specifically with the problems of coordinating federal urban development programs. The intention of Congress, as stated in the committee report, was "to provide a focal point for identifying such coordination problems and for assisting in their solution."[25] Implementation of this intention by the department continues to be a major administrative challenge.

FIELD ORGANIZATION

Attempts at federal field coordination have had a long but relatively undistinguished history. Federal regional administration continues, even today, to be characterized by a lack of consistency in the delegation of decision making among agencies and by a lack of uniformity in regional boundaries, both within and among departments. Previous attempts to rationalize field activities have been directed primarily to administrative housekeeping matters and have included: the Federal Coordinating Service of the Bureau of the Budget (1920–1933); the Federal Business Associations (1921–present); the National Resources Planning Board (1933–1943); Bureau of the Budget field offices (1943–1953); as well as the present Federal Executive Boards established in 1961. The Bureau of the Budget, in its appropriations request to the Congress, has asked for funds to re-establish a small field service. The Department of Housing and Urban Development has also sought funds to implement its authorized Metropolitan Expediter Program.

---

[25] U.S. Senate, Committee on Government Operations, *Establishment of a Department of Housing and Urban Development* (Washington: U.S. Government Printing Office, August 2, 1965), 89th Cong., 1st Sess., Report No. 536, p. 12.

Neither proposal has survived the appropriations process. Six small field offices are proposed to serve the bureau in its contact with agency field operations and with state and local governments.

SPECIAL DISTRICT SUBORDINATION

Federal grants tend to be available to special districts as well as to the cities and counties which are responsible for a far wider range of governmental functions. The special districts are increasingly being used as a legal device for financing urban development projects:

> The California speculator has recently discovered that he can employ special districts and other public agencies to provide him with a significant credit subsidy. With boundary lines artfully drawn to include only the promoter's land, a special district becomes a tightly controlled operating division of the promoter's organization—an operating division which can use its bonding powers to raise risk capital independent of the subscriber's own credit resources or capital reserve.[26]

Districts such as these are eligible to take advantage of such susceptible federal aids as community facility loans, economic development grants, Water Works and Sewage Disposal Plants in Rural Areas Program, and the Land and Water Conservation Fund.

A partial solution to the problems of urban development may lie in strengthening existing general units of government in urban areas, in making it difficult to create additional units arbitrarily, and in more closely regulating those special districts that remain.

Several trends and developments here are worthy of identification. Both federal and state aid and local "home rule" provisions in state constitutions and laws have long vested responsibility for the whole range of urban services in cities and counties. The following statistics put the "special district problem" in some perspective. Of all direct local governmental expenditures in 1964, municipalities spent 33 per cent, counties 20 per cent, townships 4 per cent, school districts 38 per cent, and all special districts only 5 per cent.[27]

The proposed Intergovernmental Cooperation Act, which passed the Senate in 1965 and is now again before the Congress with Administration support, contains a section granting local governments—cities, counties, and towns—first priority over special districts in eligibility to

---

[26] Thomas H. Willoughby, "The Quiet Alliance," *Southern California Law Review*, Vol. 38:1 (1965), p. 72.
[27] U.S. Bureau of the Census, *Governmental Finances in 1963–64* (Washington: U.S. Government Printing Office, 1965), p. 30.

receive federal loans or grants for urban development. This in no way affects the authority of any special districts to receive federal grants. If these districts desired aid, however, they would be required to provide full information concerning the request for such aid to the appropriate unit of general government in the area.

THE STATE ROLE IN URBAN DEVELOPMENT:
STATES' RIGHTS AND STATES' WRONGS

The states must bear a good share of the blame for the current fragmentation of governmental efforts in urban development. From the beginnings of the nation, the states have held the principal power to act. Certain of their powers are not available even to the federal government. These major endowments include: statewide areal jurisdiction with the attendant authority to exercise direct action and leadership; broad tax and revenue powers, limited only by interstate and federal competition; and predominance over local government organization and powers.

Today, the states are established regional forms of government, and the number of governmental services that rest primarily with them rather than the federal government is substantial. These include: the classic police powers over health, safety, and welfare; jurisdiction over the schools; and control of interstate regulations, parks and recreation, and water supply. But there is a great range of municipal services to which the states contribute little except legal power for local government to act. These include mass transportation, urban renewal, housing, planning, sewage disposal, refuse collection and disposal, air pollution control, police and fire protection, libraries, and to a large extent, public welfare and medical care facilities. The states and urban development, like Thursday's child, have far to go.

The extent of state participation in urban affairs is determined, not by legal limitations, but rather by political and administrative ability, vision, courage, and initiative. However, only isolated examples can be cited of recent state innovations which take advantage of the states' great geographic and legal powers. Relatively advanced programs of water supply and distribution are underway in New Jersey and California. A number of states have invested heavily in the development of open space and recreation. The states are establishing an increasingly respectable record of direct action in regional planning. Connecticut took the lead in this field in 1955, and fifteen regions have been defined, and seven regional planning agencies have been activated covering 80 per cent of the state's population. California's regional planning legislation states that a regional planning district will automatically be created in each of the state's regions if two thirds of the local governments declare there is a need for such a district. New York State's Office of Regional Development has recommended the designation of development regions and the creation of regional councils to prepare comprehensive regional plans. Georgia has divided the state into seventeen planning districts.

Despite these modest steps forward in intrastate planning, little progress can be cited in the cooperation between the thirty-two interstate areas, which contain 23 per cent of the nation's population. The total list of formal regional interstate agencies could include only the Delaware River Basin Commission bridging the gap between the states and the federal government in the Philadelphia metropolitan area; the Tri-State Transportation Committee in the New York metropolitan area dealing with mass transit and commuter problems; several exhortative interstate water pollution control agencies; the Port of New York Authority; the Delaware Port Authority; and the Bi-State Development Agency in the St. Louis area.

Although the Tenth Amendment to the Constitution means less than many people may think, the state does retain the residual power under our federal system. The classic rule on state-local relations as expounded by Justice Dillon, unless otherwise provided in state constitutions, is accepted as basic legal doctrine: "Municipal corporations owe their origin to, and derive their powers and rights wholly from, the legislature. It breathes into them the breath of life without which they cannot exist. As it creates, so it may destroy. If it may destroy, it may abridge and control."[28]

On the other end of the state-local power continuum, state constitutional guarantees of home rule to municipalities are creating dilemmas for local governments which are attempting to meet metropolitan-wide problems. These constitutional provisions, in essence, spell out areas of government where the state legislature may not intervene and have the effect of preventing the state and the local governments in metropolitan areas from solving their own problems. Thus, a metropolitan capital improvement district, financed by a six-county Denver

---

[28] *City of Clinton v. Cedar Rapids and Missouri River R.R.*, 24 Iowa 455, on 475 (1868).

metropolitan area sales tax, was found unconstitutional in a 1962 state court decision on the grounds that the Colorado Constitution gave home-rule cities exclusive right to govern themselves in matters of local and municipal concern. It said, further, that "The General Assembly cannot reinvest itself with any portion of the authority it lost to home-rule cities upon adoption."

The present pattern of fragmentation, overlapping, and absence of leadership in tackling area-wide problems has developed, in part, like the British Empire, in a fit of absentmindedness and, in part, because of local political gamesmanship designed to maximize revenues and minimize demands for governmental services. But here, too, the states must take the lion's share of the blame because of their excessive permissiveness in allowing new incorporations and special districts, the weaknesses built into state legislative and executive branch decision-making processes, and because of their financial arrangements that support otherwise unviable local jurisdictions.

Roscoe Martin, in what will likely be the archetype of the antistate urban volumes for some time to come, *The Cities and the Federal System,* analyzes an important aspect of our new urban federalism, the direct federal-city relationship. He finds it good and predicts its increase. Assessing the states' capacity to meet the demands of a new urban age, he concludes:

> . . . that state constitutions are outmoded and inflexible; that the legislatures, identified as the keystone of the democratic arch, are not representative; that resources, partly from deliberate choice, are inadequate; that the atmosphere is not congenial to the embrace of new programs; and that state horizons are severely limited by prevailing mythology . . . the vast new problems of urban America are unique in the experience of the states, which react to them in an impatient and sometimes a truculent manner. Nothing would please the states more than for the cities and their problems to dematerialize into thin air.[29]

WHY THE STATES WILL ACT

There is, however, increasing evidence that the states are about to come into their own in utilizing their unique governmental powers to play a crucial and positive role in urban development. There are at least four reasons why this is going to happen:

[29] Roscoe C. Martin, *The Cities and the Federal System* (New York: Atherton Press, 1965), pp. 80–81.

1. The increasing urbanization of state populations to the point of electoral superiority in every region of the country
2. The Supreme Court's decisions on reapportionment of both houses of state legislatures, and the rapid implementation of the Court's decisions
3. The incentives and support to state action that stem from federal and local efforts to meet urban citizens' needs
4. The increasing recognition of the need to prevent the present pattern of "jurisdictional fallout" in the cities coupled with the need to loose the restrictions on local powers that characterize local government today.

ONE URBAN MAN, ONE URBAN VOTE

If the Census Bureau's definition of urban population (people living in communities of 2,500 or more) is used, thirty-nine of the fifty states today are predominantly urban. In 1910 only thirteen states could be so classified. The significance of this in politics—that is, who gets what, how, when, and why—is evident. Predictably, the governors in these thirty-nine states will be the urban residents' friends; they are dependent upon urbanites for election. Few state political parties today can ignore urban needs and be successful at the polls.

It is logical, then, that one of the most significant developments in the aftermath of *Baker v. Carr*[30] and the June 1964 decisions mandating population as the basis of apportionment in both state houses has been the number of reapportionments actually accomplished or in process.

As of January 1968, virtually every state had completed the reapportionment of both houses of its legislatures. So different from the implementation record of the 1954 school desegregation decision, the rotten borough system in the state legislatures has been virtually wiped out in less than two years. Attempts to block the Court's decision such as occurred in the first session of the Eighty-ninth Congress are not likely to be seriously attempted again. The tide has turned.

While the primary beneficiaries of reapportionment will be the suburbanites, suburban-rural coalitions in the state legislature seem unlikely. Suburban problems are, in most cases, city problems and there the coalition will lie. Analysis of the *1960 Census of Population and Housing* reveals that the classic metropolitan dichotomy in which the poor, the uneducated, and the unskilled dominate the central city as

[30] *Baker v. Carr,* 369 U.S. 186 (1962).

contrasted to the comfortable suburb applies primarily to the largest metropolitan areas and to the Northeast. The fact is that, for the majority of metropolitan areas in the United States, there is not a 10 per cent difference between central cities and suburbs in their respective proportions of undereducated adults, high school dropouts, and families with low income. Unsound and low value housing is much more conspicuous in the suburbs than in the central cities.[31] In short, the central cities have no monopoly on social problems. The close-in suburbs are already beginning to look like the cities and face many of their problems. Suburban needs for state as well as federal assistance for transportation, planning, water supply and sewage disposal, air pollution control, hospitals, and education are as real as those of the cities.

REFORM OF STATE CONSTITUTIONS AND LEGISLATURES

Action on legislative reapportionment has had, perhaps, an even more useful by-product, the stimulation of interest in and opportunity for long overdue state constitutional reform. After decades of inactivity, state constitutional revision commissions have been established in California, Idaho, Kentucky, New Mexico, and Wisconsin, among others. Constitutional conventions have been called or completed in Connecticut, Michigan, New York, Maryland, and Rhode Island.

Michigan's success indicates what can be done. The Michigan Constitution, approved in 1963, established a number of state-local reforms, and it removed a number of limitations on that most hobbled level of government, the county. The grant to counties to adopt their own charters now parallels the privilege of home rule previously limited to cities. In metropolitan areas, the legislature is authorized to establish additional forms of government or multipurpose authorities with prescribed powers, duties, and jurisdiction.

In a closely related development, a number of well-financed efforts have gotten under way to salvage and reform the most scorned link in our federal system, the state legislature. A Citizens Conference on State Legislatures, supported by the Ford Foundation and the Carnegie Corporation and headed by the former Governor of Kansas, John Anderson, Jr., is dedicated to the stimulation of "grass roots" activity designed to overhaul and modernize the legislative articles of state

[31] Advisory Commission on Intergovernmental Relations, *Metropolitan Social and Economic Disparities: Implications for Intergovernmental Relations in Central Cities and Suburbs* (Washington: January 1965), pp. 8–38.

constitutions. One of their first research findings revealed that the appropriations to operate the United States Congress are more than twice the amount available for operating the 50 state legislatures combined. Implications of this statistic in terms of state legislative salaries, staff, research, reference services, and office space, are clear.

In a parallel development, the Ford Foundation is supporting a multiphased investigation by the National Municipal League of the constitutional barriers and outdated practices which interfere with state legislative effectiveness. Among other things, the league has started a newsletter, *State Legislatures Progress Reporter*. The lead article in the January 1966 issue of the newsletter described the New York State Legislature as "a sort of solid gold oxcart" with "the bulk of its practices and procedures having come down from the last century, untouched by the jet age." Still another development launched in 1965 is a two-year appraisal of state government with emphasis on the execution and administration of state services under the direction of Terry Sanford, former Governor of North Carolina.

FEDERAL-STATE-LOCAL LINKAGE

Reports of a direct federal-local tie freezing out the states may, like Mark Twain's premature obituary, be greatly exaggerated. The 1964 Air Pollution Program broke a long tradition of the Public Health Service by making grants directly to cities as well as to states. Likewise, the Economic Opportunity Act provides for direct grants to local private and public recipients, as well as to states.

On the other hand, most of the other major federal urban development programs provide either for direct administration by state agencies, financial contributions by the state, or for approval of local projects as part of a state plan. Only a few of the twenty-five new or expanded federal grant programs enacted in the first session of the Eighty-ninth Congress leave the states without a significant role to play. The direct federal-city ties established that year are limited primarily to the Housing and Urban Development Act of 1965. In federal-state-local relations, the federal agencies, and especially their lawyers, are creatures of habit. Federal grants are available for the support of counterpart state level departments and agencies in such fields as agriculture, highways, civil defense, vocational education, water pollution, hospital facilities, and public assistance. For most federal agencies, ignoring the states would be unthinkable.

STATE AIDS FOR URBAN SERVICES
The winds of change are sweeping the nation, across the prairie
and mountain states as well as the East and West Coasts. State
government expenditures continued to increase at a fairly consistent
10 per cent rate over the last fifteen years, with much of this money
being spent on urban affairs. To finance this, new or added taxes were
recommended by the governors to about half of the state legislatures
meeting in 1965. Alan Campbell has concluded that the most dynamic
part of the American economy today is not the federal government
or private enterprise but state and local government:

Although public discussion and debate about the appropriate role of
government concentrates most of its attention and fire on national government,
that level is relatively stagnant compared to state and local levels. In fact,
the rate of growth in expenditures, revenues and employment by state and
local governments outstrip the growth rate of all other parts of the economy,
public or private . . .
One indication of the comparative growth of the state and local sectors is
to relate it to the growth of the federal sector. Federal general expenditures
increased 25 per cent in the past decade while state and local expenditures
increased 128 per cent.[32]

More than half the states now have grants to local governments for
public education, health, hospitals, welfare, and highways. A lesser but
growing number make payments for libraries, fire, police, water,
pollution control, and housing. A number of new technical assistance
activities for specific urban operating programs have been authorized
in state legislatures.
A whole range of state actions have been taken since 1963 to exercise
comprehensive supervision over metropolitan affairs, to make available
an arsenal of permissive powers so that local governments may organize
better to meet public service needs, and to remove undesirable
legislative restrictions. During this period a number of state legislatures
liberalized urban annexation laws and granted to the cities across-the-
board interlocal contracting and joint enterprise authority. A number
of states extended home rule powers to existing cities while retaining
the right to act where necessary. No less than six states enacted
municipal incorporation control legislation in 1963 and 1964.[33]

[32] Alan K. Campbell, "Most Dynamic Sector," *National Civic Review,* Vol. 53:2
(February 1964), p. 1.
[33] See Norman Beckman and Page L. Ingraham, "The States and Urban Areas," *Law*

SOME FURTHER STEPS TOWARD RECONCILIATION

Additional centripetal action will be needed to bring about a
reconciliation of the demographic, social, and governmental forces
affecting urban development. It is late, but not too late, to change the
recent trends. Fortunately, there has been a badly needed redirection
of interest and talent in all fields of endeavor toward the development
of new federal, state, and local policies for meeting urban problems.
The approaches described here are representative of the directions
likely to be taken.

AREAL ADMINISTRATION

There is a need to minimize jurisdictional overlap among federally
spawned regional planning and operating agencies. Consideration should
be given to utilizing a single agency—a common administrative vessel—
to carry out such federally supported programs as those of the Economic
Development Administration, the Community Action Program of the
Office of Economic Opportunity, and regional development planning.
Grants of federal aid to regional programs of physical, economic, and
human resource planning and development should depend on administration by a single regional agency. The states could aid in this effort by
authorizing and providing financial incentives for the formation and
operation of such multifunctional agencies. Georgia, for example, now
provides state aid to regional planning and economic development
commissions and follows their boundaries in designating jurisdictional
areas for the Economic Development Administration and the
Appalachian Regional Commission. Not only do these administrative
units reverse the trends of governmental proliferation, but they also
provide a unified framework for coordinating related programs, make
the most use of limited leadership resources, and make the beginnings
of regional policy making possible. Similarly, the metropolitan planning
agency, the transportation planning program, and the regional council
of elected officials in each metropolitan area would benefit by consolidating staff resources and political leadership into a single entity.

URBAN RESEARCH

Reform in federal sponsorship of urban research is needed. Despite the
importance of a better understanding of the factors affecting urban

and Contemporary Problems (Durham, North Carolina, Winter 1965), pp. 76–102,
for additional citations of state aid for urban areas, reform of state tax and
revenue authority, exercise of state control coupled with removal of restrictions
over local government organization and powers.

social and economic well-being, a survey by the Bureau of the Budget indicates that urban research constitutes only a small fraction of all research undertaken under federal sponsorship. Only a handful of the many federal agencies affecting urban development were found to support such efforts. What research was in progress was found to be unbalanced. A relative lack at present of what might be called basic research, as distinguished from applied research, was revealed. Finally, no significant unifying focal point or coordinating machinery within the government could be identified for consideration of federally sponsored research on urban development.[34]

Some progress, however, can be cited. The Science Information Exchange of the National Science Foundation is now beginning to make available, on a more orderly and continuing basis, information on urban research currently in progress. This will start with federally supported research later to be extended to information on other public and private activities. Also, a host of research-oriented centers, mostly in universities, have sprung up in recent years, operating on an interdisciplinary approach directed toward developing a more basic knowledge of structure and functions in urban areas.

FISCAL EQUALIZATION

In order to achieve a greater equalization between local fiscal capacities and local need, the federal government has, in some cases, paid the preponderance of total urban project costs. This trend is evident in the 90–10 highway program, in urban renewal, and in government assumption of a large share of the costs of minimum payments in programs such as public assistance.

Most of these high federal support grants tend to be directed toward communities and individuals with the greatest need. Such would be the case of the unearmarked 100 per cent federal Model Cities supplemental grants.

The Elementary-Secondary Education Act, in effect, provides unmatched grants to local communities for educational services for culturally disadvantaged children. Other new federal programs, such as the Economic Opportunity Act, Appalachia, and Economic Development Programs cover 80 to 90 per cent of project costs and

[34] U.S. Senate, *Urban Research Under Federal Auspices* (A Survey Prepared by the Bureau of the Budget for the Subcommittee on Intergovernmental Relations of the Senate Committee on Government Operations, 88th Cong., 2d Sess.), April 15, 1964, pp. 5–6.

go primarily to the poorest jurisdictions for support of a range of local programs.

The states, too, can administer grants and tax sharing so that differences in local fiscal capacity and disparities in services can be minimized. In Wisconsin, for example, under its residential property tax credit system, a portion of the sales tax is channeled to localities most in need of property tax relief. This is done by using a formula which directs the greatest share to districts with the highest effective tax rates. An example of state efforts to minimize level-of-service disparities in a specific program area can be found in the field of educational grant distribution. Here, in over half the states, factors are included which measure both local tax effort and community educational requirements.

Despite these hopeful examples, almost all federal and state grant programs need to be re-examined to remove features that aggravate differences in local fiscal capacity to deal with the public service needs in metropolitan areas. As a beginning, there is need to assess the extent to which variations in local fiscal capacity should be recognized in the distribution of federal and state grant funds and to assemble the data required for measuring state-local fiscal capacity and tax effort.

METROPOLITAN PARTNERSHIP PROGRAM

A joint metropolitan goals effort should be tried, at least on a demonstration basis. The first step might be an invitation by the President to governors and mayors for partnership development of agreed-upon goals in a number of selected major metropolitan areas by key federal agencies, state representatives, and local governments. Within the framework of these agreed-upon goals, an examination might then be made of the performance of the whole range of urban functions to be followed by development of an Integrated Metropolitan Program. Such an approach would be multiprogram, multijurisdictional, and would include assurances that local government eligibility for federal aid would be dependent on participation in the program agreement. The plan would include a politically responsible comprehensive planning process, an integrated regional fiscal capital program and budgetary plan, and an agreed-upon variety of land development control mechanisms. Federal incentives to such a cooperative regional effort would have to be high and might take the form of cash contributions to help augment the regional budget needs not met by existing sources. Federal aids for councils of governments and the grant incentives for metropolitan-wide projects in the

Metropolitan Development Title of the Urban Development Act are steps in the direction of a metropolitan goals effort.

METROPOLITAN PARTY ORGANIZATION

The classic functions of political parties in the United States are to provide leadership, to crystallize issues, and to reconcile diverse community and private interests. These functions are precisely what are needed not just locally but in our metropolitan areas today. In the not too distant past, parties were well organized from ward to state level. But patronage has declined, and governmental programs today, as a matter of right rather than party favor, increasingly meet people's needs for assistance. Local political party organization in metropolitan areas today is simply a pale reflection of the existing pattern of local government.

One approach suggested in the Philadelphia metropolitan area called for supplementing existing local party structure with a unit which would attend to the political realities of today's intercounty, interstate, supercity. Within the intercounty-interstate area encompassed by urban Philadelphia, the Republican Party was represented by three men seeking seats in the U.S. Senate. Though largely facing the same problems and all campaigning within the area of influence cast by such factors as TV, there was no coordination of candidate or party activity. A minimum of coordination could have improved each campaign and could have saved money through volume purchases of time and space.

Such a council, the proposal goes on, could develop programs for a multitude of critical area-wide problems, including transportation, water resources, housing, zoning, and race relations. A similar effort is under way in the Minneapolis–St. Paul metropolitan area. Here, political leaders understand the importance of the metropolitan area to their party's future, both in terms of the proportion of the vote cast in metropolitan areas and in terms of growing urban problems. This approach has application in both parties. It can revitalize and widen the horizons of the existing central-city political machine and add structure, professionalism, and form to suburban political efforts.

PUBLIC USE OF THE PRIVATE SECTOR

It is interesting to observe that the private corporation has many of the attributes of an ideal metropolitan government. It can operate across jurisdictional and even state boundaries. It generally has broad legal authority to perform an almost unlimited variety of functions and has always attracted the bulk of the managerial and professional talent of the country. It has broad borrowing power. Its potential excesses can be controlled by government regulation. Finally, the private corporation, like the public official, is concerned with citizen reaction to its activities, its "image." These qualities should make the private corporations especially attractive to governmental officials at all levels as instruments to help carry out their programs. Many federal agencies have already, in effect, created their own private corporations, such as the RAND Corporation and the Institute for Defense Analysis. Other agencies have done likewise, but more covertly.

A number of contracts have been let under the Economic Opportunity Program with major industrial corporations to operate Job Corps training centers. Thus, the corporations can diversify their activities while OEO taps their managerial resources for public purposes.

The state of California has let contracts with some of the nation's aerospace corporations to examine the feasibility of attacking urban problems through the scientific and systems approaches developed by these firms in helping carry out the nation's defense and space programs. Taking a leaf from this experience, Lyle Fitch of the Institute of Public Administration predicts "the development of public-private 'consortiums' to meet urban social and physical needs. Government . . . might contract with industry for entire systems of urban services."[35]

Given a high degree of competence and concern with the protection of the public interest on the part of government contractors, industry is in a strategic position to make major contributions in such previously exclusive public sectors as crime and delinquency control, government information, economic development, and water supply and sewage disposal.

CONCLUSION

The current trends in the role of government in urban development might have been described in the paradoxical opening lines of Dickens' *A Tale of Two Cities*:

It was the best of times, it was the worst of times, it was the age of wisdom, it was the age of foolishness, it was the epoch of belief, it was the epoch of incredulity; it was the season of light, it was the season of darkness; it was the spring of hope, it was the winter of despair.

[35] Lyle Fitch, "Discourse," *Architectural Forum*, Vol. 124:1 (January–February 1966), p. 94.

The role of the federal and state governments continues to grow. They are helping local government do what local governments cannot do very well for themselves: raise adequate revenues and do it equitably, achieve economies of scale, administer regional programs, and provide a forum for the resolution of conflicting interests.

A new dimension in federal and state aids is likely to be demanded by local government. In an age of a $100 billion federal budget, civil rights groups are calling for an added $40 billion a year to aid economic development and racial justice in the Nation's large cities. The lesson of this new dimension of proposed financial aid will not likely be lost on urban interest groups developing their own strategy for the future.

The role of the federal government will continue to be one of acting when it is the only agency with the necessary resources, when the needed activities cannot be handled within the jurisdictional limits of smaller governmental units, when nation-wide minimum standards are justified, when state, local, or private groups are likely to take action that injures the interests of people in other states, or when basic political and civil rights are impaired.[36] The vitality of the federal response to urban problems—in voting rights, education, poverty, increased housing choice, and planning—has been demonstrated. Its role will be increasingly pragmatic and less vulnerable to traditional arguments for limitations on federal action.

Until now, the states in the federal union have exercised relatively unlimited autonomy in four major areas of governmental activity: (1) the administration of election machinery and the prescription of voter qualifications in state and local elections; (2) the financing and administration of the public schools; (3) the maintenance of law and order; and (4) the maintenance of independent tax systems. Pressured by sins of commission and omission in a handful of states, the federal government in 1965 entered three of these previously reserved fields in a substantial manner, through the Voting Rights Act, the Elementary and Secondary Education Act, the Law Enforcement Assistance Act, and the establishment of a National Commission on Law Enforcement and Administration of Justice.

Federal programs will continue to use the states, sometimes as channels as in "701" planning assistance to smaller communities, as

[36] Commission on Intergovernmental Relations, *A Report to the President for Transmittal to the Congress* (1955), p. 64.

priority-setting bodies as in sewage treatment and hospital construction grants, as planning bodies as in the Federal-Aid Highway Program, as partners as in the River Basin Commission title of the Water Resources Planning Act, and as approving bodies as in the Land and Water Conservation Fund. In large part, these differences in administrative relationships reflect subtle adaptation to political and administrative necessities, but, in larger part, they arise from piecemeal decision making and past patterns of behavior. Still needed is a federal philosophy and broad doctrine on the role of the states in federal assistance for urban development.

The states will continue to be an indispensable part of the system for a number of old reasons and for a number of new ones. The states do avoid a concentration of power, facilitate a wide participation in government, provide yardsticks and laboratories for experimentation, serve as an outlet for local grievances and for political aspirations, permit administrative decentralization and distribution of the work load, allow for diversity and regional adaptation, and help protect our two-party system. The state has ample powers and financial resources; it exists, and therefore it will be used. It will be called upon increasingly to perform the functions of regulation, leadership, technical and financial assistance, and removal of archaic restrictions on local government. With no sign of metropolitan government in sight, the governor's office and the legislatures will serve increasingly as a place for arbitration and for developing understanding among suburban and city dwellers and among the sometimes competing metropolitan area populations within the same state.

As for local government, like Shakespeare's Cleopatra, "Age cannot wither her, nor custom stale her infinite variety." It is the place where the buck stops, where ultimately most public services will be administered, and where almost all public funds, however collected, will be spent. The role of local governments in urban development will not be tidy, or even efficient, in an accountant's sense.

On the other hand, physical and administrative tidiness (and even economy) is not the only test of desired urban development. The local community action agencies spawned by the Economic Opportunity Act measure their success, in part, by the disruption of the *status quo.*

There is little indication that the local government omelet can be unscrambled. Devices such as the urban county, interlocal contracting, voluntary councils of elected officials, responsible regional development districts, liberalized annexation, municipal incorporation control, metropolitan planning, supervision of special district activities, and residual home rule powers will all help prevent the local government situation from getting worse or, at least, will slow down the rate of fragmentation. But this may be the best that can be hoped for in the way of intrametropolitan action.

Much political, professional, and administrative talent will continue to be expended just to make the interdependent metropolitan area work. At a minimum, each metropolitan area will need some form of regional governmental machinery, most likely taking the form of a council of elected officials staffed by a regional planning unit, a regional citizen information-education-response system, and an integrated regional fiscal plan, to meet agreed-upon regional goals.[37]

All three levels are developing a more discriminating form of cooperative federalism[38] to meet the needs and realities of government in metropolitan areas. In a governmental system of shared functions, frictions and anomalies will occur. There are no basic defects, however, in the federal system itself. It has met all of the challenges but one—the Civil War. The system will continue to serve for a long time to come in meeting the problems of race riots, water shortages, traffic congestion, an increasing crime rate, and contaminated air. There are no ultimate solutions in either human or governmental affairs. Consistency in urban development will, in Emerson's words, "continue to be the hobgoblin of little minds, adored by little statesmen and philosophers." The responsibility of the students and practitioners of government in keeping the system in good working order will be to help locate and oil the squeak points as they appear.

---

[37] See "The State of the Region," President's Annual Report Delivered to the Board of Trustees of the Metropolitan Fund, Inc., Detroit, Michigan, January 26, 1966, p. 5.
[38] Henry C. Hart, "The Dawn of a Community-Defining Federalism," *The Annals*, Vol. 359 (May 1965), p. 149.

7.

Inventing the Future Metropolis
Britton Harris

To be concerned with the future of the city and the metropolis is to be concerned with the future of man, and a concern with man's future cannot but lead to a concern about the future metropolis.

Most planners and many other sentient people are deeply disturbed over the present state of our great cities and metropolitan areas, and this feeling is measurably heightened by the knowledge that within the next thirty years most of them will double in population, with consequences which, though difficult to foretell in detail, are assumed to be horrendous. Let us therefore first make a brief examination of the major areas of difficulty in the present and future development of the metropolis, roughly attempting to scale the magnitude of each problem and the responsibility and involvement of the planning profession with it.

A whole group of problems regarding the metropolis do not seriously involve questions of planning at all. We have the means and intelligence, but perhaps not the nerve, to attack directly billboards, auto junkyards, filth, and abandonment. It would be only slightly more difficult to enforce adequate maintenance of existing structures, and this might have desirable indirect effects on raising the standards of new construction. All these problems present some additional difficulty when they arise out of complex social conditions where disrespect for the environment is heightened by the poverty of the environment itself and by public neglect.

At a somewhat higher level, we recognize that uncontrolled and competitive development results in an architectural jumble; yet we hesitate to permit the substitution of an arbitrary set of planners' values for the variety of arbitrary private values. Our definitions of a socially desirable aesthetic are as yet somewhat less than adequate to deal with this problem. It is then of great interest to note that the generally superior suburban environment, which has in addition a privately imposed uniformity, does not in its turn elicit widespread support. In avoiding the difficulties of the city, the suburbs are accused of contributing to urban sprawl. This accusation discloses new issues having to do with the total organization of the metropolis and with the separation of functions and distribution of activities within it.

At this scale and level we find the first real grounds for pessimism about the future of the metropolis. By comparison with cities of only a few score years ago, present urban centers bring together gigantic populations and occupy huge areas of land. Their organizational complexity—economic, social, and physical—reflects not only their great size, but also the increasing differentiation of modern society and the social problems which vex it. We face these manifestations of insensate growth and change as David faced Goliath. The implements of the planning profession as such were designed to deal with problems of an earlier era; they are almost bucolic in their picture of the world. Only very slowly are new and still inadequate policies and means of control being devised, tested, and implemented. At the same time, this process constantly founders on the Balkanization of local governments and their diversity of interests.

Uncontrolled growth is accompanied by a centrifuging of populations, a differentiation of the housing stock, and a redistribution of activities which have vast implications, mostly pejorative, for the functioning, efficiency, and amenity of the city. The problem of controlling the configuration of the metropolitan area with a view to improving the quality of life which it provides is therefore of major import.

Rapid expansion and uncontrolled growth also have significant implications in relation to the larger environment, which includes natural as well as man-made arrangements. In various particular ways, the size and organization of our population and our metropolises are pressing heavily upon that environment with pollution and destruction. We may be organizing man's habitation so as unduly to increase his separation from nature.

Finally, as a result of many forces, there is made visible and palpable in the metropolis a witch's brew of twentieth-century social problems which we have too long tried to deprecate or ignore. Although it is doubtful that the origin or the solution of these social problems is closely connected with the origin and solution of the problems of urban sprawl and environmental degradation, it is nevertheless clear that the problems are interrelated and that further deterioration of our physical and functional arrangements will probably hinder efforts to palliate or resolve our social difficulties.

BACKGROUND TO INVENTION IN THE METROPOLIS

Given the size and complexity of metropolitan problems as they are seen today and the directions in which they appear to be developing, the predictable future is sufficiently grim to have created a state of alarm within the planning profession and among the informed public. The profession now faces the problem of reducing this alarm to manageable proportions by identifying its true bases and the causes behind them, and coming to grips in a realistic way with the problem of action. Human society does not need to accept the limitations of a projected future. We can indeed talk, not about the future metropolis, but about *inventing* the future metropolis. If we conceive ourselves to be engaged in this activity, there are then three aspects of it which need to engage our attention.

First, we must recognize, as we implicitly do, that planning is oriented to the future. We have just taken a look at the present and, by projecting ourselves, have imagined that it implies an unacceptable future. We therefore wish to set ourselves to the task of devising a new future which as a result of our own willful actions will be somehow superior, and perhaps greatly so, to the one which we project. Given the historic permanence of metropolitan centers, which have perdured over centuries and millennia, and the influence which we can presently exert, one can conceive that our look into the future ought to have a very long horizon.

The second important aspect of inventing the future metropolis is that it does indeed require invention. "To invent" means "to devise in the imagination," and this is the meaning on which I intend to expand. But to invent also has an archaic meaning, "to come upon or to find," similar to another more modern meaning, "to discover." Choosing between these definitions, I believe that solutions to the problems of the metropolis must be *created in the imagination,* and are not lying around waiting to be found or discovered. The discoveries of the planner can only be compared to those of the sculptor, whose task is to discover the form of the beautiful woman who has, all along, been locked up in a block of marble.

I have so far spoken rather loosely of the "problems" of the metropolis, and of their "solutions." Perhaps more than half of the difficulty of invention for the future metropolis will actually turn out to be inventing the problems. The nature of the problems so far discussed is largely symptomatic and descriptive; the fact that we have these symptoms is problem enough, but quite clearly the symptoms are not the disease. I thus reject the rubric of problem solving as a statement of our activity. Our problem is most generally to create a better environment, and to do this we shall have to invent our own appropriate definitions of the things which stand in the way of such improvement as well as our own prefigurement of the environment as it ought to be. This job calls for a level of insight and creativity of which, if they possess it, planners may be justly proud.

If we choose to invent the metropolis of the future, we must be prepared to accept the fact that there are many possible futures. Our society must be equipped and prepared to make choices among these possibilities once they have been invented and laid before it. The choices to which I refer here have to do, of course, with broad future outlines and general directions of development. They are of a different order from the day-to-day and year-to-year administrative choices which face the planner and public-policy maker, but they clearly condition these shorter-run choices. Since society will ultimately be the judge of its own main directions, the invention of possible futures is constrained by the wishes of society. Many utopian plans which might be feasible and in many ways admirable will prove to be relatively unsuccessful in meeting the desires of society as a whole. Here a difficult distinction must be made between the planner as a technician of values, in which role he attempts to match the design of the future metropolis with the emerging wishes of the society, and the planner as a prophet who attempts to transfigure the values of society and to begin moving it in new directions. A confusion of these roles is perhaps to some extent desirable, since it may be difficult to separate innovation in design from innovation in the value system of the society itself. The planner who consciously limits himself to meeting the presently manifest desires and tendencies of society as a whole will produce plans which are flat, stale, and unprofitable. The planner whose designs embody his own value systems exclusively and whose main innovation consists in inventing new norms of behavior will find himself crying in the wilderness. Here he will have for company those critics of contemporary and foreseeable events who can say all too clearly what is wrong, but whose recommendations for action are archaic and regressive, impractical, or not publicly acceptable.

These three elements—prediction, invention, and choice—span a great range of human intellectual activity. At the one extreme, prediction involves a broad understanding of the forces and relationships which govern the development of the metropolis. This understanding must be based on the measurement of phenomena and on the establishment of causal relationships. In a word, therefore, prediction is essentially scientific. At the other extreme, choices depend on values, and values are frequently regarded as being outside of science—personal, human, and therefore humanistic. The process of social invention, mediating as it must between scientific prediction and humanistic value considerations, stands at the center of a time-honored controversy, and of the conflict between science and humanism.

RESOLVING THE CONFLICT

Curiously enough, the historic origins of science show it to be the child of humanism, and of its nurture. Renaissance science was a humanist weapon against the obscurantism and intellectual tyranny of the medieval Church. Against this background, it is not surprising that both science and humanism are deeply concerned both with truth and with the measure of the real world, and each in its way is also concerned with beauty.

Given this community of history and objectives, one may justly enquire why today one finds these two great areas of human thought and feeling in opposition to each other. It appears to me that much of the difficulty arises from the fact that early science focused on the world of nature, while early humanism was concerned with the world of man. As science has grown in stature and capability, its influence on the world of man has increased, and in the social sciences some direct concern with some of the traditional subject matter of humanism has evolved. Thus there arise a confusion of purpose and a conflict of method which are highly charged with the historical and personal views of the participants.

The scientist is viewed in the first instance as being concerned with measuring, quantifying, and mathematizing the world. The humanist feels that important areas of values, ethics, and aesthetics are not susceptible to this treatment.

The scientist is thought to be interested in generalizations and abstractions which extract from the world its juice and flavor and save only the rind. By extension, it is felt that the scientist's normative views must necessarily impose a sterile uniformity and do away with variety and individuality.

In the extreme, it is felt that the unchanging nature of humanism in the long cultural continuity of Western society may be contrasted with the changeable and hence opportunistic "progressive" nature of science. This contrast conceals deeper paradoxes. The humanist can rightly say that science, for all its progress, has been unable to deal with the most basic psychological and social issues raised since time immemorial by the humanists. The scientists, for their part, can say that today's humanists implicitly recognize that the issues of the past have really been recast in the present and that to look backward puts even humanistic problems in the framework of impotent nostalgia.

The humanist contention that scientific control over nature should have brought life and has brought death is a fearsome one. It should not go unnoticed by planners who hope to improve the lives of billions, but who might lead them to disaster. In all fairness, however, without the last century's contributions in science and technology, perhaps a half of today's world population could not survive, and the conflict and destruction which men inflict on each other arise out of problems of humanism—that is, out of human relations—as much as or more than they arise out of science itself.

Finally, therefore, in posing sharply in concept and in action the problem of the relation of the individual to the group, the humanist faction raises a dilemma which is certainly real. But the scientist, by the humanist's rules, is debarred from considering it, and the humanist by his own posture negates the possibility of a social solution. The dilemma stems from the fact that, almost unnoticeably, we have arrived at the situation in which we have universities of 30 thousand people, metropolitan areas of 30 million, nations of 600 million, and a world of 3 billion. Laws, constitutions, and modes of social interaction which were designed to cope with at most a tenth of these numbers suddenly are strained to the utmost.

We are therefore forced to the following restatement of the conflict and its solution: The humanist traditionally has been concerned with the individual and with man—and with the individual not merely for himself but as the archetype of important values and of solutions to important problems of man and society. To this extent he is also a realist and a seeker after the abstract. The scientist has been concerned with the external world and with man's manipulation of it; mastery is achieved through knowledge. The implied boundary line is now dissolving. It has become evident that society as a whole is a part of the "external" real world to which the canons of science and knowledge apply, while the most subtle and diversified aspects of men are the basic stuff of this real world, which science cannot hope to comprehend and ingest without becoming manifestly humanist.

This amounts to a joint definition of humanistic science and scientific humanism—which will probably arise within the present definition of academic disciplines in the form of a new and more complete social science. Within such a revised and renewed social science, there will be much less relative importance attached to flabby overgeneralizations such as we find today in sociology and economics. This science will and must be able to provide much finer characterizations of almost intangible qualities such as style of life, social variety, and cultural change. It must deal in both averages and differences. It must provide realistic models, many derived from current and future humanism, of how such diverse social phenomena arise. On the other hand, humanism, in its adherence to this development, will have to give up its insistence that justice, liberty, and beauty are either purely abstract values or values which can be achieved through a simple appeal to conventional wisdom. The problem of achieving them must and can be recognized as one of achieving them in a workable way without the simultaneous sacrifice of competing values and without a mistaken and fruitless appeal to nostalgia or to anarchistic self-expression.

I do not suggest that any resolution of the conflict between science and humanism will prove simple, especially because it will for a long time be perpetuated by other conflicts within our society, some of which indeed may be more fundamental. I do believe, however, that this resolution applies to the real and apparent contradictions over method in the planning profession. It is in the context of this form of resolution of our differences that I propose to develop the rest of my discussion of inventing the future metropolis.

SCALES IN PLANNING THE FUTURE

Probably the central issue of inventing the future, around which many subsidiary issues revolve, is essentially the time scale of planning. Short-run versus long-run planning seems to raise differences on many levels and in many ways. But if there is any merit in current estimates of the disastrous direction of metropolitan development, then long-run inventive planning offers the only hope for the future. I would further suggest that on detailed examination many of the conflicts between long-run and short-run planning prove to be illusory.

Perhaps the first and sharpest issue which arises in this context is a matter of planning emphasis in any functioning agency. There are a thousand problems in our metropolitan areas crying for immediate solutions. These problems touch the daily lives of millions of people, many of whom are suffering from deep social and economic stress. It is quite fashionable to place the immediate solution of these social and economic problems and of some physical problems which accompany them high on the agenda for planning action. It is also fashionable to condemn any diversion of effort to long-run investigation and to the development of policies which may be claimed to have deeper-going but slower-acting effects.

There are, I think, several answers to this position, the most important of which in no way attempts to question the imperative validity of an action approach. It seems likely that the philosophical problem would immediately disappear if we could devote sufficient resources and organizational skills to attacking the problems of planning on more than one level at once. The conflict between the long-run and the short-run approach at the practical level may reduce simply to the fact that most agencies do not have personnel or funds to work on both levels simultaneously. Even with adequate staff and funds there would be organizational and conceptual problems, but there is little excuse for using the development of long-term plans as a bar to action on immediate problems.

I particularly reject the implication that long-range planning is antihumanist and heartless. While it is true that in the long run *we* are all dead, it is hopefully far from true that in the long run *everyone* is dead. Planning for future generations, and indeed for the preservation of the total environment, must inevitably involve the diversion both of planning resources and of investment resources from present needs to future ones. As Luis Muñoz Marín has said, "Some seed for the loaf and some for the furrow." In impoverished and developing areas, this problem of providing for a better future is much more stark and demands much greater present sacrifices. On the whole, it does not seem creditable to me that in an economy as affluent as ours there should be such shrill panic in the face of immediate problems that the future must be entirely forgotten.

It is frequently argued that what is in my view a justifiable concern for the future, involving perhaps large changes of direction, will not sit well in the context of governmental decision making, that in a democracy changes can be made only incrementally, and that the appropriate activity of the bureaucrat is muddling through. The history of government as a whole seems to contradict this view at many points. If politics is the art of the possible, statesmanship is the art of the impossible, and the counsel to muddle through should only be accepted by mediocre bureaucrats. Statesmen at whatever level in government have always found ways to initiate new policies and to break sharply with the past. Nor should we underestimate the importance in this process of independent initiative from outside the government. The success at various stages of the public housing movement, with which Catherine Bauer Wurster was so deeply identified, is surely an outstanding example of this. I would like to feel that from the present agitation of the planning profession over metropolitan affairs, bold new directions will emerge which may be pursued by statesmanlike leaders of government.

There is a final and somewhat more difficult aspect of the conflict between long- and short-run planning. Those of us who are most interested in long-run planning have frequently been accused of holding up short-run decisions and actions on the grounds that the context in which they are being proposed has not been sufficiently studied and that we do not know whether the proposed action is in fact "right" in terms of long-run objectives. The analyst and scientist in the field of planning is thus represented as being "sicklied o'er with the pale cast of thought," unwilling to act and unwilling to let others act. I have no doubt that the analytic and studious aspects of planning attract their fair share of Hamlets who find this environment constitutionally more favorable to their inherent procrastination. But I do not share this notion of how long-run planning should work, and insofar as I regard some questions as presently undecided, I would willingly step aside and allow current decisions to be accepted, or step forward and oppose them on their own grounds. I put forward this position, however, with a certain qualification. An examination of the record will show, I think, that the planning profession as a whole has been slow to act and conservative—conservative both in the good sense of attempting to preserve what is valuable and in the bad sense of being loath to accept and to implement new and important ideas. This conservatism has many sources, not the least important of which is that many of our current urban actions are on a scale which creates permanent, far-reaching, and to some extent unpredictable effects. In the sense, therefore, that sound understanding and long-run analysis can elucidate more fully the effects of present decisions, the long-run and scientific approach to planning can create an enlightened rather than a timorous conservatism—a conservatism which will know more precisely what can and what cannot be permitted.

CONCEPTS OF THE PROCESS OF INVENTION

We must now face the difficult problem of defining an appropriate vehicle for the invention of the future. I do not propose to discuss this in terms of institutional or legislative forms, but primarily in a conceptual framework. What I shall propose represents essentially the merger of three very well known and variously accepted approaches to the problem.

First, I think it is clear that our vehicle must have a strong dash of utopianism. The great virtue of this is that it cuts us loose from preoccupations with the present, the pressing, the immediate, and permits us to lay out the various possible futures which might best meet the emerging needs of the community. This utopianism is, however, a practical one in at least two senses. First, the futures which are sketched should meet not only the private ideals of a master planner, but the public ideals of his clientele. These ideals may be varied and changing, and many utopias which match them are possible. Second, the utopias should be practical in the sense that they are technically feasible, that their costs are not altogether out of line with their values, and that their performance is measured and defined so as to be made a part of the image which they convey.

A second ingredient, implied by the discussion of not one but many utopias, is the procedure of sketch planning. Sketch planning in my understanding implies the preparation in preliminary form of a number of alternative plans. The preparation of these alternatives permits the planner to explore the possibilities inherent in the situation, to exercise his imagination in the search for new ideas, and to set up a basis for a comparison between different plans. The sketch planning procedure as applied to a qualified utopian view of the future should be greatly amplified and strengthened. It should become a public activity of planning agencies, research agencies, and private-interest groups, rather than a back-room practice in a few of these. Sketch planning should not be hobbled by insistence on adherence to existing norms, laws, or administrative procedures. In fact, the process of sketching plans should be a fruitful source for the suggestion and invention of new policies and procedures. Sketch plans where necessary should consist not merely of physical plans but of policy plans as well.

That is, they should have dimensions which are not necessarily best defined in designs, maps, and capital budgets. Finally, out of the many sketch plans which could be generated by this process, a substantial number should be worked up in sufficient detail so that they can be submitted to exhaustive testing and analysis for a comparison of their merits.

Properly conceived, the process of testing sketch plans for realistic utopias could lead in any metropolitan area to the establishment of a new type of master plan or comprehensive plan. For a variety of reasons, this type of plan has fallen upon evil days, and it is not my mission to rescue it from oblivion. There is, however, a very clear sense in which, if not a master plan, at least a guiding concept must be spelled out in some detail if we are to change the course of development of the metropolis. The growth and change of this gigantic organism is the result of a very large number of individual decisions, both private and governmental. Many short-run decisions are in fact permanent and irreversible. What is being decided today is a part of our future. If long-range planning is not to postpone but to facilitate decisions in the short range, it must be capable of defining a position and setting up a decision framework for all of the immediate actions which result in change. Such a framework, no matter how we twist and turn to escape the fact, will inevitably have many of the aspects of the comprehensive plan.

There is still another major aspect of our view of the world which affects many judgments as to the feasibility of long-term planning, and indeed which shapes the form in which the planning process itself is conceived and developed. This is the problem of uncertainty regarding the future. I think we may set aside as relevant to another realm of discourse those uncertainties regarding the progress of the human race in overcoming war, famine, and racial tensions on which our very survival may depend. If we succeed in solving these overriding problems, we must do so through some revolutions in social and political relations. Surely we are uncertain as to the new demands and opportunities which these changed social relations will create for the metropolis. I recommend a brief excursion into some of the future worlds of science fiction for a view of the great variety of change which might occur. Still further, our social matrix provides not only for the cultural transmission of tastes which shape demands on the urban environment, but acts as a medium in which new tastes and new desires are invented

and propagated in the form of fads, styles, and new patterns of
individual living. Have we any guarantee that changes comparable to
many which have occurred in the past do not lie ahead of us? Finally,
it is clear that the technology of the future is developing at an
accelerated pace and in ways which are completely unpredictable. It
required over fifty years from the invention of the vacuum tube to
the perfection of a marketable television system, but less than fifteen
years lay between the invention of the transistor and the perfection
of large and powerful transistorized computers. Most speculations on
future technology take their departure from presently known science,
but the technology which will be operational within our lifetimes
will be based on scientific discoveries yet to be made. This technology
will predictably have its own influence on the uncertain development
of tastes, values, and social organization through its role in creating
new possible forms of human life.

The implications of these types of uncertainty for the planning process
are quite plain. The process itself must be a continuous one which
not only is prepared to undertake periodic revisions of operating plans
and guiding concepts, but which is prepared to face and deal with the
difficult problem of deciding whether new and unforeseen developments
at various scales are temporary aberrations from planned central
tendencies or represent the appearance of new modes of behavior. In
the light of this uncertainty, further, the preparation of alternative
plans should include alternative technologies, and their evaluation
should be based on alternative patterns of behavior and of values.
Through the preparation of such alternatives, it may be possible
ultimately to design long-range plans which express the greatest
common factor of a number of alternative futures, thus minimizing
the probability that major sacrifices must be made in the event of
change. This type of design of alternative futures and alternative methods
of testing will require vivid technological and social imagination.
Finally, of course, the actual technical solutions embodied in short-
and long-range plans may be designed for future flexibility; that is,
to minimize the costs of accommodating to changes of direction. To
achieve this objective, we need not only new techniques and gimmicks
but a planning process which proceeds on the basis of a deep understanding of the functional concepts of the urban system and, indeed,
the human condition.

This last requirement implies a certain emphasis on the view, which

I find congenial, that much so-called uncertainty is superficial rather than fundamental. It might be argued with some cogency that the unchanging aspects of urban metropolitan form are more important than the changing aspects. We may suggest that in the urban area there are strong elements of constancy to the demand for shelter, for the housing of activities, for communication, and for interaction. There is also some constancy in and severe constraints upon the manner in which these functional aspects can be organized. It is quite possible that if we focus on constancy rather than change, it might be discovered that changes are due primarily to increases in per capita income, increases in total population, and a few technological innovations such as the automobile, the telephone, and the skyscraper. Even these innovations might be regarded as a response to demand rather than as sources of change. This view of the problem of change has the great virtue of narrowing the range of uncertainty and focusing our efforts to deal with it, but it may indeed be too conservative and its confirmation or denial will require much further investigation.

SUBSTANTIVE INVESTIGATIONS

The difficulties which I have reviewed regarding certain aspects of long-range planning and my sketch of the problems of the metropolis provide a setting for further consideration of the substantive fields in which we have to work to invent the future metropolis. In reviewing this substance, let us recall that we are in search of imaginative over-all approaches and not of immediate decisions, although our conclusions will strongly tend to shape those decisions. Let us also recall that although we must discuss in sequence a number of aspects of the problem, the object of planning will be to evaluate the totality of methods of dealing with all aspects, and the ways in which these interact with each other.

It is perhaps useful to start with a consideration of those aspects of planning which are involved in the preservation of the natural environment.

The unbridled continuation of urban sprawl has raised sharp issues regarding man's relationship with this environment. To a limited extent, the concentration of populations in metropolitan regions and the national decline of subsidized farming have resulted in the return of vast areas to the status of potential recreational and wilderness preservations. But the price for this gain has been very great indeed.

The energy demands of an advanced civilization have flooded canyons in the West, stripped mountains in Appalachia, and increased the danger of nuclear contamination. The dissipation of this energy in urban centers is no longer a trivial problem. The dispersal of airborne, waterborne, and solid wastes from the activities of our affluent millions has long since reached the point where pollution threatens irreversible and unbearable damage to the environment. Finally, the very process of development itself has wasted our natural heritage shamefully in precisely those areas where the largest populations are to be found. Since even at current densities the land area of our metropolises is small, the real issue is therefore not entirely the spoliation of nature itself but, at least equally, the increasing separation between man and the rest of nature which is enforced by the concentration of the national population in the sterile and polluted urban environment.

These tendencies raise subtle and complex problems of choice which need to be brought into the open. The conservationist and environmentalist movement rests on two quite distinct bases. It first holds that wherever possible the natural environment should be preserved in its original state, and second, urges that the man-made environment include certain essential aspects of the natural environment so as to minimize man's separation from nature. The immediate problems of planning the future arise because in relation to the first point, human occupancy in any form inevitably changes the natural environment, and in relation to the second point, certain aspects of economic and social efficiency are heightened by high density and increased proximity which conflict directly with the effort to maintain contact between man and nature. There also is a direct conflict between the goals of the environmentalists themselves, since if the whole of the natural environment is preserved, the space available for urban settlement is reduced and the contact between man and nature is constrained within this reduced space.

A decent respect for the environment thus provides opportunities, costs, and problems. The abatement of pollution will require resources, and will encounter political obstacles; the preservation of natural features will constrict urban land availability; and opening up the metropolis to nature may sacrifice some aspects of social and economic efficiency. Every decision here involves choices of a complex and continuous kind, but our guidelines are most frequently intuitive, judgmental, and categorical. Even to begin inventing the future we

need greatly improved knowledge of the benefits and costs of
environmental changes. This knowledge will not originate in a field
where standards are fixed, truth is by divine revelation, and decisions
are not negotiable.

Considerations of the natural environment are indeed only one aspect
of the larger problems of the density, configuration, and functional
differentiation of the metropolis. Our interst in urban sprawl is
symptomatic of our feeling that these arrangements are now the
consequences not of plans but of an uncontrolled process of short-run
private decision making. The control and direction of this process
is central to inventing the future.

In most metropolitan areas, this locational process is acting as a giant
centrifuge which separates populations in concentric layers by income,
race, and social class. The resulting social isolation presents effective
barriers to gradualist forms of social interaction, social adjustment,
and integration. Another and more subtle consequence of the extremes
of differentiation in the metropolitan area is the homogenization,
and, as many would believe, the consequent degradation of life styles
amongst the various segments of the population. Uniformity over
vast geographic areas breeds conformity and deprives the citizen of
the variety of opportunities and of interaction which it is the city's
great virtue to provide.

At the same time that residential differentiation and stultification
proceeds we have come to recognize a new level of confusion and
apparent disorganization in other aspects of location within the
metropolis. The sheer size of population and wide distribution of income
have provided a basis for new patterns of retail trade development.
The final supremacy of the automobile and the outburst of demand for
low-density housing has dissolved the former close relationships of
residential areas with a single urban center. The importance of trucking
and the proportional decline of materials handling have freed
employers from many previous locational restraints and thus contributed
to the dispersion of employment centers. The rapid growth of communications and information handling has changed and is continuing
to change the patterns of interaction between people and activities,
and among activities.

In this great flux the old central business district is indeed declining
in importance and for permanently effective reasons. At the same
time, however, it still retains some of its vitality as a center of variety

and of highly specialized activities. But the increasing geographic spread of the metropolitan area makes this center ever more inaccessible to the population as a whole and especially to the large portion of the upwardly mobile and innovative groups which have chosen to seek superior suburban residential location. This inaccessibility therefore directly contributes to the degradation of the quality of life of the metropolis. One cannot but speculate that we have failed to find a suitable form of geographic organization to contain the lives of well over 20 million residents in a single metropolis at a suitable level of variety. Nassau and Suffolk Counties on Long Island equal many small metropolitan areas, such as Buffalo, Pittsburgh, or the Twin Cities in size and income, yet they do not contain a large symphony orchestra, art museum, or many other amenities which are available in such smaller metropolitan areas. It would seem, therefore, after a certain point, that the uncontrolled consequence of growth and differentiation is the further impoverishment of life.

If we aim to invent a future in which that impoverishment can be halted or reversed, we must consider a great locational tripod which governs configurational planning. It once was said that a German could claim only two of three desirable attributes—he could not be bright, honest, and a Nazi. Similarly, we cannot give all locators in a metropolis space, choice, and convenience—or surely not at acceptable levels of cost and safety. Some balance must be struck at or near a social optimum. We can manipulate, in principle, the balance of these desired goals variously by planning the densities and character of residential development, the location of employment and other opportunities, and the connections between residence and opportunities. In so planning, we may find it necessary to modify the present manner in which many of these decisions are influenced largely or exclusively by short-run private interests.

I shall defer for a moment my consideration of the residential side of these controllable variables, and first turn to the distribution of economic activities, that aspect of planned location toward which the profession has been most negligent and compliant. It seems likely that in the future the needs and desires of the population of very large metropolitan areas could be better served, and their transportation requirements greatly reduced, if the metropolis were reorganized in a new structure around a small number of very large subcenters which would play the role of subsidiary CBDs. The superiority of such an organization of the metropolis is difficult to demonstrate, and this suggestion may be taken not as a proposal but as a hypothesis which illustrates the extent to which I feel that innovative planning should consider changing the future. In making this suggestion, I am not calling for new towns at the scale of Columbia, Reston, and Stevenage, but new cities at the scale of Hartford, Albany, and Buffalo. Quite clearly, if it could be demonstrated that this direction of development were desirable, its implementation would pose a major challenge to the planning profession.

The difficulties in so drastically altering the foreseeable growth patterns of our metropolitan areas should, of course, be matched by the possible rewards—and these can only be established by a cost-benefit comparison of probable future development and other alternative plans. A new cities movement is only one of the possible futures which would require very large-scale public actions. In the metropolitan force field, it is quite apparent that new cities of substantial size are inhibited in their growth by the existence of a powerful central business district and by the obsolescent capital structure of existing subcenters. The planning and establishment of new centers would therefore require powerful incentives and controls affecting the location of activities and quite probably the rapid provision of a new capital web constructed over an unusually short period of time.

Considering major configurational changes of this type helps to put in perspective the magnitude of forward planning for residential densities, for neighborhoods, and for amenities. The profession might well broaden its present relatively short-run view of development densities, and give detailed consideration to desirable density configurations in the relatively distant future.

A particular aspect of this scale of change and one which was a concern of Catherine Bauer Wurster revolves around the necessary reorganization of the housing market which must occur if any reorganization of employment location is to be efficient. The outward movement of employment, either on the basis of present trends or on the basis of planned relocation, tends to isolate the lower-income population in the older sections of the central city, far from new jobs. The accelerated development of new cities might exacerbate this problem. It is thus clear that a reorganization of the employment opportunities of the metropolis also implies a reorganization of the residential filtering process. These considerations bring into bold relief the

desirability, which exists in any case, of providing decentralized housing
for the low-income groups, possibly with the aid of rent subsidies,
and at the same time checking or reversing the deterioration of the
existing stock—or clearing it for redevelopment. These two measures
in a coordinated general planned development would have the effect of
leveling somewhat the quality of the housing stock, decreasing the
extreme geographic disparities of available mixes, and thus increasing
the locational freedom of choice, not only of the poor, but of the
population as a whole.

In my estimation, there are severe constraints on the ways in which
the system of transportation and communication can be used as an
instrument of improving joint choices by the metropolitan population
of place of residence and work. There are three main avenues which
need to be explored.

In only a few cities, such as Los Angeles, are transportation facilities
nearly adequate to present-day levels of income and mobility. The
modernization of transportation in most other cities, and even in places
such as Los Angeles, encounters severe difficulties and creates new
pressures on the urban environment. Therefore, even within the confines
of our present systems of individual transportation, there is room for
substantial improvement in facility and vehicle design, which will at
the same time be more respectful of the urban environment as a whole.
These improvements will be achieved only at great cost, but I believe
that the users of the systems will be prepared to pay the necessary
price for mobility and choice. Indeed, it is predictable that within
the horizon of our inventions of the future metropolis, it will be
technically feasible and economically desirable to replace present
transportation systems by entire new systems of radically different
concept. Here we are faced by technological uncertainty, by severe
problems of system compatibility, and hence by a high threshold
standing in the way of innovation, which will probably require a
national effort to surmount.

It is also predictable that the advances which are occurring in
communications will vitally affect the role of transportation in facilitating
interaction in the metropolis, and hence will affect living and working
arrangements and the nature of our choices about the future. We
must recall, however, that interaction between individuals or firms has
two components. Communication, or the transmission of information,
including television images of the actors, will undoubtedly grow. The

transmission of electrons and waves is less costly of time, of energy, and of risk than is the transmission of documents and of people. The technology of communication is inherently more susceptible of rapid development and of economies of scale than is the technology of transportation. But transportation is still required to move materials and to move people where the requirements of interaction demand face-to-face contact or the assembly in one place of any numbers—as at a political rally, in a factory, or on a date. The growth of communications will therefore gradually reduce the growth of demand for transportation, but it will not eliminate it entirely, and it may very well not reduce the total demand. This demand, however, may shift from the economic and workaday interactions of people toward their social and leisure-time activities.

As I have already indicated, in spite of the importance and magnitude of problems of the physical arrangements for living and working in the metropolis, the future also involves the solution of social problems which will be only partly affected by physical arrangements. There is a strong temptation to consider planning the whole of the society of the metropolis. On a worldwide basis the growth in numbers of the metropolitan areas, the deepening of social and economic special-ization, and vast movements of populations of divergent economic and social backgrounds have resulted in a new constellation of forces. If we are not faced with major problems of social disorganization and alienation, at least we have widely divergent patterns of social development and cultural differentiation with great potential for conflict and stress. Such internal division is not new, and indeed has humbled civilizations as proud as our own. What is new, however, is the sheer scale of the problem and its appearance at a critical moment in the development of mankind. Today a distraught Samson can pull not the Temple but the world down around our heads. Thus, while we recognize a larger societal problem embedded in the metropolis and exacerbated by the pattern of metropolitan growth, we should not conclude that the improvement or the redesign of the metropolis will itself resolve these issues. Meeting these difficulties may require new forms and new levels of societal planning in the metropolitan framework.

It is quite obvious that a considerable portion of this needed social planning will proceed in the national and metropolitan context relatively divorced from physical planning. Such social action will create very heavy demands for national and metropolitan resources, and in this sense will be competitive with physical planning. At the same time, it will also develop certain clear demands on the physical arrangements of cities, and it will change the matrix of social values and objectives in which both social and physical plans are evaluated. Thus, in the context of all the objectives of our society, it is impossible to make a complete separation between social policy planning and the planning of metropolitan arrangements, but it remains to be decided whether these activities will be conducted as a unified whole or separately but in close relation to each other. Since in both spheres we need much more exploration of the limits and potentialities of planning, this question must be left for future resolution.

SOME CONCLUSIONS ABOUT METROPOLITAN INVENTION

In such a whirlwind tour of this vast continent, I cannot devote the attention I would like to most of the difficult problems of implementation which flow from my ideas of inventing the future and securing broad acceptance for this invention. In particular I must neglect the impotence which comes from the diffusion of power in the metropolis, and the role of minority interests in blocking action, frequently where it is most needed. Let my awareness of these problems be recorded, together with my view that by having a better product, we may overcome much sales resistance. I will however pause to consider some other conclusions which flow more naturally from my view of the total problem.

I have already emphasized my belief that our failure to attain a better future in some automatic fashion is the outcome of our failure to control or direct in desirable fashions the process of private investment. These investments are therefore made in a short-run and opportunistic way, leading to urban sprawl and unstructured development. But this is not an evidence of the failure or iniquity of private enterprise; it represents rather its success and its virtue, but in a public environment which is itself inadequately structured and controlled. It is entirely possible that a more conscious effort to devise systematic and well-designed taxes and incentives could redirect private development energies in publicly desired directions. The polemically popular alternatives of greatly expanded public actions and much more rigorous controls are not without dangers: these avenues almost inevitably lead to inefficiencies and uniformities which are less prevalent in the private sector, and which do not accord well with our objectives of instrumental freedom and increased public choice.

We have still another recourse in a different context and direction. If in a sense the private market is too efficient, it is unfortunate that the markets for public services are too imperfectly developed. This is particularly the case with a publicly produced commodity like transportation services, whose availability in the metropolis no longer depends in the main on a recognition of its widespread social effects but on individual demand. This market could be more differentiated, more flexible, and more "economic." We ought, moreover, to give much more thought to the pseudo markets which we create when we impute costs and benefits to the external effects of activities which are undertaken either privately or publicly—this is the whole basis for many transfer taxes and incentives to private activities, for compensations to property owners and private parties injured by development, and for at least a part of social decision making. Insofar as we can create a market, at least in principle, for all aspects of public actions, and enforce the influence of this market as it would act on private decision makers, we need not be afraid of the consequences of transfering decisions to the public from the private sphere. At least in judging the desirability of such transfers, we can apply a test of arbitrariness and lack of variation, in comparison with an existing, a hypothetical, or a possible market situation.

THE COMPETENCES OF INVENTORS

We may now turn to some of the competences which it appears that our foregoing statement of the problem would require the planning profession to expand or to develop in order to meet the challenge of inventing the future.

I would like to start at the end of the process, when society with the assistance of the planner must make a choice amongst possible futures. This starting point is suggested by the desirability of emphasizing that choice and the desires of society are the most general framework in which the process of planning may be embedded. It is perhaps important to note that the process as I have outlined it envisages not a series of sequential choices, perhaps of the type which pave the road to hell, but a grand choice of a total future. Such a grand choice implies a much more sophisticated knowledge of the value system of society and its dynamics than we presently possess, and the planner can only hope to elucidate these problems in cooperation with the type of revitalized social science that we have postulated above.

When we consider the values of society as a whole, we find that ends and means are not clearly separated. Unlike any single organization within the society, the goals to be pursued are in no wise externally imposed, but arise out of some internally generated valuation of objectives. The retention of the means which might be expended to achieve one end may be another end in itself. Thus we have a set of interacting values which are mediated by technical and societal relations which determine rates of tradeoff.

The possibility of making choices directly implies that the tradeoffs between values can be estimated, and that the degree of satisfaction of these values can be measured commensurately. Yet it is precisely in the realm of values that we are prone to talk about things which are unmeasurable, intangible, and not comparable. It is apparent to me that the planner or the politician who actually makes decisions does in fact measure these values and that the comparison of values is the essence of judgmental decisions. I would suggest, moreover, that it is now appropriate to talk about displaying and defining these measurements objectively and in the public view, so that decision making is no longer a private and arcane matter but one in which society as a whole can increasingly participate. The whole process of formalizing these measurements will expose the fundamental problems raised by dissimilar value systems in a pluralistic society. The planner can, upon a serious consideration of this exposure, find some measures which will reduce conflict by exploiting the complementary pluralistic nature of the metropolitan environment. In the final analysis, however, he must participate with the public and with other social scientists in formulating decision rules which permit resolving Arrow's paradox in ways acceptable to a democratic society.

The preparation of useful alternative plans and the spelling out of their consequences as a basis for evaluation and choice requires an expanded understanding of the metropolitan system. We may define that understanding in slightly more specific terms. The planner inventing the future will have at his disposal a large number of planned configurations and policy variables, as well as variable assumptions about behavior and technology. These are assumed to have diverse effects upon the growth of the metropolis, or its functioning at some future date, or both. To lay a basis for informed public choice, the planner must make conditional predictions as to the consequences of each postulated set of policies and assumptions. This type of conditional prediction is essentially scientific in nature, since the aim of science is to provide general theories on which we can base relatively firm conclusions about the consequences of conditions—that is to say, laws of cause and effect. The science here being considered, however, is social science and is unusually rich in humanistic content. The immediate objective of the exercise should be not only to produce a factual description of the consequences of plans, but, as a bridge into the evaluation process, measures of the satisfactions derived by various groups within the population from the proposed arrangements. This amounts to a greatly enriched and multidimensional benefit-cost analysis which depends on a more thorough understanding of people's goals and desires, in their diversity as well as in their communality. There is also a deeper issue of the same type. Since many of the decisions relevant to the growth and functioning of the metropolis are made by individuals but have mass effects, it is likely that the conditional predictions which we need will be unsuccessful or suspect if they are not based on an understanding of these individual decisions. There is thus a complementary relationship between prediction and plan evaluation, owing to the fact that both are properly based on a profound understanding of individual needs, desires, and behavior, and on their social interaction.

I have suggested that the competence involved in prediction and evaluation as a major part of planning has an overwhelming scientific component, but that this science will fall short of its purposes if it is simplistic, mechanical, and not illuminated by a humanist understanding of the diversity and the fundamental needs and aspirations of people. Dealing with the realistic aspects of these problems in a systematic way will sharpen and improve the intrinsically important creative parts of planning in the same sense that laboratory experience heightens the creative parts of the scientific endeavor—or wide acquaintance with people, with cultures, and with ideas heightens literary and artistic creativity. I should like, however, to specify more exactly the nature of two important aspects of planning creativity.

The first such aspect derives from very simple ideas in a somewhat surprising fashion. If we review the alternatives open to the planner in assembling a sketch plan, we can systematically express these in terms of "Yes" or "No" decisions—that is, binary choices. Such choices might include redevelopment versus rehabilitation in specific areas, to build or not to build a particular transit line, to build or not to build a specific expressway, and to permit one of two density levels in a specified zone. It is easy to imagine many scores of such binary decisions in confecting any one sketch plan. The effects of these decisions are not independent. Redevelopment with transit differs in its effects from redevelopment without transit, and, to a greater or less degree, every subset of possible policy choices displays interactions. Thus a complete evaluation of all possible plans cannot be achieved by the short-cut method of evaluating the effect of each policy separately and adding the results. It follows that even if there are as few as twenty binary decisions, there are over a million possible plans. The planner must choose a few such plans, certainly less than a hundred, for exploration and evaluation, and he thus stakes his reputation that not one of the 999,900 rejected combinations is greatly superior to his one hundred selections. The creative courage required for such an act is perhaps analogous, in this example, to writing the perfect three-word advertising slogan out of 1,000 given English words. Certain combinations are obviously preposterous (and others may be obscene), but facility in exploring the remaining possibilities requires some considerable skill. In terms of the reality which may involve not twenty, but a thousand binary choices, the problem is perhaps closer to writing a good sonnet. This is not a job which we assign to a roomful of monkeys with typewriters, or even key-punch machines.

The most important creative aspect of planning is invention itself. If we push our analogy toward the breaking point, the planner must not only discover poems, but he can, and indeed is required to, invent new words which improve the quality of the poem. Indeed, insofar as he invents problems in the sense that I defined earlier, he not only invents new words but new meanings for words. There is thus a three-cornered tension between the planner, his medium, and his audience which is in every way analogous to the situation of the creative artist. The analogy is constrained, however, by the fact that most creative artists act at the small scale, and individual successes and failures are relatively insignificant. The planner works at the scale of the metropolis, and his successes or failures enhance or diminish in measurable proportion society's total stock of resources and of the fruits of its endeavors.

The planner is therefore compelled to succeed in three major activities. First, he is part of a great social process, and in his role must be in tune with the values and objectives of society. Second, he is dealing with complex phenomena of a social and behavioral nature whose understanding requires powerful means of analysis and participation in the development of a substantially new science. Finally, he is engaged in a creative activity which depends on his personal qualities and on his capacity to organize interaction with his fellow professionals and with others. In maintaining an appropriate balance between these aspects of his work, he must beware that his scientific interest does not stultify his inventiveness, that invention does not egotistically override knowledge and understanding, and that the importance of the individual and the profession in science and creativity does not negate the overriding interests of society as a whole. If we can achieve this balance as a profession and effectively deal with the processes which I have sketched, we may reach that happy state in which our preoccupation with a better future and our profession are both going concerns.

Bibliography of Books and Articles
by Catherine Bauer Wurster *

"Machine-Age Mansions for Ultra-Moderns: French Builders Apply Ideas of the Steel and Concrete Era in Domestic Architecture," *New York Times Magazine,* Vol. 10:1 (Apr. 15, 1928), pp. 10, 22.

"Prize Essay: Art in Industry," *Fortune,* Vol. 3:5 (May 1931), p. 94.

"Who Cares About Architecture?" *New Republic,* Vol. 66:857 (May 6, 1931), pp. 326–327.

"Americanization of Europe," *New Republic,* Vol. 67:864 (June 24, 1931), pp. 153–154.

"Goût Américain, Demi-Sec," *New Republic,* Vol. 69:886 (Nov. 25, 1931), pp. 45–46.

"Indian Tribal Arts," *New Republic,* Vol. 69:891 (Dec. 30, 1931), pp. 191–192.

"Are Good Houses Un-American?" *New Republic,* Vol. 70:900 (Mar. 2, 1932), p. 74.

"Exhibition of Modern Architecture, Museum of Modern Art," *Creative Art,* Vol. 10 (Mar. 1932), pp. 201–206.

"Architecture," *Arts Weekly,* Vol. 1 (Mar. 18–Apr. 2, Apr. 23–May 7, 1932), pp. 30, 50, 75, 151, 177–178, 192–193.

"Photography: Man Ray and Paul Strand," *Arts Weekly,* Vol. 1 (May 7, 1932), p. 193.

"Swiss Family Borsodi," *Nation,* Vol. 137:3564 (Oct. 25, 1933), pp. 489–491.

"Slum Clearance or Housing," *Nation,* Vol. 137:3573 (Dec. 27, 1933), pp. 730–731.

Modern Housing. Boston: Houghton Mifflin, 1934.

Clarence Stein, joint author, "Store Buildings and Neighborhood Shopping Centers," *Architectural Record,* Vol. 75:2 (Feb. 1934), pp. 174–187.

"Slums Aren't Necessary," *American Mercury,* Vol. 31:123 (Mar. 1934), pp. 296–305.

"Machine-Made," *American Magazine of Art,* Vol. 27:5 (May 1934), pp. 267–270.

"Housing: Paper Plans or a Workers' Movement," in Carol Aronovici, ed., *America Can't Have Housing.* New York: Museum of Modern Art, [c. 1934], pp. 20–23.

"Toward a Concrete Housing Program," in National Association of Housing Officials, Joint National Conference on Housing, *Proceedings, 1935.* Chicago, Ill.: 1935, pp. 80–87.

"Should the Administration's Housing Policy be Continued?" *Congressional Digest,* Vol. 15 (Apr. 1936), p. 118.

"Modern Architecture in England," in The Museum of Modern Art, *Modern Architecture in England.* New York, 1937, pp. 19–23.

* These works are arranged chronologically, according to date of publication.

" 'Art-for-Art's Sake' Approach to Architecture No Longer Possible, Says Houser," *Architectural Record,* Vol. 81:1 (Jan. 1937), pp. 8–9.

Ruth M. Carson, joint author, "Land for Your House," *Collier's,* Vol. 99 (May 15, 1937), p. 19.

"Now-at-Last: Housing: The Meaning of the Wagner Steagall Act," *New Republic,* Vol. 92:1188 (Sept. 8, 1937), pp. 119-121.

Labor and the Housing Program. Washington: U.S. Housing Authority, Division of Research and Information, [1938].

"A Few Facts about the Housing Problem," in U.S. Bureau of Labor Statistics, *Labor Information Bulletin,* Vol. 5:1 (Jan. 1938), pp. 3–7.

"Housing Progress and the Southeast," speech before the Conference of Southeastern Housing Authorities . . . , Atlanta, Georgia (August 5, 1938).

"A Year of the Low-Rent Housing Program," *Shelter,* Vol. 3:4 (Nov. 1938), pp. 4–6.

"Architectural Opportunities in Public Housing," *Architectural Record,* Vol. 85:1 (Jan. 1939), pp. 65–68.

"Low-Rent Housing and Home Economics," *Journal of Home Economics,* Vol. 31:1 (Jan. 1939).

"European Housing: Post-War to Pre-War," in U.S. Housing Authority, Press Section, *Release,* No. 416 (Nov. 10, 1939).

A Citizen's Guide to Public Housing. Poughkeepsie, N. Y.: Vassar College, 1940.

Jacob L. Crane, joint author, "What Every Family Should Have: Two Federal Experts Tally Up the Standards, from Cellar to Garret, from Neighborhood to Community, That We Mean When We Discuss Everything from Our Own Homes to Homes Fit for a Democracy," *The Survey Graphic* Vol. 29:2 (Feb. 1940), pp. 64–65, 136–139.

'A Balance Sheet of Progress,' in "Planned Large-Scale Housing, a Building Types Study," *Architectural Record,* Vol. 89:5 (May 1941), pp. 89–105.

"Sources of Information on Housing," *Architect and Engineer,* Vol. 150:2 (Aug. 1942), p. 13.

"Columbia Basin: Test for Planning," *New Republic,* Vol. 107:10 (Sept. 7, 1942), pp. 279–280.

"War-Time Housing in Defense Areas," *Architect and Engineer,* Vol. 151:1 (Oct. 1942), pp. 33–35.

"Public Housing," in Anthony Adamson, ed., *Homes or Hovels.* Toronto: Canadian Institute of International Affairs and the Canadian Association for Adult Education, [1943], pp. 21–32.

"Urban Redevelopment: Crisis in Land Economics Produces Hansen-Greer Plan and Others," *Public Housing Progress,* Vol. 9:1 (Jan. 1943), pp. 2, 5.

"Housing: a Memorandum," *California Arts and Architecture,* Vol. 60 (Feb. 1943), pp. 18–19.

"Cities after the War: a Challenge to American Enterprise," in Philadelphia Housing Association, Annual Luncheon and Conference, *Proceedings, 1943.* Philadelphia, [1943], pp. 2–5, Appendix II, and *passim.*

Sara White, "A Home of Tomorrow: Land Ownership to Pose Problem," interview in *Boston Traveler* (June 17, 1943), p. 4.

'Memorandum on Basic Weaknesses in Current Legislative Proposals for Urban Redevelopment,' in article "N[ational] H[ousing] C[onference] Attacks 3 Errors in Postwar Bills," in *Public Housing,* Vol. 9:6 (June 1943), pp. 2, 7.

"Outline of War Housing," *Task,* No. 4 [c. 1943], pp. 5–8.

"Cities in Flux: A Challenge to Postwar Planners," *American Scholar,* Vol. 13:1 (Winter 1943–1944), pp. 70–84.

"Planning is Politics . . . but . . . Are Planners Politicians?" *Pencil Points,* Vol. 25:3 (Mar. 1944), pp. 66–70.

"Toward a Green and Pleasant England? Critical Review of English Publications on Postwar Planning," *Pencil Points,* Vol. 25:4 (Apr. 1944), pp. 78, 94, 100, 102, 104.

"Start Tax Reform in Redevelopment Projects," *Tomorrow's Town,* Vol. 2:2 (May 1944), p. 8.

"Baldwin Hills Village: Description and Appraisal," *Pencil Points,* Vol. 25:9 (Sept. 1944), pp. 46–60.

"We Present Catherine Bauer in Her Own Words," *Journal of Housing,* Vol. 1:2 (Nov. 1944), pp. 27, 31.

"An Editorial: for Edith Elmer Wood," *Public Housing,* Vol. 11:6 (June 1945), pp. 3, 5.

". . . Housing in the United States: Problems and Policy . . . ," *International Labour Review,* Vol. 52:1 (July 1945), pp. 1–28.

Review of Louis Mumford's *City Development: Studies in Disintegration and Renewal,* in *Journal of the American Institute of Planners,* Vol. 11:3 (July–Aug.–Sept. 1945), pp. 36–40.

"Good Neighborhoods," *Annals of the American Academy of Political and Social Science,* Vol. 242 (Nov. 1945), pp. 104–115.

"Saneringsforhold i U.S.A.," in Boligkommission, *Aarsberetning.* Copenhagen, 1946, pp. 23–37.

"Is Urban Redevelopment Possible under Existing Legislation?" in American Society of Planning Officials, *Planning, 1946.* Chicago, 1946, pp. 62–70.

"Garden Cities and the Metropolis: A Reply," *Journal of Land and Public Utility Economics,* Vol. 22:1 (Feb. 1946), pp. 65–66.

"Restrictive Covenants," *Architectural Forum,* Vol. 84:3 (Mar. 1946), p. 38.

"Europe vs. America in the Housing Crisis," *Journal of Housing,* Vol. 4:5 (May 1947), pp. 137, 154–155.

"Comment on Article Regarding Death of Howard Myers," *Architectural Forum,* Vol. 87:5 (Nov. 1947), p. 22.

"Catherine Bauer Speaks," *Issues,* Vol. 5:11–12 (Nov.–Dec. 1947), p. 4. [Résumé of address at Women's University Club, Philadelphia, Nov. 11, 1947.]

National Association of Housing Officials and National Public Housing Conference, Joint Committee, *A Housing Program for Now and Later,* Washington, D.C., 1948.

"Reconstruction," *Task,* Nos. 7–8 (1948), pp. 3–6.

"Reconstruction: France," *Task,* Nos. 7–8 (1948), p. 34.

"Freedom of Choice: Report of National Association of Housing Officials and National Public Housing Conference," *The Nation,* Vol. 166:20 (May 15, 1948), pp. 533–537.

"The Current Change in Civic Hopes and Attitudes," in Dept. of Social Affairs, United Nations, *Housing and Town and Country Planning* (Bulletin No. 1). Lake Success, N.Y., Nov. 1948, pp. 35–37.

"Some Notes on Social Research re Community Planning," for Philadelphia, Pennsylvania, Citizens' Council on City Planning, Cambridge, Feb. 1949.

"Housing and Health: The Provision of Good Housing," *American Journal of Public Health,* Vol. 39:4 (Apr. 1949), pp. 462–466.

"Local Environment," in Council for Planning Action, Boston, Symposium I, "Debunk: A Critical Review of Accepted Planning Principles," Cambridge, Mass., Littauer Center, Harvard University, May 7, 1949, pp. 18–22.

"Middle Class Needs Houses Too," *New Republic,* Vol. 121:9 (Aug. 29, 1949), pp. 17–20.

"Social Research as a Tool for Community Planning," in Leon Festinger *et al., Social Pressures in Informal Groups: A Study of Human Factors in Housing.* New York: Harper, 1950, pp. 181–201.

"Some Background References to Clarify the Social Issues Involved in Housing and Community Development in the United States," Cambridge, 1950.

"Social Questions in Housing and Community Planning," *Journal of Social Issues,* Vol. 7:1,2 (1951), issue entitled "Social Policy and Social Research in Housing," pp. 1–34.

"Redevelopment and Public Housing," in American Society of Planning Officials, *Planning 1950.* Chicago, 1951, pp. 39–44.

"What Boston Can and Must Do Now," in Council for Planning Action, Boston, Symposium II, "Metropolitan Planning," Cambridge, Mass., Graduate School of Design, Harvard University, Mar. 1951, pp. 31–32.

"Housing, Planning and the New Emergency," *Community Planning Review,* Vol. 1:3 (Aug. 1951), pp. 78–82.

"Housing Progress and the Architect," excerpts from a speech at a dinner of the Detroit Chapter, American Institute of Architects, 1952, *Monthly Bulletin of the Michigan Society of Architects* (Apr. 1952), p. 9.

"The Social Responsibility of the Planner," *Town and Country Planning,* Vol. 20:96 (Apr. 1952), pp. 169–173.

"Clients for Housing: the Low-Income Tenant: Does He Want Supertenements?" *Progressive Architecture,* Vol. 33:5 (May 1952), pp. 61–64.

Review of Nathan Strauss's *Two-Thirds of a Nation: A Housing Program,* in *Land Economics,* Vol. 28:2 (May 1952), p. 188. See also "Addendum from C.B.," pp. 190–191, in reply to review by Leo Grebler, pp. 188–190.

"Low Buildings? Catherine Bauer Questions Mr. Yamasaki's Arguments," *Journal of Housing,* Vol. 9:7 (July 1952), pp. 227, 232, 246.

"Are There Comparable Costs on High- and Low-Rise?" *Journal of Housing,* Vol. 9:9 (Sept. 1952), p. 322.

"Housing Policy: Toward Feudalism or Democracy? (Or Old Cities Face New Problems)," in National Committee Against Discrimination in Housing, Fourth Annual Conference on Discrimination in Housing, *Proceedings, May 1952.* New York, [1952], pp. 43–49.

"The Home Builders Take a 'New Look' at Slums—and Raise Some Questions," *Journal of Housing,* Vol. 10:10 (Nov. 1953), pp. 371–373, 389.

"Redevelopment: A Misfit in the Fifties," in Coleman Woodbury, ed., *The Future of Cities and Urban Redevelopment.* Chicago: University of Chicago Press, 1953, pp. 7–25.

Davis McEntire, joint author, *Relocation Study, Single Male Population: Sacramento's West End* (Report No. 5). Sacramento, Calif.: Redevelopment Agency, 1953.

"Social Effects of Decentralization," in University of California, First Conference on City and Regional Planning: Problems of Decentralization in Metropolitan Areas, Berkeley, Calif., *Proceedings, 1953.* Berkeley, Calif., 1954, pp. 41–46.

"Swing Low, Sweet Architect: The First Lady of Housing Discusses Flaws in Public and Private Design," in National Housing Conference, *The Housing Yearbook,* 1954, pp. 40–41.

"Economic Progress and Living Conditions," *Town Planning Review,* Vol. 24:4 (Jan. 1954), pp. 296–311.

"Three-Way War in Housing: Lenders v. Builders v. Reformers," *Reporter,* Vol. 10:13 (June 22, 1954), pp. 18–21.

Review of Maurice Parkins' *City Planning in Soviet Russia,* in *Social Forces,* Vol. 33:1 (Oct. 1954), pp. 94–95.

"The Case for Regional Planning and Urban Dispersal," in M.I.T., The Albert Farwell Bemis Foundation, Burnham Kelly, ed., *Housing and Economic Development.* Cambridge, Mass.: M.I.T. School of Architecture and Planning, 1955, pp. 39–51.

Commentaries to R. M. Fisher, ed., *The Metropolis in Modern Life.* Garden City, N.Y.: Doubleday, 1955, pp. 369–372.

"What's Wrong With Our Redevelopment? Catherine Bauer's Answer: We Have the Tools, but Not the Know-How," *Architectural Forum,* Vol. 102:2 (Feb. 1955), pp. 151–152.

"Housing, Planning and Public Policy," *Marriage and Family Living,* Vol. 17:2 (May 1955), pp. 101–102.

"Housing Policy and the Educational System," *Annals of the American Academy of Political and Social Science,* Vol. 302 (Nov. 1955), pp. 17–27.

"Economic Development and Urban Living Conditions: An Argument for Regional Planning to Guide Community Growth," a rough draft prepared for United Nations, Bureau of Social Affairs, Housing, Building, and Planning Branch, New York (May 1956).

"The Pattern of Urban Economic Development: Social Implications," *Annals of the American Academy of Political and Social Science,* Vol. 305 (May 1956), pp. 60–69.

"First Job: Control New-City Sprawl," *Architectural Forum,* Vol. 105:3 (Sept. 1956), pp. 105–112.

Review of Lloyd Rodwin's *The British New Towns Policy: Problems and Implications,* in *Journal of the American Institute of Planners,* Vol. 23:1 (Winter 1957), pp. 43–45.

"Do Americans Hate Cities?" *Journal of the American Institute of Planners,* Vol. 23:1 (Winter 1956), pp. 2–8.

"The Dreary Deadlock of Public Housing," *Architectural Forum,* Vol. 106:5 (May 1957), pp. 140–142, 219, 221.

"Leadership Responsibilities in Planning for Human Needs," speech before American Municipal Association, 34th Annual Congress, San Francisco, Calif. (Dec. 2, 1957), pp. 22–32.

William W. Wurster, joint author, "Indian Vernacular Architecture: Wai and Cochin," *Perspecta,* No. 5 (1959), pp. 36–48.

Ernest van den Haag, José Luis Sert, Louis I. Kahn, joint authors, "The New Art of Urban Design: Are We Equipped?" New York: Columbia University, Dec. 8, 1960. "Framework for an Urban Society," in U.S. President's Commission on National Goals, *Goals for Americans.* New York: Prentice-Hall, 1960, pp. 223–247.

"The Optimum Pattern of Urbanization: Does Asia Need a New Type of Regional Planning?" *Community Development,* No. 7 (1961), pp. 197–213.

"Urban and Regional Structure: The Belated Challenge and the Changing Role of the Physical Planner," keynote address before the American Institute of Planners, Washington (1961), pp. 2–13.

"Urban Living Conditions, Overhead Costs and the Development Pattern," in Roy Turner, ed., *Seminar on Urbanization in India: India's Urban Future.* Berkeley, Calif.: University of California Press, 1961, pp. 277–298.

"The Urban Octopus," in David Brower, ed., *Wilderness, America's Living Heritage.* San Francisco, Calif.: Sierra Club, 1961, pp. 117–122.

Review of Maurice R. Stein's *The Eclipse of Community* and Bennett M. Berger's *Working-Class Suburb,* in *Journal of the American Institute of Planners,* Vol. 28:1 (Feb. 1962), pp. 46–47.

"Four Trends," reported at Harvard University, Graduate School of Design, Sixth Urban Design Conference, Cambridge, Mass. (1962), in *Progressive Architecture,* Vol. 43:8 (Aug. 1962), p. 109.

"The Form and Structure of the Future Urban Complex," in Lowdon Wingo, Jr., ed., *Cities and Space.* Baltimore: Johns Hopkins Press, 1963, pp. 73–102.

Housing and the Future of Cities in the San Francisco Bay Area. Berkeley, Calif., Institute of Governmental Studies: University of California, 1963.

Introduction to Melvin M. Webber *et al., Explorations into Urban Structure.* Philadelphia: University of Pennsylvania Press, 1964, pp. 9–13.

"Can Cities Compete with Suburbia for Family Living?" *Architectural Record,* Vol. 136:6 (Dec. 1964), pp. 149–156.

"Social Front of Modern Architecture in the 1930's," *Journal of the Society of Architectural Historians,* Vol. 24:1 (Mar. 1965), pp. 48–52.

Biographical Notes on Authors

Lisa Redfield Peattie is a Lecturer in Urban Anthropology at the M.I.T. Department of City and Regional Planning, and Research Associate at the Joint Center for Urban Studies of M.I.T. and Harvard University. Her recent book *The View from the Barrio* is based on field research in Venezuela, where she was anthropologist on the Joint Center's Guayana Project from 1962 to 1964. Dr. Peattie has also done field studies on American Indians and in New York City schools. She is the author of articles dealing with relationships between anthropology, action, and values, and on the development process in Venezuela. She received her doctorate in anthropology from the University of Chicago.

Charles Abrams is Chairman of the Division of Urban Planning at Columbia University and was formerly a Visiting Professor at M.I.T. His career spans a wide range of experience in housing and urban affairs. He helped draft the law establishing the New York City Housing Authority in 1934, served as legal counsel for the Authority, and, with Catherine Bauer Wurster, he belonged to the group of reformers who helped establish public housing and other national programs in the 1930's. Later he served as chairman of the New York State Rent Commission and the State Commission Against Discrimination, and as president of the National Committee Against Discrimination in Housing. He has also had extensive experience in real estate.
  In another facet of his career, Professor Abrams has done pioneering work in housing problems of developing countries. As a United Nations advisor, he has worked in Ghana, Turkey, India, Ireland, Barbados, and other countries. His book *Man's Struggle for Shelter in an Urbanizing World* is the definitive study of this subject.
  His other books include *The City is the Frontier, Forbidden Neighbors,* and *The Future of Housing.*

Thomas F. Pettigrew, Professor of Social Psychology at Harvard University, has specialized in race relations throughout his academic career. In addition to his research on race in the United States, he has studied racial conflict in South Africa. He has served as consultant to the U.S. Commission on Civil Rights and other federal and local government agencies. He is co-author of *Christians in Racial Crisis* and author of *A Profile of the Negro American*. Recently he was president of the Society for the Psychological Study of Social Issues and held a Guggenheim Fellowship. He received his doctorate in social psychology from Harvard University.

Edward P. Eichler was director of the Community Development Project at the University of California, Berkeley, a study of privately developed new communities in the United States. His book *The Community Builders* (with Marshall Kaplan) reports on the results of this research. He is currently Vice President of Exchange Building Corporation in San Francisco. Formerly he was Vice President of Reston, Virginia, Inc., a new community, and previously was Vice President of Eichler Homes, Inc., in California.

He has also been chairman of the California Governor's Advisory Commission on Housing Problems and Lecturer in Urban Economics at the University of California, Berkeley, and at Stanford University.

Lowdon Wingo, Jr., is Director of the Program of Urban and Regional Studies at Resources for the Future, Inc., in Washington. He has worked as a city planner and as a researcher concerned with problems of urban and regional development in the United States and in the developing nations. Recently he has been involved in the study of urbanization in Latin America. During 1964–1965 he was in Santiago, Chile, doing research on investment in urban infrastructure with the Latin American Institute of Social and Economic Planning. He is the author of *Transportation and Urban Land* and editor of *Cities and Space*. He has also written articles on urban transportation and land use planning, outdoor recreation, metropolitan development, urban renewal, and urbanization of developing countries.

Norman Beckman is Director of the Office of Intergovernmental Relations and Planning Assistance in the U.S. Department of Housing and Urban Development. This office is responsible for helping state and local governments to work cooperatively in resolving urban problems, supporting the development of urban manpower through fellowships and grants to states, and providing aid to state and local governments for comprehensive urban planning.
Formerly Mr. Beckman was Assistant Director of the Advisory Commission on Intergovernmental Relations, where he was responsible for work on governmental structure and functions and on metropolitan area problems. Prior to that he held staff positions with the federal Bureau of the Budget, the Public Health Service, and New York State government. He has lectured at George Washington University and American University and has written extensively for professional journals.

Britton Harris is a Professor of City and Regional Planning at the Institute for Urban Environmental Studies and the Department of City and Regional Planning at the University of Pennsylvania. His recent research and consulting work have focused on the design of simulation models of urban development. He has served as research coordinator of the Penn Jersey Transportation Study and consultant to several governmental and private organizations concerned with urban development. Formerly, Professor Harris was a member of the Delhi Master Planning team sponsored by the Ford Foundation in India, and he was chief of the Office of Economic Research, Economic Development Administration, Government of Puerto Rico.
He was guest editor of a special issue of the *Journal of the American Institute of Planners* (May 1965) dealing with urban development models and is author of many technical reports and articles in professional journals. He has contributed chapters to *Elements of Regional Accounts* and *India's Urban Future*. Professor Harris has recently served as President of the Regional Science Association.

Index